D1168247

SCIENCE FICTION

This is a volume in the
Arno Press collection

SCIENCE FICTION

ADVISORY EDITORS

R. Reginald

Douglas Menville

See last pages of this volume
for a complete list of titles

Into Other Worlds

Space-Flight in Fiction, from Lucian to Lewis

ROGER LANCELYN GREEN

ARNO PRESS

A New York Times Company

New York — 1975

ALBRIGHT COLLEGE LIBRARY

Reprint Edition 1974 by Arno Press Inc.

Copyright © 1958 by Roger Lancelyn Green

Reprinted by permission of Abelard-Schuman

Reprinted from a copy in The University
of Illinois Library

SCIENCE FICTION
ISBN for complete set: 0-405-06270-2
See last pages of this volume for titles.

Manufactured in the United States of America

————◆————

Library of Congress Cataloging in Publication Data
Green, Roger Lancelyn.
    Into other worlds.

    (Science fiction)
    Reprint of the ed. published by Abelard-Schuman,
London, New York.
    Bibliography: p.
    1. Science fiction--History and criticism.
2. Space flight in literature. I. Title. II. Series.
[PN3448.S45G67 1974   809.3'876   74-15976
ISBN 0-405-06329-6

808.3
G797i

164658

Into Other Worlds

ROGER LANCELYN GREEN

Into
Other
Worlds

Space-Flight in Fiction,
from Lucian to Lewis

What if within the Moones fair shining spheare,
What if in every other starre unseene
Of Other Worldes we happily should heare?
SPENSER

ABELARD-SCHUMAN
LONDON AND NEW YORK

FIRST PUBLISHED 1958

ⓒ COPYRIGHT 1958 BY ROGER LANCELYN GREEN
Library of Congress Catalog Card No. 58-5441

Printed in Great Britain by
PURNELL AND SONS LTD., PAULTON (SOMERSET) AND LONDON *for*
ABELARD-SCHUMAN LIMITED
38 RUSSELL SQUARE, LONDON, W.C.I, *and*
404 FOURTH AVENUE, NEW YORK 16, N.Y.

To

C. S. LEWIS

CONTENTS

PREFACE

Coming out of the British Museum after reading the Great Lunar Hoax of 1835, I bought an evening paper and, opening it, found the first chapter of 'Venture to the Moon'; a glance down any advertisement page of 'Books to Come' shows several works of 'Science Fiction'. The theme of the cosmic voyage, of a journey into other worlds, is more alive today than at any time in the past; with the promise of actual space-flight before the century is out, imaginary voyages to the Moon and the planets take on an added interest.

Yet, though there has been considerable literature of this kind, little seems to be known about it by most readers of this or any other sort of fiction. Jules Verne is, in this context, now little more than a name; H. G. Wells has still some readers; many children still visit the Moon with Dr. Doolittle, and in our 'teens we may follow John Carter's thrilling adventures on Mars—but that is all, until we come to the last two decades.

In 1948 Marjorie Nicolson, one of America's greatest scholars, published her *Voyages to the Moon*, a work of great learning and interest which traces the theme of Space-flight through literature to the middle of the eighteenth century. Her volume stands alone, nor has it been published in England—but my book is not intended in any sense as a rival to it: both the scope and the treatment are utterly different, though I have learnt much from her and take this opportunity of acknowledging my debt.

Into Other Worlds is an attempt to describe the outstanding journeys to the Moon and the planets in the writings of storytellers from Lucian the Greek near the beginning of the Christian era, to those of our contemporary Professor C. S. Lewis. As most of these books are hard to find, I have quoted freely from them, and I have tried to show how each author thought the voyage might be made, and what he imagined his voyagers would find at their journey's end. Where, as we near the present, these books become better known and more easily obtainable, my quotations are fewer, and I have tried rather to set the books in their true place in the tradition of the cosmic voyage than to describe them—or give away their plots.

In the main, however, my work is descriptive rather than critical: Space-flight has usually been a minor form of literature, with relatively little development in the medium. The chief interest lies in what has been imagined, and from that point of view my pilgrimage through the planets has proved most exciting—not least in the literature of the last hundred years, an almost completely unexplored territory in the realm of fiction.

I must add that this book professes no absolute completeness. I hope that few stories of any interest, written in English, have escaped me before the beginning of the present century, though there may well be some in the Victorian period where the research has proved most difficult. But I have not attempted to include all those in foreign languages which have not been translated, and have no apparent influence on this type of literature in England or America.

Finally, to end on a personal note, the idea of making this book is by no means new and is certainly not impelled by the modern outburst of Science Fiction. A schoolboy devotion to Jules Verne and Edgar Rice Burroughs set me off on the quest for other books in the same genre: and I might claim this to be the work of twenty-five years, since the early interest in extra-terrestrial adventure, while finding its completest satisfaction when the planetary romances of C. S. Lewis first came my way, has continued with me since those early days. My search of late years has been among the authors of the past rather than of the present, and just for that reason I feel called upon now to share the delights of half-forgotten fancies with readers who can then turn with a new interest to the rich harvest of the present.

How rich that harvest is, and how provocative a challenge it offers to the novelists and storytellers of today, may be gathered by reading Mr. Patrick Moore's *Science and Fiction*, published early in 1957 some months after I had finished writing my own book. Although Mr. Moore covers the history of Space-flight in fiction in his early chapters, he does no more than sketch the achievements of the more important writers such as Kepler, Godwin, Verne and Wells, passing others with a brief mention and omitting altogether many of whom I have treated fully. But indeed his real interest, and that of his excellent little book, begins where mine ends: in the application of scientific accuracy to 'Science Fiction' (not only of the inter-planetary kind), how it has been applied during the last thirty years, and what fields lie open to the writers of the future, who, he thinks, should restrict themselves to the possibilities which we may live to see realised.

If, however, we feel that more scope should be given to the fancy and the imagination than he allows, we should at least look back to see the achievements of the past and how both imagination and scientific knowledge may be wedded together by a writer of genius to produce, even in the present century, such outstanding books as *Voyage to Arcturus* and *Perelandra*.

At the least, this journey Into Other Worlds is offered as a footnote to our literature—the fingerpost inviting us to an absorbing and little-known byway.

June 1957   ROGER LANCELYN GREEN

CHAPTER ONE

LUCIAN THE LOFTIE TRAVELLER

Sing of Selenē the fair-faced, wide-winged Moon, ye Muses, sweet-voiced daughters of Zeus the son of Cronos, accomplished in song! The heavenly gleam from her immortal head circles the earth, and all beauty arises under her glowing light, and the lampless air beams from her golden crown, and the rays dwell lingering when she has bathed her fair body in the ocean stream, and clad her in shining raiment, divine Selenē, yoking her strong-necked glittering steeds. Then forward with speed she drives her deep-maned horses in the evening of the midmonth when her mighty orb is full; then her beams are brightest in the sky as she waxes, a token and a signal to mortal men. . . .'

So sang the poet of the Homeric Hymn to the Moon about the seventh century before Christ, and so a recent poet, Andrew Lang, renders it in a suitably lofty style; but it may be that the ancient Greek who wrote thus of Selenē no more believed in her anthropomorphic character than Lang spoke habitually in the poetic prose of which he was so rare a literary master.

Six or seven hundred years later when, in the second century of our era, Lucian the Greek satirist wrote the first space-voyages that have come down to us, he was perfectly well aware that he or his hero, ascending to the Moon, would find himself in another world, and not an uninvited passenger in Selenē's silver chariot.

The Homeric Hymn may have reflected popular belief, as it must certainly have derived its mythology from the guesses of early man: but in the same century as the Hymn's probable date, Anaximander (born about 610 B.C.) was putting forward one of the earliest scientific theories of the Moon's construction.

Myth and folk-tale continued, of course, in popular belief long after the beginnings of scientific theory. What tales were told in the lonely valleys of Arcadia or the mountain fastnesses of Thessaly we can only guess, turning to the early mythology of other peoples tapped by anthropologists at various stages in their development.

The Moon, to primitive man, was nearly always a woman, though one Australian myth tells of an old man who climbed a tree to pick gourds; while he was engaged in this task his sons, apparently in a mere spirit of mischief, caused the tree to grow up into the sky with their aged parent still perched at the top of it. The tree withered away in the course of time, but the old man remained in his elevated position —as the Moon.

The Eskimos, too, thought of the Moon as a man, and not a very pleasant specimen at that. For, so they said, he became enamoured of his sister the Sun and tried to violate her on a dark night. But she resisted him and, in order to identify her assailant, smeared his face with ashes so that she should recognise him when next they met. As the Moon's face obviously *is* smeared with ashes, said the Eskimos, this tale must be true.

Selenē, however, was a goddess, sister of Helios the sun, so perhaps the savage ancestors of the Greeks believed once, like the natives of Encounter Bay, that she was a woman of no virtue at all. Mistress Moon, so they fabled, passed such a gay life among men that she wasted away until her paramours drove her out into the desert. This happened regularly once a month, for the Moon, during her period of exile, took a strict diet of nourishing roots until she became plump, lovely and desirable once more.

As a transition from Moon-maid to Lunar world came legends of the Man or Woman in the Moon, folk-tales that are still cherished in our nurseries. Such a tale the old Nokomis told the little Hiawatha when he saw the flecks and shadows on the full Moon at its rising:

> Once a warrior, very angry,
> Seized his grandmother and threw her
> Up into the sky at midnight;
> Right against the Moon he threw her;
> 'Tis her body that you see there.

The people of Malay, on the other hand, pointed out a banyan tree growing on the Moon, under which was visible an old hunchback and a rat. The old man, they said, was weaving a fishing-line, and when it was completed he would fish up everything on earth; but the rat always gnawed through the line just when the ancient angler was ready to make his first cast. (Readers of Rudyard Kipling's Just-so Story of 'The Crab that Played with the Sea' will remember what happened when the rat ceased to meddle with the line and the Fisherman caught the Sea itself.)

When Greek literature begins, round about 1000 B.C., the Earth appears as a flat disc surrounded by the waters of the Ocean Stream, with Tartarus and the Realm of Hades hollowed under it, and the Sky set above it like a hollow dish-cover studded with stars. In some sense Sky and Earth (Uranus and Gaea) were living creatures, but they had ceased to be anthropomorphic in the way that Helios and Selenē still were. These titans rode between Earth and Sky in their chariots, Helios crossing the Heavens each day, and then sailing in a golden boat round the Ocean Stream during the hours of darkness. He could be approached, since Prometheus, lurking on Mount Olympus, stole fire for mankind from his chariot; and on a certain occasion Phaethon, the mortal son of Helios by a human mother, drove his father's chariot with such disastrous results that when half the earth was already parched and burnt up into the desert of Sahara, Zeus only saved the rest by his prompt action with his ever-ready thunderbolt. The luck- less Phaethon fell like a meteor into the river Eridanus, to be mourned with tears of amber by his sisters, and Helios became once more the charioteer of the Sun.

Selenē herself 'white-armed Goddess, gentle of heart and fair of tress', was the beloved of Zeus himself in the morning of time and bore him a lovely daughter called Pandia. Later she was loved in vain by Pan; but her own preference was for the divine young Endymion whom she cast into an endless sleep upon Mount Latmos where she might visit him, ageless for ever, when each sky-journey was done.

But while the bards were polishing and beautifying the old tales and beliefs, the scientists were viewing the heavenly bodies with a purely Platonic love, and by Lucian's day had arrived at a surprisingly accurate degree of knowledge. Some even went so far as to suggest that Earth herself was a planet revolving round the Sun.

There were degrees, however, in the growth of Astronomy, and that early scientist Anaximander was of the opinion, in about 540 B.C., that 'the Moon is a circle nineteen times as large as the Earth; it is similar to a chariot-wheel, the rim of which is hollow and full of fire, like the circle of the Sun, and it is placed obliquely like the other. It has one vent like the tube of a blowpipe. The eclipses of the Moon depend on the turnings of the wheel . . . The Moon is eclipsed when the opening in the rim of the wheel is stopped up'.

Whatever Anaximander meant precisely by this, he is at least putting the wheel before the chariot, and is well on his way from the myth of

Selenē to the opinion of Anaxagoras a century later, who held that 'the Sun, the Moon, and all the stars are stones on fire, which are carried round by revolutions of the aether . . . The Sun is a red-hot mass, or a stone, on fire . . . It is larger than the Peloponesse . . . The Moon is of earthy nature . . . an incandescent solid, having in it plains, mountains and ravines'.

A little later comes Philolaus, a contemporary of Socrates and follower of Pythagoras, who maintained that: 'the Moon has an earthy appearance because, like our Earth, it is inhabited throughout by animals and plants, only larger and more beautiful than ours: for the animals on it are fifteen times stronger than those on the Earth . . . and the day in the Moon is correspondingly longer.'

The last writer worth mentioning here is the historian Plutarch (A.D. c.46–120) who died only a few years before the birth of Lucian. Among his many and varied works is one *Of the Face appearing in the Orb of the Moon*, which is a garrulous discussion on Lunar Astronomy giving many details of the various theories about the Moon already put forward by scientists and philosophers. One suggestion finds an echo even in recent Moon romances: 'as this Earth on which we are has in it many great Sinuosities and Vallies, so 'tis probable that the Moon also lies open, and is cleft with many deep Caves and Ruptures, in which there is Water, or very obscure Air, to the bottom of which the Sun cannot reach or penetrate. . . .'

But even more interesting is the discussion as to whether the Moon is habitable or not: 'I would gladly first understand something concerning those who are said to dwell in the Moon; not, whether there are any persons inhabiting it, but whether 'tis impossible there should be any; for if 'tis not possible for the Moon to be inhabited, 'tis also unreasonable to say that she is [an] Earth: otherwise she would have been created in vain and to no End; not bearing any Fruits nor affording a Place for the Birth or Education of any Men, for which Causes and Ends this Earth, wherein we live, was made and created. . . . For those who . . . inhabit her, 'tis said, that being ty'd and bound, like a sort of *Ixions*, they are with so much Violence turn'd and whirl'd about, as if they were perpetually in danger of being flung out . . . Wherefore 'tis not greatly to be admir'd, if thro' Violence of her Motion there sometime fell a Lion from her into *Peloponnesus*, but 'tis rather to be wondred that we do not daily see ten thousand Falls of Men and Women, and Shocks of other Animals tumbling down thence with their Heels upwards on our heads—for it would be a

Mockery to dispute about their Habitation there, if they can have there neither Birth nor Existance.'

This was the background of suggestion and objection against which Lucian was able to build his slight but amusing card-castles of fiction and satire. He had an even more important source, a fictitious travel book, *Of the Wonderful Things Beyond Thule*, which included a voyage to the Moon: but unfortunately this, perhaps the oldest of Moon-romances, has not survived, nor is even the date of its author, Antonius Diogenes, known for certain, though some authorities place him as early as the reign of Alexander the Great, while others make him actually a contemporary of Lucian. All that remains of this interesting work is a short précis of the story included in the *Bibliotheca* of Photius, who scornfully dismisses the incident of the visit to the Moon with: 'But what most completely exceeds all belief is that travelling North-wards they came to the Moon, a land of especial purity, and reaching it saw what it was likely that a man who constructed such extravagant fictions should see.' A very tantalising summary for us who cannot turn to the original.

Properly speaking, however, the story of journeys into other worlds begins with Lucian, who was a Syrian of Samosata born about A.D. 125. He began life as apprentice to his uncle, who was a sculptor, but not caring for such a pursuit, he turned to the study of Rhetoric, which was then the most popular branch of the literary profession. An ordinary rhetorician's job was to plead in court or prepare pleas for others—but Lucian followed the practice of the more literary rhetoricians, travelling from place to place and, in his case, from country to country, displaying his prowess as a public speaker. Lucian visited Ionia, Greece, Italy and even Gaul in this way, and many of his lectures are still extant. Later in life he studied philosophy—and many philosophers and their tenets come in for mockery in his *Dialogues*, as do also the classical gods and most of the popular religions and superstitions of his day.

The Dialogue which concerns us here is called *Icaro-Menippus*, which its first translator, Mr. Francis Hickes of Oriel College, Oxford, gives the sub-title of 'The Loftie Traveller', and I quote the relevant passages from his version, which first appeared in 1634, only sub-stituting the correct Greek names for the ill-fitting Roman with which it was then customary to equate them.

Menippus, a Cynic philosopher, is walking in the market place at Athens, and a friend overhears him talking to himself:

'*Menippus:* By this account, from the Earth to the Moone can be no lesse than three thousand furlongs, where wee tooke up our first lodging: from thence upwards to the Sunne, are about five hundred leagues: and from the Sunne to the heigth of Heaven, and the sublime seat of Zeus himselfe, is as farre as a swift Eagle is able to reach in a whole dayes flight.

Friend: How now Menippus? are you trading in Astronomie, and practising Arithmeticall conclusions so closely by your selfe? For as I followed after you, mee thought I heard you talk strangely of Suns and Moones, and leagues, and lodgings, and I cannot tell what.

Menippus: Marvell not good friend, though I talke transcendently, and above the pitch of our common region, for I am making a summarie computation to my selfe of my late peregrination.

Friend: Why, good Sir, did you travell like a Phenician, and score out your way by the course of the Starres?

Menippus: I tell you no: for my journey lay among the very Starres themselves. . . .'

The friend tells Menippus that he has been dreaming, but the philosopher sticks to his story, declaring that he did not need the Eagle of Zeus which carried Ganymede up into Heaven, nor even the wax-bound wings which Daedalus made for his son Icarus—yet he *did* fly by means of wings:

Friend: And how durst thou put thy selfe upon such an adventure, for feare of falling into the Sea, which after thy name might be called the Menippian Sea, as the other was called the Icarian?

Menippus: I was secure of that: for Icarus's wings were cemented with waxe, which dissolving with the Sunne, he cast his feathers and could not chuse but fall: but my feathers were joynted with no such matter.

Friend: How then? for by little and little thou hast screwed me up, I cannot tell how, to imagine there may be some truth in thy narration.

Menippus: Thus I did, I tooke a good bigge Eagle, and a strong Vulture, and cut their wings at the first joynt . . . I cut off the right wing of the one, and the left wing of the other which was the vulture, as handsomely as I could, and buckling them about mee, fastened them to my shoulders with thongs of strong leather, and at the ends of the uttermost feathers made mee loopes to put my hands through, and then began to trie what I could do, leaping upwards at the first withall, and sayling with my armes. . . .'

At first Menippus could only fly with his feet just above the ground, but soon, growing bolder, he flew down from the Acropolis, landing without mishap in the theatre of Dionysus. After this he began flying to the tops of mountains, beginning with easy ascents such as Parnes and Hymettus, and finally soaring triumphantly to the top of Taygetus and Olympus. And it was from Olympus, when he had loaded himself with food for his expedition, that Menippus at length set out on his journey to Heaven for his interview with Zeus.

'At the first,' he goes on, 'the distance made me somewhat dizzie for a time, but afterwards I endured it well enough: when I was got up as high as the Moone, by making way thorough so many cloudes, I found myselfe wearie, especially upon the left wing, which was of the Vulture: I therefore sate me down upon it to rest my selfe. . . .'

Once settled on the Moon, Menippus says that 'shee travelled with mee in her usuall course, and holp me to survey all earthly things: and at the first, me thought I saw a very little kinde of Earth, far lesse than the Moone: and thereupon stooping downe, could not yet finde where such Mountaines were, or such a Sea. . . . At the last, the glittering of the Ocean by the Sunne beames shining upon it, made me conjecture it was the Earth I saw . . . '.

The only inhabitant of the Moon whom Menippus met was the Earthly philosopher Empedocles, no ghost but the man himself: 'I am the physicall Empedocles, that tumbled myselfe headlong into the tunnells of mount Aetna, and was thence cast out againe by the strength of the smoake, and tossed up hither, and now dwell in the Moone; and am carried about in the aire as shee is, feeding only upon the dew.' Empedocles showed Menippus how to obtain an eagle-eye view of all that is happening on Earth, where mankind looks of no more importance than ants in an ant-hill—which affords good scope for Lucian's satire. Finally Menippus was ready to continue on his way: 'When I had thus seene enough to serve my turne, and satisfied my selfe with laughter at it, I set my wings together againe, to take my flight to the habitation of heavenly Zeus . . . and so struck up directly towards Heaven, and had soone lost sight of all that was done either by men or beasts, and within a while the Moone itself began to be lessened, and the Earth was utterly hid from me: then I left the Sun upon my right hand, and taking my flight thorow the Starres, the third day I arriv'd at Heaven.'

Here he was kindly received, watched Zeus deciding which prayers to grant, participated in an Olympian banquet, and told the gods of the absurd and contradictory statements and beliefs being put forward by the various philosophers, giving weight to his complaints with a message from the Moon who had spoken to him 'with a Feminine voice' as he was flying away from her, begging him to tell Zeus that she was tired to death of the theories about herself which were constantly being propounded by the wise men on Earth. Zeus then pronounced impending doom on all false philosophers—particularly the Epicureans—deprived Menippus of his wings, and bade Hermes carry him back to Earth and deposit him gently in the Street of the Tombs at Athens—where his friend found him at the beginning of the Dialogue.

Lucian's other Moon-voyage is more properly a romance than *Icaro-Menippus* and forms part of his *True Historie* which is the first in the long line of tall tales that includes *Mandeville's Travels, Gulliver,* and the doings of *Baron Munchausen*—or rather it is really the second, for the lost work of Antonius Diogenes, *Of the Wonderful Things Beyond Thule,* is said to have been Lucian's model, though it seems to have been far inferior to the delightful nonsense of the *True Historie.*

Lucian begins by mentioning other travellers whose stories do not bear the stamp of truth, the chief, in his opinion, being Odysseus when he came to narrate his adventures to Alcinous in the *Odyssey,* and this study of poetic and other fictions, he said, made him jealous:

'This made mee also ambitious to leave some monument of my selfe behinde mee, that I might not be the onely man exempted from this libertie of lying: and because I had no matter of veritie to imploy my penne in, (for nothing hath befalne mee worth the writing), I turned my stile to publish untruthes, but with an honester minde than others have done: for this one thing I confidently pronounce for a truth—that I lie!—and this I hope may be an excuse for all the rest, when I confesse what I am faultie in: for I write of matters which I neither saw nor suffered, nor heard by report from others; which are in no beeing, nor possible ever to have a beginning: let no man therefore in any case give any credit to them.'

After this propitious beginning, Lucian tells how he set sail from Gibraltar out into the Western Ocean and came after many days to an island which had been visited in past ages by the two great travellers of mythology, Heracles and Dionysus. Here he and his companions find rivers of wine, creatures half women and half trees, and other wonders, before they put to sea again in search of new adventures.

And they had scarcely lost sight of land when: 'upon a suddaine a whirlewinde caught us, which turned our shippe round about, and lifted us up some three thousand furlongs into the aire, and suffered us not to settle againe into the sea, but wee hung above ground, and were carried aloft with a mightie wind which filled our sailes strongly. Thus for seven daies space and so many nights, were wee driven along in that manner, and on the eighth day, wee came in view of a great countrie in the aire, like to a shining Island, of a round proportion, gloriously glittering with light, and approaching to it, we there arrived, and tooke land, and surveying the countrie we found it to be both inhabited and husbanded. And as long as the day lasted we could see nothing there, but when night was come many other islands appeared unto us, some greater and some lesse, all of the colour of fire; and another kind of Earth underneath, in which were cities and seas and rivers and woods, and mountains, which we conjectured to be the Earth by us inhabited. And going further into the land, we were met withall and taken by those kind of people which they call Hippogypians ["Flying Dragoons"—literally "Horse-Vultures"]. These are men riding upon monstrous vultures, which they use instead of horses— for the vultures there are exceeding great, every one with three heads apiece; you may imagine their greatnesse by this: every feather in their wings was bigger and longer than the mast of a tall ship. Their charge was to flie about the countrie, and all the strangers they found to bring them to the King; and their fortune was to seize upon us, and by them we were presented to him. As soone as he saw us, he conjectured by our habit what country-men we were, and said: "Are not you strangers Grecians?" Which when we affirmed, "And how could you make way," said hee, "thorow so much aire as to get hither?" Then we delivered the whole discourse of our fortunes to him; whereupon he began to tell us likewise of his owne adventures, how that hee also was a man, by name Endymion, and rapt up long since from the Earth, as he was asleep, and brought hither, where he was made King of the Countrie, and said it was that region which to us below seemed to be the Moone. . . .'

At the time of Lucian's arrival at the Moon, Endymion was about to engage in battle with Phaethon, King of the people of the Sun— also an inhabited world, according to certain Stoic Philosophers. The reason of the quarrel was that some years earlier Endymion decided to plant a colony of his poorer subjects on another, uninhabited world, the Morning Star—presumably identical, even to Lucian, with the planet

Venus; but out of jealousy Phaethon had prevented Endymion's attempt at empire-building, and beaten him in battle, since when a state of war had existed between their two worlds.

Lucian and his companions agreed to join Endymion's army, were at once supplied each with a suit of armour and a royal vulture, and on the morrow set forth to battle. The forces to which they were joined consisted of various incredible regiments with ingenious names: besides the Vulture Dragoons were the Grassplume-riders, mounted on large birds with grass instead of feathers and wings like lettuce-leaves. There were also the Millet-shooters and the Garlic-fighters, besides the Flea-archers who came from the Great Bear and whose mounts were as large as twelve elephants. Phaethon's army consisted of Ant Dragoons and Sky-mosquitoes whose mounts were of a similarly outrageous size; Sky-dancers and Stalk-mushrooms were his infantry, and from the Dog Star came the dog-faced Puppy-corns, together with the Cloud-centaurs, who only turned up after the battle. But when they did turn up, they completely routed the Selenites (until then victorious), Lucian and his companions were taken prisoner, and Phaethon built a wall to keep the sun's light from shining on the Moon—thus causing a total eclipse. Endymion begged for terms, and the Moon became a tributary to the Sun, the Peace Treaty being a parody of that between Athens and Sparta as recorded by Thucydides.

Lucian gives no description of his short sojourn in the Sun, but his account of the world in the Moon and its inhabitants is full and fantastic.

The Selenites, he tells us, are all men, and their children are either born from the calf of the leg, or else grown upon trees and released from acorns a cubit in length—rather like the Plant Men in Edgar Rice Burroughs's Martian stories—and they do not die, but dissolve into air when they arrive at the correct age.

As for other peculiarities . . . 'they hold it a great ornament to be bald, for hairie persons are abhord with them . . . such beards as they have, are growing a little above their knees; they have no nailes on their feete, for their whole foote is all but one toe', and they have tails like cabbage-leaves which are not damaged however often they fall on them.

'One kinde of food is common to them all: for they kindle a fire and broyle frogges upon the coales, which are with them in infinite numbers flying in the aire; and whilst they are broyling, they sit round about them, as it were about a table, and lappe up the smoake that riseth from them, and feast themselves therewith—and this is all their feeding. For their drinke, they have aire beaten in a morter, which yeeldeth a kinde of moysture much like unto dew. . . .' Instead of grapes for wine-making, they have hailstones growing on vines, which produce nothing but water.

More wonderful still, 'they have eyes to take in and out as please themselves: and when a man is so disposed, hee may take them out and lay them by till hee have occasion to use them, and then put them in and see againe. Many, when they have lost their owne eies, borrow of others: for the rich have many lying by them . . . I saw also another strange thing in the same court: a mightie great glasse lying upon the top of a pit of no great depth, whereinto, if a man descend, hee shall heare everything that is spoken upon the Earth; if he but looke into the glasse, he shall see all cities, and all nations as well as if hee were among them. There had I the sight of all my friends, and the whole countrie about: whether they saw mee or not, I cannot tell; but if they believe it not to be so, let them take paines to goe thither themselves, and they shall find my words true . . .'.

So Lucian ends his adventures on the Moon; Endymion presents him and his companions with Lunar robes made of spun glass and woven bronze, and their ship is guided back into the terrestrial ocean by a regiment of Vulture Dragoons, there to meet with adventures that leave Odysseus or the Argonauts well in the shade. But they did not again visit the Moon, nor any other of the heavenly bodies.

CHAPTER TWO

SAINTS AND SCIENTISTS

THE translation of Lucian by Francis Hickes in 1634 came at a date when popular belief in the Copernican Astronomy was spreading and the time was ripe for the serious, or fictitious, consideration of a voyage to the Moon.

But in England, as in Greece, Lunar folklore still lingered in the country districts, and was finding its way into the nursery, and thence to literature.

The tale was already old of that ancient stick-gatherer who insisted upon pursuing his otherwise harmless profession even on the Sabbath day. How, one unlucky Sunday he had the misfortune to meet an Angel unawares, that Heavenly Visitant being concealed by an impenetrable disguise.

'Hallo, old man, what are you up to—gathering sticks on the Sabbath?' cried the Celestial Stranger, duly horrified at what he saw.

'None of your business,' growled the stick-gatherer, who was obviously unrelated to Wordsworth's sublime peasants. 'Sunday or Monday, it makes no difference to me! I'll gather sticks just when I choose!'

'Not so!' cried the Heavenly Visitant sternly, as he flung off his disguise. 'If you cannot keep even a Sunday here, you shall keep an eternal Moon-day in the skies!'

And up went the old man, complete with his bundle of sticks, to say nothing of the dog, who takes the place of the Malayan rat.

'All that I have to say is, to tell you that the lantern is the moon; I, the man-i'-th'-moon; this thorn-bush, my thorn-bush; and this dog, my dog,' as Starveling told his audience at the court of Duke Theseus on the memorable occasion when he came in 'to disfigure or to present the person of moonshine'.

Nursery-lore in the eighteenth century brought the old man back to Earth before he was wanted:

> The Man in the Moon
> Came down too soon,
> And asked his way to Norwich.

He went by the south
And burnt his mouth
With supping hot pease porridge!

His customary diet was given as early as 1660 in a ballad which ends:

The Man in the Moon drinks Clarret;
With Powder-beef, Turnep and Carret,
A Cup of old Malago Sack
Will fire his bush at his back.

The Man in the Moon might come down to Earth, but visits to his abode were unknown in the Middle Ages, until Lucian's works came back with the Renaissance. But they cannot have seemed strange, since during preceding centuries several Saints, and a more mundane traveller or two, had made voyages almost as remarkable.

Visits to Heaven and Hell are, strictly speaking, outside the scope of this book, and so is St. Brandan's Atlantean isle somewhere between Moy Mell, home of the Daoine Sidh of Gaelic tradition and the Garden of the Hesperides of which Homer told.

But the Apocalyptic Journey into Space has a certain connection with the voyages of such adventurers as Domingo Gonsales and Cyrano de Bergerac. These stem from the Revelation of St. John, who became almost a professional guide to such travellers, though the Patriarch Enoch in a Jewish work of much the same date was led by the Angel Raphael. Enoch came, on his way through the circles of Heaven, 'far to the east of the earth, and I came to the Garden of Righteousness'.

This is the Earthly Paradise, usually situated at the world's eastern verge, and tenanted by the Phoenix who sits on his Tree above the Well at the World's End. But there was some confusion of paradises, and a charming Anglo-Saxon writer, in a work known as 'The Phoenix Homily', told how the angel took St. John and brought him to Paradise ('Neorxenewange') which is neither 'in Heaven nor on Earth', but 'hangeth most wonderfully between Heaven and Earth', and is forty fathoms higher than the highest level reached by Noah's flood. 'Therein is neither frost nor snow nor hail nor rain, but there is *fons vite*, that is to say, the Well of Life', which at stated times floods all the land. 'And there is a fair wood that is called "Radion *saltus*" [the shining grove]; and there is a tree, so erect, so straight, so high,

23

ALBRIGHT COLLEGE LIBRARY 164658

that no earthly man may see how high, nor can he say what kind of tree it is.'

Here no leaves fall, and the birds sing; the sun shines always, and is seven times more bright than upon this earth. The Phoenix dwells in this grove, 'lord over all the bird kind. Once each week this fair fowl bathes himself in the Well of Life; and then flieth the fowl and sits upon the highest tree, over against the hot sun. Then shineth he like the sunlight, and glittereth as if he were of gold. His feathers are like the feathers of angels, his breast and bill shine bright'. After a thousand years the Phoenix grows old: 'then he gathers together from all over Paradise the most precious twigs, and heaps up the same, and by God's might and the light of the Sun the heap is kindled. Then falleth the Phoenix into the midst of that great fire, and is burned all to dust. Then on the third day ariseth the fair fowl Phoenix from the dead, and groweth young again, and fareth to the Well of Life, and bathes himself therein, and waxeth fair of feather, as he were ever the fairest.'

The Apocalyptic journey died hard, and when Ariosto came to send his brave and adventurous knight Astolpho to the Moon in his chivalric epic *Orlando Furioso* at the beginning of the sixteenth century, the influence was still strong—and St. John was still the Heavenly Guide.

Astolpho made his journey in search of the lost wits of the unfortunate Orlando who had been driven mad by his unlawful love for a Paynim maid. Riding upon his hippogryph—a winged horse like Pegasus— Astolpho came to Paradise, on the summit of a great and unscalable mountain. After stopping for a while to admire the beauties and the wonders of this other Eden, the jewels spread everywhere in rich profusion, the brightly coloured birds, the perfection of eternal Summer, he entered the great shining palace—glowing more crimson bright than any carbuncle—and found St. John waiting for him there. The aged apostle told him that they must journey to the Moon, the nearest planet to this Earth, for there all things lost here were stored, Orlando's wits amongst them.

When evening came, accordingly, they entered into the very chariot which had carried Elias up to Heaven. To it were harnessed four goodly coursers more red than flame, and as soon as St. John had gathered up the reins in his hands, away they flew, rising at a steep angle and then spiralling up until they came to the Region of Fire which was popularly supposed to surround the Earth. The burning properties of this belt were miraculously suspended for the saint and his companion to pass in safety.

> *Through all this elemental flame they soar'd,*
> *And next the circle of the Moon explor'd,*
> *Whose spheric face in many a part outshin'd*
> *The polish'd steel from spots and rust refin'd:*
> *Its orb increasing to their nearer eyes,*
> *Swell'd like the Earth, and seem'd an earth in size,*
> *Astolpho wondering view'd what to our sight*
> *Appears a narrow round of silver light:*
> *Nor could he thence, but with a sharpen'd eye*
> *And bending brow, our lands and seas descry,*
> *The lands and seas, which, lost in vap'rous shade*
> *So far remote, to viewless forms decay'd.*
> *Far other lakes than ours this region yields,*
> *Far other rivers, and far other fields;*
> *Far other valleys, plains, and hills supplies,*
> *Where stately cities, towns and castles rise;*
> *Where lonely woods extensive tracts contain,*
> *And sylvan nymphs pursue the savage train.*

Landed on the Moon, Astolpho followed his divine guide through the Lunar scenery, which was of a classical nature with wooded parkland 'where nymphs forever chased the panting prey'. They came at last to a wide valley, stored in marvellous fashion with all things lost on Earth—from fame, fortune, empty desires, broken vows, to crowns, bribes, the 'lays of venal poets', women's wiles, and finally sense itself stored in vessels ranging from tiny vials to great vases.

There Astolpho came upon Orlando's missing wits, set carefully in a great heroic vase as became the lost senses of so great a paladin. By them he found a smaller vial which held such senses of his own as he had already lost in the ordinary course of life; and this, by the grace of the Saint who accompanied him, Astolpho raised to his nostrils, and straightway all wisdom returned to him, nor did he lose any of it again in after days.

Then, carrying with difficulty the great vase which held Orlando's scattered wits, Astolpho followed his divine guide once more, and came next beneath 'a stately dome' where sit for ever the Three Fates spinning the lives of all men, both living and to come; and in this House of Fortune the knight saw many wonders to interest both him and Ariosto's contemporaries.

When these marvels were exhausted, St. John led Astolpho once more to the flying chariot, and they returned to Earth as swiftly and easily as they had come, 'The wheels smoothe turning through the yielding air,' and brought back sanity to the stricken Orlando.

By the end of the sixteenth century the idea of the Moon and even the planets as inhabited worlds was becoming an accepted theme, the thought that the Moon might be visited almost a legitimate aspiration. Spenser voiced this feeling in *The Faerie Queene* when he wrote:

> *Why then should witlesse man so much misweene*
> *That nothing is but that which he hath seene?*
> *What if within the Moones fair shining spheare,*
> *What if in every other starre unseene*
> *Of other worldes he happily should heare?*
> *He wonder would much more: yet such to some appeare.*

Visits, however, were still divine or visionary: the serious scientist and astronomer Johann Kepler wrote a Moon-voyage in the guise of a *Somnium* in or shortly after 1608, which circulated in manuscript though it was not published until 1634, some years after his death.

Its hero, Duracotus, is taken in Kepler's dream by a Daemon or Spirit of the Moon to this new world of Levania. There is little to interest us in the voyage, but Kepler's description of the Moon itself is more vivid than any in literature before H. G. Wells made Professor Cavor and Mr. Bedford his First Men in the Moon at the beginning of the present century—which owes much to Kepler.

With vivid, rather nightmare-like reality Kepler describes the Lunar night of fifteen days' duration, 'dreadful with uninterrupted shadow'; the intense cold of this long night and the merciless heat of as long a day; the exaggerated height of the mountains, the unbelievable depths of valleys and fissures in the rock. In Levania whatever is born is of monstrous size—creatures and plants that flower and fade in a single Moon-day, reptilian echoes of the antediluvian world, who, if they are to live through the night, must seek shelter from the cold in vast subterranean caves, or beneath the waters of the deep Lunar seas.

Kepler's voyage to the Moon was a dream, however accurate the descriptions of the Lunar landscape, and Duracotus had a Spirit for his guide. Even as late as 1656 the Jesuit, scientist and traveller Athanasius Kircher sent his hero Theodidactus on a tour of the Heavens accompanied, and apparently carried, by the angel Cosmiel. The object of this work is to teach the system of astronomy propounded by Tycho Brahe, and oppose that of Copernicus on theological grounds, and the book is full of diagrams and scientific technicalities. Only at one moment is there any feeling of a visit to a real world, after a long dissertation by Cosmiel.

'Scarcely had he spoken,' says Theodidactus, 'when lo! and behold, I found myself deposited on the Moon. Oh Lord! What sights do I gaze upon never beheld ere this!'

'Bear up!' replies Cosmiel, 'and let us hasten, so that everything may appear more clearly at close quarters.'

'So speaking,' continues Theodidactus, 'he set me on the highest peak of a Lunar mountain, and a new and unaccustomed world met my eyes. Here everything was novel and unexpected, and a spectacle was opened up before me utterly different in all respects from what is found on earth. There were deep valleys, mountain chains, a vast expanse of ocean, of seas and of lakes; there were islands set in the ocean and surrounded by lofty mountains; rivers breaking out of the mountains emptied themselves into the sea by winding courses. . . .'

The idea that the Moon was a habitable world with seas and rivers endured for a long time, and began with Galileo: it was still credited by the unscientific at the time of the Great Lunar Hoax in 1835.

Milton, who had visited Galileo, compared Satan's shield in *Paradise Lost* to

> *The Moon, whose orb*
> *Through optic glass the Tuscan artist views*
> *At evening, from the top of Fesole,*
> *Or in Val d'Arno, to descry new lands,*
> *Rivers, or mountains, on her spotty globe.*

And Kepler, Galileo's contemporary, was even more definite: 'I take the dark areas to be seas, I take the bright to be land,' he declared.

Hevelius, another serious astronomer, prepared a Map of the Moon in 1647, in his great work *Selenographia*, many names on which are still in use, in spite of our knowledge that the Moon is dry and waterless. You may still find on Moon-maps 'The Sea of Clouds', 'The Sea of Dews', 'The Sea of Nectar', 'The Sea of Fruitfulness', or 'The Sea of Tranquillity'; and there is 'The Lake of Dreams' as well as 'The Lake of Death'; there is 'Rainbow Bay' and 'The Gulf of Surges', besides 'The Pool of the Mists' and 'The Pool of Sleep'.

On dry land you can find some four hundred mountains and craters all duly named: Plato, for example, has a crater of a hundred miles in diameter, the darkest spot on the Moon, and Copernicus, a mere fifty-six miles across, but with sheer cliffs and precipices rising to some twelve thousand feet in height.

The Moon seemed very accessible in the seventeenth century, and it was even included in such a World Geography as that of Peter Heylyn in 1652—though, to be sure, he adopted a sceptical attitude and grouped it with such more or less imaginary lands as Australia, New Guinea, the Solomon Islands, Utopia, New Atlantis and Fairyland.

'The New World in the Moon,' says Heylyn, 'was first of Lucian's discovering . . . But of late times, that World which he there fancyed and proposed but as a fancy only, is become a matter of more serious Debate; and some have laboured with great pains to make it probable that there is another *World* in the Moon, inhabited as this is by persons of divers Languages, Customs, Politics and Religions; and more then so, some means and ways proposed to Consideration for maintaining an entercourse and Commerce betwixt that and this. . . .'

Conditions on the Moon, and the possibility of getting there were treated seriously by a learned Bishop of Chester, John Wilkins, in 1638, his interesting book bearing the typically descriptive title of the period: *A Discovery of a New World, or, A Discourse Tending to prove, that 'tis Probable there may be another Habitable World in the Moon. With a Discourse Concerning the Probability of a Passage thither. Unto which is Added, A Discourse Concerning a New Planet, Tending to prove, That 'tis Probable Our Earth is one of the Planets.*[1]

While Wilkins maintained that the Moon was inhabited, he would not commit himself about the inhabitants—'concerning whom there might be many Difficult Questions raised; as, whether that place be more Inconvenient for Habitation than our World (as Kepler thinks); whether they are the Seed of Adam, whether they are in a Blessed Estate, or else what means there may be for their Salvation? with many other such Uncertain Enquiries, which I shall willingly Omit'.

Troubled by the absence of Scriptural authority regarding the spiritual state of the Moon men, Wilkins felt that it 'may be more Probable that the Inhabitants of that World are not Men as we are, but some other kind of Creatures which Bear some Proportion, and

[1]This is the title-page of the fourth edition (1684), the first differed very slightly.

Likeness to our Natures. Or it may be, they are of a quite Different Nature from anything here Below, such as no Imagination can Describe, our Understandings being Capable only of such things as have Entered by our Senses, or else such Mixed Natures as may be Composed from them. Now, there may be many other Species of Creatures beside those that are already known in the World; there is a great Chasme betwixt the Nature of Men and Angels; It may be the Inhabitants of the Plannets are of a Middle Nature between both these. 'Tis not Improbable that God might Create some of all Kinds, that so he might more Compleatly Glorifie himself in the Works of his Power and Wisdom'.

Having dismissed the Moon's inhabitants with these sensible words, Wilkins went on to comment that 'All that hath been said, Concerning the People of the New World, is but Conjectural, and full of Uncertainties; nor can we ever look for any Evident or more Probable Discoveries in this kind, unless there be some hopes of Inventing means for our Conveyance thither'.

Wilkins was serenely hopeful of this consummation: 'Time will come,' he declared, 'when the Indeavours of after Ages, shall bring such things to Light as now lie hid in Obscurity. Arts are not yet come to their Solstice. But the Industry of Future Times, Assisted with the Labours of their Fore-Fathers, may reach that Height which we could not Attain to.'

Some Drake or Columbus of the air will surely come, declared Wilkins, and 'when ever that Art is Invented, or any other, whereby a Man may be Conveyed some Twenty Miles high, or thereabouts, then, 'tis not altogether Improbable that some or other may be Successful in this Attempt'.

Wilkins then went on to list the difficulties to be overcome: the natural heaviness of a man's body which makes it unsuitable for flying; the great distance to the Moon; the extreme coldness of the upper air, and the extreme thinness of it.

Even supposing a man could fly a thousand miles in a day, reasoned Wilkins, it would take him half a year to reach the Moon, and 'how were it Possible for any to Tarry so long'.

'For Diet,' observed Wilkins, 'I suppose there could be no trusting to the Fancy of Philo the Jew who thinks that the Musick of the Sphears should supply the Strength of Food. Nor can we well Conceive how a Man should be Able to Carry so much Luggage with him as might serve for his *Viaticum* in so Tedious a Journey.

'But if he could: he must have some time to Rest and Sleep in. And I believe he shall scarce find any Lodgings by the Way. No Inns to Entertain Passengers, nor any Castles in the Air, unless they be Inchanted ones.'

Nevertheless Wilkins did not despair, for he was of the opinion that at a certain distance above the Earth all gravity would cease, and that 'without the Sphere of the Earth's Magnetical Vigor', which he placed at twenty miles high, 'a Man might there stand as firmly in the Open Air, as now upon the Earth. And if he might Stand there, why might he not also Go there? And if so, then there is a Possibility likewise of having other Conveniences for Travelling'.

Wilkins went on to reason that if there was no gravity, we need expend no energy; and if no energy were expended, might we not be able to do without food—just as people do when plunged in a long sleep or insensibility, or as animals do who hibernate: 'Or, if we must needs Feed upon something else, why may not smells nourish us? Plutarch and Pliny, and divers other Ancients, tell us of a Nation in India that lived only upon Pleasing Odors.' Or even, he ended, 'The Purity of the Aethereal Air, being not mixed with any Improper Vapours, may be so Agreeable to our Bodys, as to yeeld us suficient Nourishment.'

Finally, after considering the thin air likely to be encountered on the journey—against which he suggested moistened sponges—Wilkins came to the all-important question of the method of travelling to the Moon.

There seemed to him to be three possible methods: ' 'Tis not perhaps impossible that a Man may be able to Fly, by the Application of Wings to his own Body; As Angels are Pictured, as Mercury and Daedalus are feigned, and as hath been attempted by divers, particularly by a Turk in Constantinople, as Busbequius relates.'

For the second means, 'If there be such a great *Ruck* [the 'Roc' of *The Arabian Nights*] in Madagascar, as Marcus Polus the Venetian mentions, the Feathers in whose Wings are Twelve Foot Long, which can scoop up a Horse and his Rider, or an Elephant, as our Kites do a Mouse; why then 'tis but Teaching one of these to carry a Man, and he may Ride up thither, as Ganymed does upon an Eagle.

'Or if neither of these Ways will serve: Yet I do seriously, and upon good Grounds, affirm it possible to make a Flying Chariot, in which a Man may sit, and give such a Motion unto it, as shall convey him through the Air. And this perhaps might be made large enough to carry divers Men at the same time, together with Food for their *Viaticum*, and Commodities for Traffique . . . I conceive it were no difficult matter (if a Man had leisure) to shew more particularly the means of composing it. . . .

'So that notwithstanding all these seeming impossibilities, 'tis likely enough, that there may be a means invented of Journeying to the Moon. And how happy shall they be that are first successful in this attempt!'

CHAPTER THREE

HOW GONSALES VISITED THE MOON

IT was to be expected in the early years of the seventeenth century, when so many people, from eminent scientists and theologians down, were discussing the probability that the Moon was inhabited, and the possibility of visiting it, that writers of fiction should try their hands at describing imaginary voyages to this new world.

Ariosto and Kepler, with their supernatural means of transport, were the only imaginary visitors since Lucian, so far as Bishop Wilkins knew when he published his *Discovery of a New World . . . in the Moon* in 1638; but in that very year appeared the first, and one of the most important Space-flights in English.

In his third edition in 1640 Wilkins added a couple of pages in reference to this little volume: 'Having thus finished this Discourse, I chanced upon a late fancy to this purpose under the fained Name of *Domingo Gonsales*, written by a late Reverend and Learned Bishop: In which there is delivered a pleasant and well contrived Fancy concerning a Voyage to this other world.'

This 'fancy' was *The Man in the Moone, or A Discourse of a Voyage Thither* (1638), and its concealed author was Francis Godwin (1562–1633), Bishop first of Llandaff, and then of Hereford. He was the author of *A Catalogue of the Bishops of England* (1601) which was revised from time to time by him, and was a standard work for many years. He also wrote (in Latin) an anonymous pamphlet called *Nuncius Inanimatus*—'The Mysterious Messenger'—by 'Ed. M. Ch.', published in 1629 with the whimsical imprint 'In Utopia' which deals with the sending of secret messages and messages requiring speed. After dealing with pigeon-post and messages sent by swallows, Godwin becomes mysterious about his own supposed invention—'an Inter-Nuncio, who is not a Bird, neither is he winged, no not so much as a living Creature, and yet notwithstanding by many degrees goes beyond any Creature whatsoever, though never so swift in celerity of motion'. But the whole work seems to be an elaborate hoax, for we are never told what Godwin's messenger is, though he can carry a message from London to Bristol, Wells or Exeter in a few moments: 'This he will do, will do it I say, if there be need, or else I am the vainest person of all that know how either to speake or write.'

When *The Man in the Moone* was written is uncertain, some of Godwin's contemporaries placing it before 1600, while internal evidence suggests that it was at least revised during the last few years of his life. But from its publication in 1638 it became a popular favourite for two centuries, and was read, quoted and sometimes imitated by writers from Cyrano de Bergerac to Jules Verne.

The story tells of the adventures of the noble Spaniard Domingo Gonsales, who ran away from the University of Salamanca and became a gentleman of fortune in the Low Countries where he finally killed a man in a duel and went hastily to sea on a voyage to the East Indies.

Grievously sick on the return voyage, he was put ashore with his trusty native servant Diego on the island of St. Helena—'the only paradice, I thinke, that the earth yeeldeth, of the healthfulnesse of the Aire there, the fruitfulnesse of the soile, and the abundance of all manner of things necessary for sustaining the life of man'.

Here Gonsales and Diego remained for a year with all that they could wish in the way of flowers and fruits, animals and birds. Among the latter Gonsales noticed 'huge flocks of a certaine kinde of wild *Swans* that like unto our *Cuckoes* and *Nightingales*, at a certaine season of the yeare doe vanish away, and are no more to be seen'.

It should be noted that in Godwin's day there was much speculation as to where migrating birds went to spend the winter.

On the island Gonsales and Diego lived at some distance from one another, and signalled messages across several miles by lights, smokes and finally with the aid of birds. For this last method Gonsales needed to catch his messengers young; and seeking for suitable chicks, he narrates how 'I found great store of a certaine kinde of wild *Swan* (before mentioned) feeding almost altogether upon the prey, and (that which is somewhat strange), partly of *Fish*, partly of *Birds*, having (which is also no lesse strange) one foote with Clawes, talons, and pounces, like an *Eagle*, and the other whole like a Swan or water fowle'.

Of these 'Gansas' as he calls them, Gonsales took some thirty or forty young ones, bred them up by hand, and taught them 'to come at call affarre off, not using any noise but onely the shew of a white Cloth', and by the time they were six months old they would carry messages and small parcels between Gonsales and Diego.

'Having prevailed thus farre,' says Gonsales, 'I began to cast in my head how I might doe to joyne a number of them together in bearing of some great burthen: which if I could bring to passe, I might enable a man to fly and be carried in the ayre.'

Gonsales, after several experiments, constructed with the aid of pulleys a machine which successfully carried a lamb into the air, 'whose happinesse I much envied, that he should be the first living creature to take possession of such a device'.

It was not long now before Gonsales made his first experiment in taking the place of this fortunate lamb: 'having provided all things necessary, I placed my selfe with all my trinckets upon the top of a rocke at the Rivers mouth, and putting my selfe at full sea upon an Engine [of which a delightful wood-cut is supplied] I caused *Diego* to advance his Signall: whereupon my Birds presently arose, 25 in number, and carried mee over lustily to the other rocke on the other side, being about a Quarter of a league. . . . When I was once over in safety, O how did my heart even swell with joy and admiration of mine owne invention!'

Not long after his first successful flight the Spanish fleet arrived, and took off Gonsales and Diego, complete with the flying-machine and twenty-five Gansas. But on the voyage to Spain 'we encountred with a fleet of the *English* some 10 leagues from the *Island* of *Tenerik*, one of the *Canaries*'.

Gonsales escaped from the ship by means of his flying-machine, and landed on the high mountain of El Pico. To his distress he found that 'it is inhabited by a Savage kinde of people that live upon the sides of that hill, the top whereof is alwayes covered with Snow, and held for the monstrous height and steepnesse not to be accessible either for man or beast'.

To escape from the savages, Gonsales mounted once more upon his machine—but there befell him 'the strangest Chance that ever happened to any mortall man', for the Gansas 'like so many horses had gotten the bitt betweene their teeth', and flew with him to the top of El Pico 'where they say never man came before, being in all estimation at least 15 leagues in height perpendicularly upward above the ordinary levell of the Land and Sea'.

This was startling enough, but more amazing things were to follow. The Gansas, realising that it was now their time to migrate, 'as our Cuckoes and Swallowes doe', set out once more and 'to my unspeakable feare and amazement strooke bolt upright, and never did linne towring upward, and still upward for the space, as I might guesse, of one whole hower; toward the end of which time mee thought I might perceive them to labour lesse and lesse; till at length, O incredible thing, they forbare moving anything at all, and yet remained unmoveable, as stedfastly as if they had beene upon so many perches; the Line slacked, neither I nor the Engine moved at all, but abode still as having no manner of weight'.

Gonsales had, in fact, passed beyond the magnetic attraction of the Earth, as it was sometimes believed to be in the days before gravity was properly understood.

'Truly I must confesse, the horror and amazement of that place was such, as if I had not been armed with a true *Spanish* courage and reso-lution, I must needs have died there with very feare!' The voyage of Gonsales is indeed one of the most awe-inspiring in all the fiction of Space-flight, since he alone of more serious astronauts travelled virtually without any car or flying chariot. As he sat on his tiny piece of wood, dangling on thin cords from his flock of Gansas, he was more isolated in the vastness between the Earth and the Moon than even the scientifically equipped adventurers of the latest 'scientifiction' venturing outside their Space-ship in their brightly coloured Space-suits.

'The next thing that did most trouble me,' continues Gonsales, 'was the swiftnesse of Motion, such as did even almost stop my breath. If I should liken it to an Arrow out of a Bow, or to a stone cast downe from the top of some high tower, it would come farre short, and short.'

Another thing which troubled Gonsales for a while, which later astronauts were spared, was his passage through Limbo, the region immediately outside the Earth's magnetism, where he was plagued with 'the Illusions of Devills and wicked spirits, who, the first day of my arrivall, came about mee in great numbers, carrying the shapes and likenesse of men and women, wondring at mee like so many Birds about an Owle, and speaking divers kindes of Languages.

'And here I saw onely a touch of the Sunnes absence for a little while once, ever after having him in my sight——', when he came beyond Limbo and was free once more of the plaguing spirits.

'Now shall I declare unto you the quality of the place in which I then was. The Clouds I perceived to be all under me, betweene mee and the earth. The starres, by reason it was alwaies day, I saw at all times alike, not shining bright, as upon the earth we are wont to see them in the night time, but of a whitish Colour, like that of the Moone in the daytime with us.

'Againe I must tell you that whether I lay quiet and rested, or else were carryed in the Ayre, I perceived myselfe still to be alwaies directly betweene the Moone and the earth. Whereby it appeareth that my *Gansas* took none other way than directly toward the Moone. . . .

'The ayre in that place I found quiet without any motion of wind, and exceeding temperate, neither hot nor cold. . . . Lastly now it is to be remembred that after my departure from the earth, I never felt any appetite of hunger or thirst.'

Meanwhile, being well past the region of the evil spirits, 'my *Gansas* began to bestir themselves, still directing their course toward the Globe or body of the Moone. And they made their way with that incredible swiftnesse as I thinke they gained not so little as Fifty Leagues in every hower. In that passage I noted three things very remarkable: one that the further we went, the lesser the Globe of the Earth appeared unto us, whereas still on the contrary side the Moone shewed her selfe more and more monstrously huge.

'Againe, the Earth (which ever I held in mine eye) did as it were mask itself with a Kind of Brightnesse like another Moone; and even as in the Moone we discerned certaine spots or Clouds, as it were, so did I then in the earth. But whereas the forme of those spots in the Moone continue constantly one and the same, these little and little did change every hower. The reason thereof I conceive to be this, that whereas the Earth according to her naturall motion, (for that such a motion she hath, I am now constrained to joyne in opinion with *Copernicus*,) turneth round upon her owne Axe every 24 howers from the *West* unto the *East*.

'There is yet one accident more befell me worthy of especiall remembrance: that during the time of my stay I saw as it were a kind of cloud of a reddish colour growing toward me, which continually growing nearer and nearer, at last I perceived to be nothing else but a huge swarme of Locusts———' Thus Gonsales solved the problem of whence the locusts came: it was from the Moon.

'After Eleven daies passage in this violent flight, I perceived that we began to approach neare unto another Earth, if I may so call it, being the Globe or very body of that starre which we call the Moone. . . . I perceived also that it was covered for the most part with a huge and mighty Sea, those parts only being drie Land which shew unto us here somewhat darker than the rest of her body. . . . As for the part which shineth so clearly in our eyes, it is even another Ocean, yet besprinckled heare and there with *Islands* which, for the littlenesse, so far off we cannot discern.

'The Earth by turning about had now shewed me all her parts twelve times when I finished my course: For when by my reckoning it seemed to be (as indeed it was) Tuesday the Eleventh day of *September* [1599], (at what time the Moone being two daies old was in the Twentieth degree of *Libra*), my *Gansas* staied their course as it was of one consent and tooke their rest for certaine howers; after which they tooke their flight, and within lesse then one hower set me upon the top of a very high hill in that other world, where immediately were presented unto mine eyes many most strange and unwonted sights.

'For first I observed that although the Globe of the Earth shewed much bigger there then the Moone doth unto us, even to the trebling of her diameter, yet all manner of things there were of largenesse and quantity 10, 20, I think I may say 30 times more then ours. Their trees at least three times so high as ours, and more then five times the breadth and thicknesse. So their herbes, Beasts and Birds; although to compare them with ours I know not well how, because I found not any thing there, any *species* either of *Beast* or *Bird* that resembled ours any thing at all, except *Swallowes*, *Nightingales*, *Cuckooes*, *Woodcockes*, *Batts*, and some kindes of wild *Fowle*, as also of such *Birds* as my *Gansas*, all of which (as I now well perceived) spend the time of their absence from us even there in that world.

'No sooner was I set downe upon the ground, But I was surprised with a most ravenous hunger and earnest desire of eating. Wherefore stepping unto the next tree, I fastened thereunto my engine, with my *Gansas*.

'Now while I stood musing and wondering, I heard my *Gansas* upon the sudden to make a great fluttering behind me. And looking back, I espied them to fall greedily upon a certaine shrub within the compasse of their lines, whose leaves they fed upon most earnestly; where heretofore I had never seene them to eat any manner of greene meate whatsoever. Whereupon stepping to the shrubb, I put a leafe of it between my teeth. I cannot expresse the pleasure I found in the tast thereof; such it was I am sure as if I had not with great discretion moderated my appetite, I had surely surfetted upon the same.'

'Scarcely had I ended this banquett, when upon a sudden I saw myselfe environed with a kind of people most strange, both for their feature, demeanure, and apparell. Their stature was most divers, but for the most part twice the height of ours; their colour and countenance most pleasing, and their habit such as I know not how to expresse. For neither did I see any kind of *Cloth*, *Silke*, or other stuffe to resemble the matter of that whereof their Clothes were made, neither (which is most strange of all other) can I devise how to describe the colour of them, being in a manner all clothed alike. It was neither blacke, nor white, yellow, nor redd, greene nor blew, nor any colour composed of these.

'But if you aske me what it was, then I must tell you it was a colour never seen in our earthly world, and therefore neither to be described unto us by any, nor to be conceived of one that never saw it. For as it were a hard matter to describe unto a man borne blind the difference betweene blew and Greene, so can I not bethinke my selfe any meane how to decipher unto you this *Lunar* colour, having no affinitie with any other that ever I beheld with mine eyes. Onely this I can say of it, that it was the most glorious and delightfull that can possibly be imagined; neither in truth was there any one thing that more delighted me, during my abode in that new world, than the beholding of that most pleasing and resplendent colour.

'It remaineth now that I speake of the Demeanure of this people, who presenting themselves unto me upon the sudden and that in such extraordinary fashion as I have declared; being strucken with a great amasement, I crossed my selfe, and cried out "*Jesus Maria!*"

'No sooner was the word *Jesus* out of my mouth, but young and old fell downe upon their knees, (at which I not a little rejoyced) holding up both their hands on high, and repeating all certaine words which I understood not.

'Then presently they all arising, one that was farre the tallest of them came unto me, and embraced me with great kindnesse, and giving order (as I partly perceived) unto some of the rest to stay by my *Birds*, he tooke me by the hand and leading me down toward the foote of the hill, brought me to his dwelling, being more than half a league from the place where I first alighted.

'It was such a building for beauty and hugenesse as all our world cannot shew any neere comparable to it. Yet such I saw afterwards elsewhere, as this might seeme but a Cottage in respect of them. There was not a doore about the house that was not 30 foote high, and twelve in breadth. The roomes were between 40 and 50 foote in height, and so all other proportions answerable. Neither could they well be much lesse, the Master inhabiting them being full 28 high.

'After I had rested myselfe with him the Value of one of our dayes, he ledd me some Five leagues off, unto the *Palace* of the *Prince* of the Country.

'This *Prince* whose stature was much higher than the former is called (as neere as I can by Letters declare it, for their sounds are not perfectly to be expressed by our characters) *Pylonas*, which signifieth in their Language *First*, if perhaps it be not rather a denotation of his dignity and authority, as being the prime Man in all those parts.

'In all those parts, I say. For there is one supreme *Monarch* amongst them, of stature yet much more huge then hee, commanding over al that whole *Orbe* of that world having under him 29 other Princes of exceeding great power, and every of them 24 others, whereof this *Pylonas* was one.

'The first ancestor of this great *Monarch* came out of the Earth (as they deliver) and by marriage with the inheretrice of that huge Monarchy, obtaining the government, left it unto his posteritie—who ever since have held the same, even for the space of 40 thousand daies or *Moones*, which amounteth unto 3077 yeeres.

'And his name being *Irdonozur*, his heires, unto this day, doe all assume unto themselves that name, hee, they say, having continued there well neere 400 *Moones*, and having begotten divers children, returned (by what meanes they declare not) unto the Earth againe. I doubt not but they may have their Fables, as well as we.'

Nevertheless Gonsales felt that this story might be true, since the Lunarians set such a high value on truth and knowledge, and since some of them lived to be a thousand years old by Earthly notation.

Pylonas, who was about seven hundred years old, received Gonsales graciously, and so did the Queen and the Princes, all of whom, from the highest to the lowest, fell upon their knees and prayed in their own language when Gonsales again spoke 'the holy name of our *Saviour*'. Gonsales then ran through a list of saints, but only when St. Martin was named 'they all bowed their bodies, and held up hands in signe of great reverence: the reason whereof I learned to bee that *Martin* in their language signifieth God'.

Pylonas, to whom Gonsales made a present of jewels, instructed a hundred of his followers to attend to his every want, to look after the precious Gansas, and in particular to teach him the Lunar language— but not to tell him certain secret things, 'marry, what those particulars were I might never by any means get knowledge'.

'Being dismissed,' Gonsales continues, 'I was affoorded all manner of necessaries that my heart could wish, so as it seemed unto me I was in a very *Paradise*, the pleasures whereof notwithstanding could not so over come mee as that the remembrance of my wife and children did not trouble mee much.'

Gonsales, however, began his sojourn on the Moon by sleeping for a fortnight, for, as he discovered, 'it commeth to passe there by a secret power and unresistable decree of nature, that when the day beginneth to appeare, and the Moone to bee enlightened by the *Sunne* beames, (which is at the first Quarter of the Moon) all such people as exceed not very much our stature inhabiting those parts, they fall into a dead sleepe, and are not possibly to be wakened till the *Sun* be sett and withdrawne out of their sight, even as *Owles* and *Batts* with us cannot indure the light, so wee there at the first approach of the day, begin to be amazed with it, and fall immediately into a slumber, which groweth by little and little into a dead sleepe, till this light depart from thence againe, which is not in 14 or 15 daies, to wit untill the last quarter.

'Mee thinkes now I heare some man to demand what manner of light there is in that world during the absence of the *Sunne*: to resolve you for that point, you shall understand that there is a light of two sorts. One of the *Sun* (which I might not endure to behold), and another of the Earth. That of the Earth was now at the highest, for that when the Moone is at the Change, then is the Earth (unto them in the Moon) like a full Moone with us; and as the Moone increaseth with us, so the light of the Earth decreaseth with them. I then found the light there (though the Sunne were absent) equall unto that with us in the day time, when the *Sun* is covered with clouds; but toward the quarter it little and little diminisheth, yet leaving still a competent light, which is somewhat strange.

'But much stranger is that which was reported unto me there, how that in the other Hemispheare of the *Moone* (I meane contrary to that I happened upon), where during halfe the Moone they see not the sunne, and the Earth never appeareth unto them, they have notwithstanding a kinde of light (not unlike by their description to our Moon light) which it seemeth the propinquitie of the starres and other Planets (so much neerer unto them then us) affordeth.

'Now give mee leave to settle my selfe to a long nights sleepe. My attendants take charge of my *Birds*, prepare my lodging, and signifie to mee by signes how it must bee with mee. It was about the middle of *September* when I perceived the Ayre to grow more cleare then ordinary, and with the increasing of the light I began to feele my selfe first dull, then heavy and willing to sleepe, although I had not lately been hindred from taking mine ease that way. I delivered my self at last into the custody of this sister of Death, whose prisoner I was for almost a fortnight after. Awaking then, it is not to bee beleeved how fresh, how nimble, how vigorous I found all the faculties both of my bodie and minde.'

Restored by this long sleep, Gonsales set himself to learn the Lunar language, which was current throughout the whole of this new world: not, he felt, so greatly to be wondered at as three quarters of the Moon's surface consisted of water. The language he found extremely difficult, as it resembled no language of this world, consisting 'not so much of words and Letters, as of tunes and uncouth sounds that no letters can express'.

Nonetheless, in two months' time Gonsales could converse reasonably well with his strange hosts, and at once began to enquire into their customs.

He found the Moon very much of a Utopia, or even of a Paradise: 'There is no want of anything necessary for the use of man. Food groweth every where without Labour, and that of all sorts to be desired.' The manufacture of clothes, houses or anything else is so easy that 'they doe nothing but as it were playing, and with pleasure'.

The women are so beautiful that no man could ever be false to his wife; and murder is unheard of—and indeed impossible 'for there is no wound to bee given which may not bee cured', and even a man's head can be joined onto his body again in the space of a few hours, aided by 'the juyce of a certaine herbe there growing'. But of all this absence of evil and crime 'the chief cause is that through an excellent disposition of that nature of people there, all, young and old, doe hate all manner of vice, and doe live in such love, peace, and amitie, as it seemeth to be another Paradise'.

True, there are a few who are born sinners; but the fact can be recognised at birth, and in some way which Gonsales could never discover these evilly disposed babies were sent to the Earth as changelings. Most of them were deposited in North America 'whose people I can easily beleeve to be wholly descended of them, partly in regard of their colour, partly also in regard of the continuall use of Tobacco which the *Lunars* use exceeding much'.

There is no need of Government on the Moon, nor of Courts of Justice, any more than of Physicians. When the inhabitants die, they celebrate their departure to a happier state with great joy, both on the part of the dying man and of those left behind. And the body does not decay, but is placed in storage so that 'most of them can shew their Ancestors bodies uncorrupt for many generations'.

Gonsales did not enter into many more details about the world in the Moon, as he tells us that he was keeping most of his information for a second book. During his stay he visited Irdonozur, the Monarch of the Moon, but was unable to explore a holy place called 'The Island of God', since anyone less than twenty-seven feet tall falls asleep as soon as he reaches it. This island was alone not under Irdonozur's jurisdiction, its ruler being Hiruch, the oldest man on the Moon, aged about five thousand years; Gonsales was also unable to meet the spiritual potentate Imozes; but with Irdonozur he got on well and received a present of three wondrous jewels called Poleastis, Machrus and Ebelus.

The first of these, which was the size of a hazel nut, and black in colour, had the property of retaining heat. If once placed in the fire these stones remained so hot (though still black) that 'they will make red hot any mettall that shall come within a foot of them, and being put in a Chimney will make a roome as warme as if a great Fire were kindled in the same'. The heat of the Poleastic was quenched in any kind of liquid, but it could be reheated any number of times.

The Machrus was more precious still; though only the size of a bean, this topaz-coloured stone was 'so shining and resplendent as, being placed in the midst of a large Church in the night time, it maketh it all as light as if a 100 Lamps were hanged up round about it'.

Yet the third stone, the Ebelus, was most precious of all. In size and shape it resembled a thick gold coin, but was of the indescribable Lunar colour, and 'so incredibly beautifull as a man should travell 1000 Leagues to behold it. . . . The one side of this, which is somewhat more Orient of Colour then the other, being clapt to the bare skin of a man, in any part of his bodie, it taketh away from it all weight or ponderousnesse; whereas turning the other side it addeth force unto the attractive beames of the Earth either in this world or that, and maketh the bodie to weigh halfe so much againe as it did before'.

One other interesting item in Moon-life was recorded by Gonsales: the Lunar method of transport: 'Now when I shall declare unto you the manner of our travell, you will say you scarce ever heard any thing more strange and incredible.

'Unto everyone of us there was delivered at our first setting forth two Fans of *Feathers*, not much unlike to those that our Ladies doe carrie in *Spaine* to make a coole Ayre unto themselves in the heat of *Summer*. The use of which Fans before I declare unto you, I must let you understand that the *Globe* of the *Moone* is not altogether destitute of an attractive Power; but it is so farre weaker than that of the earth, as if a man doe but spring upward with all his force, (as Dancers doe when they shew their activity by capering), he shall be able to mount 50 or 60 foote high, and then he is quite beyond all attraction of the *Moones* earth, falling downe no more, so as by the helpe of these Fans, as with wings, they conveigh themselves in the Ayre in a short space (although not with that swiftnesse that Birds doe) even whither they list.'

So Gonsales continued his interesting stay on the Moon for over a year and a half, until 'the moneth of *March* in the yeare 1601, at what time I earnestly besought *Pylonas* (as I had often done before) to give mee leave to depart, (though with never so great hazard of my life) backe into the Earth againe'.

Pylonas tried to persuade him to remain, pointing out how much happier life on the Moon was to that on Earth. But Gonsales professed anxiety to see his wife and children again, and was also filled with ambition to enjoy the fame and glory that would be his as the first man to visit the Moon, and he pointed out, when begged to stay at least another year, how 'my *Birds* began to droope, for want of their wonted migration, 3 of them were now dead, and if a few more failed, I was for ever destitute of all possibilitie of returning'.

With much ado Gonsales persuaded Pylonas who, having received permission from Irdonozur, at last consented. 'I trimmed up mine Engine, and took my leave of *Pylonas* who (for all the courtesie hee had done mee) required of mee but one thing, which was faithfully to promise him that, if ever I had meanes thereunto, I should salute from him *Elizabeth*, whom he tearmed the great *Queene* of *England*, calling her the most glorious of all women living, and indeed hee would often question with mee of her, and therein delighted so much as it seemed hee was never satisfied in talking of her.

'Upon the 29 day of *March*, being Thursday, 3 dayes after my awakeing from the last Moones light, I fastened my selfe to mine Engine, not forgetting to take with mee, besides the Jewels *Irdonozur* had given me, a small quantitie of Vitual . . .

'I let loose the raines unto my *Birds*, who with great greedinesse taking wing quickly carried mee out of their sight. It fel out with me as in my first passage, I never felt either hunger or thirst, till I arrived in *China* upon a high mountain some 5 Leagues from the high and mighty City of *Pachin*.

'This Voyage was performed in lesse then 9 dayes. I heard no newes by the way of these ayrie men which I had seen in my ascending.

'Nothing stayed my journey any whit at all: whether it was the earnest desire of my *Birds* to return to the Earth, where they had missed one season, or that the attraction of the Earth, so much stronger then that of the Moone, furthered their labour; so it came to passe, although now I had 3 *Birds* wanting of those I carried forth with mee.

'For the first 8 dayes my *Birds* flew before, and I with the Engine was as it were drawne by them.

'The Ninth day when I began to approach unto the Clouds, I perceived my selfe and mine Engine to sincke towards the Earth, and go before them.

'I was then horribly afraid, lest my *Birds* not being able to beare our weight, they being so few, should bee constrained to precipitate both mee and themselves headlong to the Earth. Wherefore I thought it no lesse then needfull to make use of the *Ebelus*, (one of the stones bestowed upon me by *Irdonozur*), which I clapped to my bare flesh within my hose; and it appeared manifestly thereupon unto mee that my *Birds* made their way with much greater ease then before, as being lightned of a great burthen; neither doe I thinke it possible for them to have let mee downe safely unto the Earth without that helpe.'

And so ended Gonsales's strange journey. For in China he was seized and imprisoned as a magician, and was still there, though allowed a great measure of freedom, when he wrote the account of his wonderful experiences and sent it by the help of some Jesuit missionaries in Pekin, to be published 'as a forerunner of my return. . . . With them also did I lay a foundation for my returne, the blessed houre whereof I doe with patience expect; that by inriching my Country with the knowledge of hidden mysteries I may once reape the glory of my fortunate misfortunes'.

CHAPTER FOUR

CYRANO IN THE MOON AND SUN

Francis Godwin's account of Gonsales's adventures is the most important journey into other worlds before the nineteenth century, and its influence—direct or indirect—continued to be apparent until recent times: it was probably only Jules Verne and H. G. Wells who completely superseded him.

But *The Man in the Moone's* influence was deflected from the straight path of adventure and fantasy by the brilliant satirical inventions of the French wit Cyrano de Bergerac, that almost legendary Gascon who is best known now as the hero of Rostand's play.

Cyrano de Bergerac (1619–1655), the superb swordsman with the big nose, might have been a character in a romance by Dumas or Stanley Weyman: indeed he was a member of the Gascon Guard of the period described in *The Three Musketeers* and *Under the Red Robe*: he fought more duels than D'Artagnan and gambled as wildly as Gil de Berault. But after being seriously wounded on active service in 1639 and again in the following year, he forswore the military life, and allied himself instead with the wits and scholars of the day—though he did not cease to use his sword when occasion demanded.

Many of Cyrano's works circulated in manuscript years before they were printed. Some were ephemeral political pamphlets; there were occasional verses, a comedy, a verse tragedy. There was also *Histoire Comique. Contenant les Estats et Empires de la Lune*, first published in 1657 but written nearly ten years earlier and read widely before publication. In 1662 his last, unfinished work was added, which described a similar voyage to the Sun. The Moon book was translated into English in 1659, and the two together in 1687 in what became the popular edition for over a century.

Cyrano knew Godwin's book well (*The Man in the Moone* was translated into French in 1648), and probably derived the idea of his own Space-flights from it. But his purpose was quite different from Godwin's, since once he had reached the Moon or the Sun he used his new worlds merely for the purpose of satirising the old—an unfortunate departure, however well he did it, which was to influence the stories of journeys into other worlds for nearly two centuries.

Cyrano took his voyage to the Moon, so he tells us, because when he told his friends that the Moon was a world just like ours, they merely laughed at him, and were not even impressed when he quoted to them the opinions of Copernicus and Kepler.

So, full of his determination to make the voyage and prove his friends in the wrong, Cyrano retired to a house in the country to study the problem. He soon thought of several excellent methods, and began without any very careful consideration of the consequences to put the easiest into practice.

He collected dew enough to fill a number of small bottles which he fastened about his waist: for the Sun, he had observed, always drew up the dew. He was not mistaken: up went the dew, taking the bottles with it; and up went the bottles, carrying Cyrano triumphantly into the sky.

But when he was well above the clouds he suddenly realised that he was being pulled faster and faster towards the Sun. This was not at all what he wanted, so he began breaking the bottles until the dew in the remainder was not sufficient to keep him up and he sank gently back to Earth.

Here a surprise awaited him: he was no longer in Paris, but in a wild land where naked savages gathered round him. After frightening these away he came upon a band of French soldiers from whom he discovered that he was not in France at all, but in Canada. Then he realised that the Earth had turned under him, so that naturally he had gone straight up in Paris and come straight down a few hours later on the other side of the Atlantic.

Cyrano was kindly entertained by the Viceroy of 'New France', but still hankered after the Moon. So at night he went out to study the satellite, and to construct a flying-machine which had wings and a 'spring', though he gave no description of how it worked.

On St. John's Eve, the Moon being full, Cyrano set out again. But when he cast himself in his machine from the top of a cliff, he found that he had made a miscalculation again, and that both he and his invention merely crashed to the ground. Much bruised, Cyrano retired to his room, comforted himself with a bottle of cordial, and rubbed his bruised body all over with beef-marrow.

Quite eased of his discomfort, Cyrano set out to recover his flying machine. But to his consternation he found that the soldiers of the garrison had carried it into the middle of the market place of Quebec and fastened rockets all round the back of it. Their idea was to launch it into the air, when the 'spring' would move its great wings, and the rockets make everyone who saw it take the thing for a fire-breathing dragon.

They were actually lighting the fuses when Cyrano reached the market-place, and 'the pain of seeing the work of my hands in such peril affected me so much that I rushed forward to grasp the arm of the soldier who was about to fire it. I seized his slow-match and cast myself furiously into the machine to break off the fireworks which surrounded it; but I came too late, for I had scarcely set my two feet in it when I was carried off into the clouds.

'The fearful horror that dismayed me did not so thoroughly overwhelm the faculties of my soul but that I could recollect afterwards all that happened to me at this moment. You must know then that the flame had no sooner consumed one line of rockets (for they had placed them in sixes by means of a fuse which ran along each half-dozen), when another set caught fire and then another, so that the blazing powder delayed my peril by increasing it. The rockets at length ceased through the exhaustion of material and, while I was thinking that I should leave my head on the summit of a mountain, I felt (without my having stirred) my elevation continue; and my machine, taking leave of me, fell towards the Earth'.

But Cyrano continued gloriously on his way, for the Moon having just begun to wane drew up the beef-marrow with which he had anointed himself so liberally, and of course drew him with it. (That the waning Moon sucked up the marrow of animals was a popular superstition very firmly held at the time.)

When he was three-quarters of the way between the Earth and the Moon, Cyrano suddenly turned a violent somersault, and began falling towards the new world, on which he landed with such force that he was knocked insensible. When he recovered consciousness, 'I found myself under a tree, entangled with three or four rather large branches which I had snapped off in my fall and my face moistened with an apple which had been crushed against it.

'As you shall know very soon, this place was happily the Earthly Paradise and the tree I fell on none other than the Tree of Life. You may well suppose that without this miraculous chance I should have been dead a thousand times'.

Whether the Earthly Paradise might not be in the Moon was seriously debated by the learned at the beginning of the seventeenth century, and Marmaduke Carver as late as 1666 in *A Discourse of the Terrestrial*

Paradise complained that 'some have sought for Paradise under the orb of the Moon, or far above the tops of the highest mountains, without the vierge of this habitable world. . . . And indeed where not, where a wanton fancy or an ignorant imprudence is pleased to place it? But (which is worst of all) beside the mischief hereby occasioned to believers, it hath opened the mouths of atheists and infidels to impeach the Holy Scriptures of falsehood'. Cyrano was one of the worst of those whom Carver attacked, for his account of the Moon is largely a satire on the Book of Genesis—neither funny, nor in good taste.

On the Moon Cyrano met Elijah, who informed him that he had got there by the simple method of making an iron chariot, sitting in it, and holding a large magnet at arm's length above his head, and sometimes tossing it before him. He was bent double by the end of his journey, because 'the movement of the iron to join with the magnet was so vigorous,' and did not dare to risk travelling in that way again.

After some time in the Earthly Paradise, Cyrano was so foolish as to eat an apple from the Tree of Knowledge, and at once found himself alone in the Lunar wilderness. Here he was captured by some of the real Lunar people, who turned out to be a vulgar parody of those described by Godwin. They put Cyrano into a cage and carried him off, saying that he was certainly 'the female of the Queen's little animal'.

When Cyrano reached the court, he was moved into a bigger cage with 'the Queen's little animal', who turned out to be 'a man about my own size', who 'told me he was an European, a native of old Castile, that by means of birds he had conveyed himself to the world of the Moon wherein we now were, that he fell into the Queen's hands and she had taken him for a monkey, because it happens they dress their monkeys in Spanish clothes.'

Much of the rest of the book is taken up with the satirical arguments and conversations which Cyrano had with Gonsales, and also with a Moon 'demon'. There is very little description or invention of a real Lunar world: the language, as Gonsales had found, consisted of musical sounds rather than words, and to this Cyrano added one pleasant touch—an early kind of gramophone or musical box which took the place of books on the Moon.

'It is a book indeed, but a miraculous book without pages or letters; in fine, it is a book to learn from which eyes are useless, only ears are needed. When someone wishes to read he winds up the machine with a large number of all sorts of keys; then he turns the pointer towards the chapter he wishes to hear, and immediately, as if from a man's mouth or a musical instrument, this machine gives out all the distinct and different sounds which serve as the expression of speech between the noble Moon-dwellers.'

Cyrano returned to Earth in a highly original manner. While arguing with one of his Lunar friends, Cyrano grew more and more pious and his friend more and more blasphemous, until on a sudden the devil himself rushed in, seized the Lunarian, and dashed up the chimney with him. Cyrano grabbed his friend by the foot, and was whisked away too. In a moment they were in the clouds, and Cyrano had to hold on tight to save himself from falling.

Away they went at an incredible speed in the direction of Earth, and Cyrano could already make out Italy beneath him, 'when my heart told me that this Devil was no doubt carrying my host to Hell, body and soul, and that he was passing by way of our Earth, because Hell is in its centre'.

The devil made a dive for Mount Vesuvius as the shortest way in to Hell, but Cyrano let go in time, and was later picked up by Italian shepherds and entertained kindly by them.

Not so by their dogs, however, who bayed furiously and attacked Cyrano fiercely, until he realised that he smelt of the Moon, and dogs 'are accustomed to bay at the Moon on account of the pain she causes them from so far'.

A good sun-bath cured Cyrano of this Lunar curse, and he was soon ready to return to France and surprise his friends with the narration of his startling experiences in the Moon.

Cyrano's second, unfinished cosmic voyage was to the Sun—a heavenly body which he alone of space-travellers seems to have visited, if we exclude Sydney Whiting's fantasy *Heliondé* of two centuries later. But apparently the Sun had been thought of as inhabitable by as early a writer as Nicholas de Cusa who, in 1440 in his *De Docta Ignorantia*, wrote (so Wilkins translates him): 'We may Conjecture the Inhabitants of the Sun are like to the Nature of that Plannet, more clear and bright, more Intellectual than those in the Moon where they are nearer to the Nature of that duller Plannet, and those of the Earth being more gross and material than either; for that these Intellectual Natures in the Sun are more form than matter, those in the Earth more matter than form, and those in the Moon betwixt both. This we may guess from the Fiery Influence of the Sun, the Watery and Aereous Influence of the Moon, as also the Material Heaviness of the Earth.'

Cyrano went there by mistake. After his return from the Moon he boasted so much about his exploits that he was seized and imprisoned as a magician. While confined, however, he was allowed visits from his friends who brought him all that he needed for his 'mechanical inventions' and experiments to which his gaolers made no objection.

At length he planned an escape from prison, and spent eight days in constructing a flying-chariot to carry him from the roof of his prison to his friends in the village of Colignac.

'It was a large very light box which shut very exactly. It was about six feet high and three wide in each direction. This box had holes in the bottom, and over the roof, which was also pierced, I placed a crystal vessel with similar holes made globe shape but very large, whose neck terminated exactly at and fitted in the opening I had made in the top. The vessel was expressly made with several angles, in the shape of an icosahedron [twenty-sided solid], so that as each facet was convex and concave my globe produced the effect of a burning mirror.'

None of the gaolers took any notice of Cyrano's labours, and at nine o'clock in the morning Cyrano placed his machine on the top of the tower in which he was imprisoned, in such a way that no air could get into it except through the two openings. Then he seated himself inside, on a plank which was its only furnishing, and awaited results.

These were not long in coming. As soon as the sunbeams began to shine strongly onto the icosahedron they created a void inside it: consequently 'a furious abundance of air' was attracted through the hole in the bottom of the chariot to fill this vacuum—which was immediately renewed, and 'the horrible wind which rushed through the hole could not reach the roof except by passing furiously through the machine and thereby lifting it up'.

Away went Cyrano in his aerial car, faster and faster, until Toulouse from which he had come was out of sight, and the wind had torn away the sail by which he proposed to steer in the direction of Colignac. In less than an hour he found himself well above the clouds, and was watching the rain and hail falling far beneath him. When he got beyond the region of winds, he was still moving so fast that the vacuum continued to be created and filled in the crystal icosahedron and so his voyage went on uninterruptedly.

Cyrano felt no hunger on his long journey, his only refreshment was from 'a bottle of essence I always carried with me', and the nearer he came to the 'flaming world', the stronger he felt. Nor did he suffer from the heat of the Sun, for which unexpected phenomenon he produced several very specious arguments: 'I approached the Sun without being burned', his reasoning concludes, 'because that which burns is not fire, but the matter to which it is attached, and because the Sun's fire cannot be mingled with any matter.'

On his journey Cyrano passed near the Moon, left Venus on his right hand, and obtained a good view of Mercury. From what he saw he concluded that the Copernican astronomy was correct and that the Earth and the planets revolved round the Sun and 'are globes without light of their own and are only capable of reflecting what they borrow'.

After travelling for about four months Cyrano arrived at 'one of those little Worlds which fly around the Sun, called by Mathematicians "Spots".' On this he landed with ease since the clouds kept the heat of the Sun from his mirrors sufficiently for his cabin to sink gently onto a hill-top on this new earth.

Cyrano did not find any of the lessening of gravity on his little Asteroid which we might expect; on the contrary he could scarcely walk 'on account of the thickness of the soil'. The only inhabitant of this unusual 'Spot' appears to have been a 'Natural Man' whom Cyrano found wallowing naked in a bog and who conversed with him by a kind of thought-reading which made any language readily understandable.

After a long philosophical argument with this singular character, Cyrano re-entered his cabin, which already showed signs of restlessness as the clouds grew thinner, and continued on his way.

Further and further he journeyed until the Earth dwindled from the size of the Moon to the appearance of a planet, and then disappeared altogether. Now he was drawing nearer to the Sun, and various changes began to make themselves apparent.

To begin with, his flying cabin became transparent and for a time completely invisible, owing to the purity of the Sun's light; and in time he himself became transparent also. Then he found that he was moving more and more slowly as the air became stiller and more rarefied the nearer he approached to 'the Source of the daylight'. At last his cabin came to a complete standstill 'on account of the serenity of the ether', but he was able to move it towards the Sun by the ardour of his will.

Finding the cabin weigh heavily on his head, Cyrano finally got out into Space where he had the misfortune to break the now invisible icosahedron, which caused his cabin to fall back towards the Earth, becoming visible again as it went.

But Cyrano continued on his way without it, drawn to the Sun by the very strength of his will, and arrived there safely after a journey of twenty-two months. He landed happily 'at the great plains of Day' in a land that looked 'like flakes of burning snow, so luminous it was', and where he walked so lightly that he only touched the ground with the points of his feet, and often rolled like a ball without finding it any less comfortable to walk on his head than on his feet.

Almost 'ashamed to walk upon the daylight', Cyrano wandered for fifteen days until he came to a slightly less resplendent district where he lay down to sleep in a bare desert of sand.

When he woke, however, it was to find himself under a tree of tremendous height with trunk of gold, branches of silver and leaves of emerald, while its fruits and flowers were of various precious stones.

As he gazed up into the tree Cyrano was interested but hardly surprised to see a beautiful pomegranate grow swiftly and easily into a little dwarf, detach itself from the tree, and walk lightly towards him.

And so Cyrano entered upon another series of adventures which served to satirise various people and opinions which he desired to attack in contemporary France.

After the plantmen Cyrano visited the Kingdom of the Birds, ruled over by the Phoenix who, so he fables, flies to the Sun as soon as it has brought forth its egg in the midst of the embers of its Earthly pyre. And with the Birds he spent most of his time on the Sun, only leaving them to visit talking trees, to witness the battle of the Fire-Beast and the Ice-Beast (which Andrew Lang turned to much better use in his fairy-story of *Prince Prigio*), and to meet and argue with the ghosts of the Utopian writer Campenella and the philosopher Descartes.

And here Cyrano's *Voyage to the Sun* breaks off suddenly, since he died before he could conclude it, and there is no indication of how he returned to Earth.

The satirical use made of the journey into other worlds by Cyrano de Bergerac was speedily followed in a variety of ways. *The Government of the World in the Moon* was translated into English by Thomas St. Serf in 1658, and the two voyages as *The Comical History of the States and Empires of the Worlds of the Moon and Sun* by A. Lovell in 1687. The second of these inspired a variety of satirical plays such as

Thomas D'Urfey's *Wonders in the Sun, or The Kingdom of the Birds* (1706), while Elkanah Settle and Mrs. Aphra Behn both produced similar works based on Godwin and Cyrano, which have no real place except as curiosities in the fiction of Space-flight.

The more serious and scientific aspects of life on the Moon and the Planets was popularised in 1686 by Bernard le Bovier de Fontenelle whose work *A Plurality of Worlds* was first translated into English two years later by John Glanvill, and appeared in numerous versions and editions throughout the eighteenth century.

This book consists of a series of dialogues between Fontenelle and the 'Countess of D.' as they gaze up at the night sky and speculate about the possibilities of life on the Moon and the planets, Fontenelle tending to damp the ardour of Her Ladyship's flights of fancy, as when he suggests that the 'Seas' on the Moon may really be craters and cavities.

'But what do you think then of the Inhabitants of *Mercury*?' he asks. 'They are yet nearer to the Sun [than those of Venus], and are so full of Fire that they are absolutely mad. . . . The Day there is very short, and the Sun appears to them like a vast fiery Furnace at a little distance whose Motion is prodigiously swift and rapid; and during their Night, *Venus* and the Earth (which must appear considerably big) give light to them.' No chance of life as we know it on Mercury, thinks Fontenelle, but maybe 'the inhabitants of *Mercury* may have no occasion either for Rain or Salt-Petre. If it is a certain truth that Nature gives life to any Creature but where that Creature may live, then thro' Custom, and Ignorance of a better Life, those People may live happily.

'After *Mercury*,' continues Fontenelle, 'comes the Sun, but there is no possibility of peopling it, nor no room left for a wherefore. By the Earth which is Inhabited, we judge that other Bodies of the same Nature may be likewise inhabited; but the Sun is a Body not like the Earth or any of the Planets, the Sun is the source or Fountain of Light. . . . It seems the Sun is a Liquid Matter, some think of melted Gold which boils over continually. . . .'

For the rest 'let us leave *Mars*, he is not worth our stay', and the outer planets Jupiter and Saturn are things of beauty, but too cold for any life which we can imagine.

Christian Huygens, a more formal astronomer, in his *Cosmotheoros*, 1698 (translated into English anonymously the same year as *The Celestial World Discover'd*), held out even less hope of the planets being inhabited, and was certain that on the Moon there were no seas or rivers, and indeed no air at all.

'I cannot imagine,' he concludes, 'how any Plants or Animals, whose whole nourishment comes from liquid Bodies, can thrive in a dry, waterless, parch'd Soil. . . . And yet 'tis not improbable that those great and noble Bodies have somewhat or other growing and living upon them, tho very different from what we see and enjoy here. Perhaps their Plants and Animals may have another sort of Nourishment there. . . .'

Yet the sober facts of the scientists did not hinder writers of fiction from sending their heroes to the Moon, though perhaps in deference to them they used their voyages almost exclusively for the purposes of satire for nearly two centuries after Godwin's classic appeared.

Thus in 1690, between the appearance of the planetary guides of Fontenelle and Huygens, Gabriel Daniel produced his charming *Voyage du Monde de Descartes*, Englished by T. Taylor of Magdalen College, Oxford, in 1692 as *A Voyage to the World of Cartesius*.

The book is to some extent a satire on Descartes' theory of the separation of 'mind' and 'matter'. Descartes had reached his new world by an act of will, and was not dead; his disciple, the hero of the story, has not so strong a 'will', but with the aid of a peculiar kind of snuff concocted by Descartes himself, 'I sneezed (God bless me) three or four Times with mighty Violence. Hereupon I fell into a swoon like that of *M. Descartes* I described before, and in an instant my Soul, by the only Act of Will, perceived her enlargement from the Body'.

Guided by his mentor, Father Mersennus, 'we steered towards the *Globe* of the *Moon*. My Soul perceived an unspeakable Pleasure to scud it in the Air, and to wander in those vast Spaces she could only travel with the Eye before, when united with the Body'.

So they came swiftly and easily to the World of the Moon, only stopping to argue with the disembodied Souls of various philosophers that they met on the way.

'The *Moon* is a Mass of Matter much like that of which the *Earth* is compos'd. There you have Fields and Forests, Seas and Rivers. I saw no Animals indeed, but I am of Opinion if there were some transported they would thrive and probably multiply. 'Tis false that there are men there as Cyrano reports; but 'twas undesignedly that he deceiv'd us, having first been deceiv'd himself.'

There are no men, but there are Spirits, and several of these took on the shapes of men to deceive Cyrano: 'But 'tis worth the knowing that some Fopperies he has inserted he brought not from that Country, as the Soul assur'd me: and that many Profane Allusions and Libertine Reflections he there makes were only the Fruits of a debauch'd Imagination and a corrupt Mind such as was that *Historian's*, or of the Imitation of an *Author* yet more Atheistical than himself—I mean *Lucian*, one of whose Works was made the Plan to his *History* of the *Moon*.

'The Inequalities we found in the *Globe* of the *Moon* are partly Isles wherewith the Seas there are pleasantly chequer'd, and partly Hills and Vallies in its Continent. They belong to several famous *Astronomers* or *Philosophers* whose Names they bear, and who are the high and mighty States there. We landed in *Gassendi*, a Seat extraordinary fine and very apposite, and such in a word as an *Abbot* like *Monsieur Gassendus* could make it. . . .'

'From *Gassendi*, *Father Mersennus* conducted us to the *Land* that bears his Name. It is very conveniently situate upon the same Coast as *Gassendi*, bordering upon the *round* sea, which others call the *Sea of Humours* . . . at the end whereof, Northwerds, is a *Peninsule* call'd *Dream-land*. . . .'

On a voyage of exploration across the hemisphere of the Moon which always faces the Earth, 'We cross'd the *great Ocean*, leaving on our left hand *the Isle of Winds* and on the right that of *Copernicus*, and passed over that of *Pitheas*, still pushing on quite to the *Sea of Rains* which is bounded by a vast *Land* stretch'd from East to West, much like that of *America* as it is decypher'd in the Maps.

'Towards the middle of that Land, upon the shore of the *Sea of Rains*, we discover'd a kind of a large Town, of an oval Figure, which we had the Curiosity to go to see. But we found all the Avenues guarded with Souls who deny'd us Entrance, tho' civilly and obligingly enough. We demanded of one of them, What Town that was, and why there was no Admission? He answer'd it was call'd *Plato*, and was the same where that *Philosopher* whose Name it bore had establish'd his *Commonwealth*.

'So we went on our Journy, dissatisfied enough, from the *Republick* of Plato', and 'travell'd over all that Land from North to South, after which we discover'd another Sea, call'd the *Sea of Cold*, in which stood a very fair *Island* which they said was *Aristotle's*'.

After a full description of this 'Lyceum of the Moon', the travellers 'pass'd through *Thales*, and drove on quite to *Zoroaster*; from whence we made a double towards the West, through desert Lands, where we saw the ruins of some ancient Towns, as of *Atlas, Cepheus, Hermes*, without meeting Man, Woman or Child, till we came to the *Lake of Dreams*'.

A glance at a modern Map of the Moon will reveal nearly all the places named by Gabriel Daniel not far from the Moon's north pole, and his journey can be followed quite easily. So can the rest of his wanderings on the Moon, which consisted of various other visits to the dwelling places of the Souls of Philosophers.

Nevertheless when the party left for the real World of Cartesius in 'the Third Heaven', they had been only seven hours absent from the Earth.

'So we left *Mersennus*, and departed from the *Moon* by the Northside of that Globe; we made towards the *Starry Heaven* with all the Speed we were capable of, that is to say in one Minute we compass'd many thousand Leagues.'

And so we must leave Daniel to visit the Soul of M. Descartes and learn from him a philosophy which (so he demonstrates on his return to Earth) would prove that the stars are invisible, that the Moon cannot revolve round our planet, nor his satellites round Jupiter, that heavy bodies do not fall to the ground but are attracted to the Sun, that there are no tides in the sea, and that, in short, he had demonstrated 'The General Principle of all the Physical Effects of the lower World quite over-turned', with the corollary that Copernicus was right and Descartes was wrong.

CHAPTER FIVE

A LUNATICK CENTURY

THE eighteenth century, though it may have been the Century of Reason, abounded in extravagant fancies with regard to other worlds and the various means of reaching them—though it usually sent its heroes across Space solely for purposes of satire.

The earliest astronaut of the century, David Russen of Hythe, in his heavy and humourless *Iter Lunare: or, A Voyage to the Moon* (1703) took even Cyrano de Bergerac seriously, complaining that it was an insult to subtitle it 'a comical history' as it was really most rational and probable, even the most exaggerated and most ribald passages of smut and satire concealing deep scientific or philosophical truths.

The only interesting passage in Russen's book is the description of his machine for reaching the Moon, a gigantic catapult set up on a high mountain. 'Since springiness is a cause of forcible motion,' he argues in all seriousness, 'and a Spring will, when bended and let loose, extend itself to its length: could a Spring of well-tempered Steel be framed, whose Basis being fastened to the Earth and on the other end placed a Frame or Seat, wherein a Man, with other necessaries, could abide with safety, this Spring being with Cords, Pullies, or other Engins bent and then let loose by degrees by those who manage the Pullies, the other end would reach the Moon, where the Person ascended landing, might continue there, and according to a time appointed, might again enter into his seat, and with Pullies the Engin may again be bent, till the end touching the Earth should discharge the Passenger again in safety.'

Every bit as lucid as this scientific suggestion was Daniel De Foe's purely allegorical and satirical space-ship the Consolidator invented by that ingenious Chinaman Mira-cho-cho-lasmo as described in a book printed 'two thousand years before the Flood'.

'Above all his inventions for the making the voyage,' commented De Foe, 'I saw none more pleasant or profitable than a certain engine formed in the shape of a Chariot, on the backs of two vast bodies with extended wings, which spread about fifty yards in breadth, composed of feathers so nicely put together that no air could pass; and as the bodies were made of Lunar earth, which would bear the fire, the cavities were filled with an ambient flame, which fed on a certain spirit deposited in a proper quantity to last out the voyage; and this fire so ordered as to move about such springs and wheels as kept the wings in a most exact and regular motion, always ascendant; thus the person being placed in this airy Chariot drinks a certain dosing draught that throws him into a gentle slumber, and dreaming all the way, never wakes till he comes to his journey's end. These engines are called . . . in English a Consolidator.'

This promising suggestion of a petrol-engine a couple of centuries too soon is shown in its true light in the next paragraph: 'The number of feathers,' De Foe explains, 'are just 513, they are all of a length and breadth exactly . . . only there is one extraordinary feather, which, as there is an odd one in the number, is placed in the centre, and is the handle, or rather rudder of the whole machine. . . . Nor are these common feathers, but they are picked up and culled out of all parts of the Lunar country by the command of the prince; and every province sends up the best they can find, or ought to do so at least, or else they are very much to blame; for the employment they are put to being of so great use to the public, and the voyage or flight so exceeding high, it would be very ill done if, when the King sends his letters about the nation to pick up the best feathers they can lay their hands on, they should send weak, decayed, or half-grown feathers, and yet sometimes it happens so.'

The Consolidator, in fact, represents the House of Commons; the feathers are the Members, the guide-feather is the Speaker, and the King's letters are the writs for new elections.

De Foe goes on to describe with much detail everything to do with his Consolidator before embarking on his journey to the Moon: 'The first voyage I ever made to this country,' he then tells us, 'was in one of these machines, and I can safely affirm I never waked all the way; and now having been as often there as most that have used that trade, it may be expected I should give some account of the country, for it appears I can give but little of the road. Only this I understand, that when the engine, by help of these artificial wings, has raised itself up to a certain height, the wings are as useful to keep it from falling into the Moon as they were before to raise it and keep it from falling back into this region again.'

'I was no sooner landed there and had looked about me, but I was surprised with the strange alteration of the climate and country and particularly a strange salubrity and fragrancy in the air, I felt so nourishing, so pleasant, and delightful, that though I could perceive some small respiration, it was hardly discernible, and the least requisite for life supplied so long that the bellows of Nature were hardly employed.'

But this was the only difference De Foe found between our world and that in the Moon. The first Lunarian he met took him for the Man in the Moon, growing very angry when De Foe tried to persuade him that they were actually standing on the Moon and looking up at the Earth, and not vice versa, as the Lunarians most firmly believed.

Following up this idea, De Foe was able, with the aid of a few Luna pseudonyms, to present the politics and abuses of his own day as those of the Moon, which he continues to do throughout the volume.

'Never was there such a couple of people met,' he says of his first Luna acquaintance. 'He was the Man in the Moon to me, and I the Man in the Moon to him. He wrote down all I said and made a book of it, and called it *News from the World in the Moon*; and all the town is like to see my minutes under the same title. Nay, I have been told he published some such bold truths there, from the allegorical relations he had of me from our world, that he was called before the Publick Authority, who could not bear the just reflections of his damned satirical way of writing,' and was pilloried—just as De Foe had been two years earlier for his pamphlet *The Shortest Way with the Dissenters*.

De Foe followed *The Consolidator, or Memoirs of Sundry Transactions from the World in the Moon* (1705) with several more Luna pamphlets of a similar satirical nature, of no interest from the point of view of journeys into other worlds, though it is amusing to notice that in one of them, having ascended to the top of a Castle in the Air (he lived, he tells us, in a country where an abundance of such *Chateaux en Espagne* are daily built), 'one Day as I was Gazing about, in order to find out some new Discovery, I fell down directly upon the *World in the Moon*'.

Just as De Foe had satirised the political abuses of 1705 in his Moon-world, so, twenty-one years later, Swift far more brilliantly pilloried abuses of all kinds in *Gulliver's Travels*. The worthy Captain Gulliver did not travel further away from this Earth than to the flying island of Laputa, but his voyages and the Lunar expedition of De Foe were imitated in 1727 by 'Captain Samuel Brunt' (probably a pseudonym, though the real author has not been identified) who in that year gave to the world his account of *A Voyage to Cacklogallinia*.

This is an earthy Cloud-cuckoo-land, a Kingdom of the Birds such as Aristophanes had invented and Cyrano de Bergerac translated to the

Sun for satirical exploitation by himself and such imitators as D'Urfey and Mrs. Aphra Behn. The abuse which Captain Brunt satirises in his 'Description of the Religion, Policy, Customs and Manners' of Cacklogallinia is the craze for speculation which led to the bursting of the South Sea Bubble in 1720. Captain Brunt, after various adventures, became the protégé of the Chief Minister of Cacklogallinia, a country of the birds which merely satirises England under Walpole's ministry with less skill and less ruthlessness than Swift does, in reverse, in the Land of the Houyhnhnms.

The Cacklogallinians were as obsessed with 'Projects' and speculations as were Brunt's contemporaries in England, and after many had been tried unsuccessfully, one wise bird called Volatilio suggested an expedition to the Moon to extract gold from its mountains which would bring enormous wealth to Cacklogallinia.

Captain Brunt argued strenuously against this scheme, citing scientific objections to the practicability of a voyage to the Moon. But the Bird Emperor over-ruled him, declaring that 'I look upon the Distance, which you have computed to be about 179,712 Lapidians (answerable to so many English miles) to be none at all, since we have Cacklogallinians who, with provisions for a Week, will fly 480 Lapidians a Day, and hold it for many Days'.

So Brunt consented to head the expedition, and was himself transported in a specially designed 'Palanquin' which was lined with feathers to keep out the 'extream coldness' that he expected on the voyage, and which was 'made sharp at each End, to cut the Air'.

Before setting off, Brunt and his convoy of birds went up onto a high mountain where the adventurers experimented with the rarefied atmosphere until at length Volatilio returned from his longest flight to announce 'I have pass'd the Atmosphere, and, by Experience, have found my Conjecture true: for being out of the magnetick Power of the Earth, we rested in the Air, as on the solid Earth, and in an Air extreamly temperate, and less subtle than what we breathe.'

And so Brunt set off in his palanquin, and found the journey simple and uninteresting except for the moment when, after less than an hour and a half's flight, Volatilio 'folded his Wings, and came to me on Foot, and told me I might get out and stretch my Limbs. My Palanquineers stood still, and confirmed what he said; and more, that they had not for a Quarter of an Hour past been sensible of my Weight, which had lessen'd by Degrees, so as not to be felt at all'.

Out got Brunt in consequence, and found that weight had quite ceased: he could lift the palanquin with its load of provisions weighing five hundredweight as easily as he could raise a feather on Earth.

Brunt's adventures on the Moon itself were of little interest, and added nothing to the accepted picture of Cyrano and the playwrights. He failed to get the Lunar gold, since the inhabitants were such idealists that wealth meant nothing to them and they could not even see the point of trade and commerce, and politely but firmly requested him to depart from their world, which he did in company with Volatilio, to land in Jamaica and set out by himself for England.

Even less interesting was Murtagh McDermot's *Trip to the Moon, containing some Observations and Reflections made by him, during his stay in that Planet, upon the Manners of the Inhabitants* in 1728. After being blown to the Moon in a whirl-wind, McDermot found there a drearily satiric world, which he proceeds to describe without one gleam of originality.

But his return journey was performed in a novel manner: instead of Russen's 'spring', he had recourse to gunpowder—which so far only Cyrano had used, and that by chance in the rockets attached to his flying machine by the French soldiers in Quebec.

'We already know,' declared this mad Irishman, 'the Height of the Moon's Atmosphere, and know how Gun-powder will raise a Ball of any Weight to any Height. Now I design to place myself in the Middle of ten wooden Vessels, placed one within another, with the Outermost strongly hooped with Iron, to prevent its breaking. This I will place over 7,000 Barrels of Powder, which I know will raise me to the Top of the Atmosphere. . . . Before I blow myself up, I'll provide myself with a large pair of Wings, which I will fasten to my Arms in my Resting-Place, by the help of which I will fly down to the Earth.' Which hazardous return to Earth he accomplished in safety.

Later in the century an anonymous author made *A New Journey to the World in the Moon* (the first edition does not seem to be extant, but the second is dated 1741) which was based closely on *The Consolidator*, but with an interesting difference.

The author begins his little book of eighty-four pages with a dissertation on Space-travel in which he points out that it is absolutely impossible: 'a Passage thither is altogether impracticable by the Help of any *Machine*, however contrived to float in the Atmosphere; or of *artificial Wings*, could they even carry us through the Regions of the

Clouds, and round our own Globe: for a Journey thither would require a Passage through a vast *Abyss*, or *Vacuum*, between the Atmospheres of this Globe and the *Moon's*, which could not be subsisted in by any living Inhabitant of this Globe, who require a sufficient Quantity of Air to breathe in to support the Union of Animal Life.

'The Vessel also wou'd not be out of the Attraction of the Body of the Earth, if it was possible to carry it beyond its Atmosphere, and therefore its flight must necessarily be there unsupported. . . . Nor cou'd any, either artificial or natural wings whatsoever carry any Body farther or higher than a sufficient Quantity of Air wou'd support it.'

After showing more knowledge of the difficulties of Space-flight than any author before Jules Verne, and pointing out that Bishop Wilkins's ideas were just as impracticable as the bird-drawn machine on which Gonsales travelled, he continues:

'As then no material Engines nor any possible Inventions can ever convey our Bodies to the World in the Moon, the only Converse we can have with this Lunar World, is, while awake, to observe the near Affinity of the Make and Shape of the Moon with our Globe the Earth, and by Help of Glasses observe her Lands, and Waters, Hills, Mountains, and Vallies; and by this observe that it is properly fitted for Inhabitants in all Respects as this Globe we live upon is. From whence we naturally conclude that the Wise Author of the Creation has not only fitted it for, but has also furnish'd it with *Inhabitants* like our selves and Fellow Animals.

'But as I have found that a proper bodily Conversation cannot be come at with the *Inhabitants of the Lunar World*, I have renounc'd all Attempts of a Journey thither in any of the Ways hitherto proposed by others, and have taken another Method of my own, to visit these Regions by a *spiritual Analogy* in a profound Silence from the Hurry of the Affairs of our Globe. To prepare for which, I fix'd myself upon an high Mountain at the time of the Full-Moon, when the bright Sun had withdrawn his illustrious Rays from our Horizon, but cast them on the *Rising Moon* with the most splendid Brightness; which strengthen'd my Curiosity to fix my Thoughts wholly upon that *Globe* and sub-tract them from my own: when setting myself wholly to shut out of my thinking Faculty all manner of other Cogitations, I found my Imagination drawn in a direct Line to the World in the *Moon*, and so left the Machine of my Body in a sound Repose, being almost in-stantaneously arrived at my desired Port, *viz. The Lunar World*.'

Arrived in the Moon by the exact method which was to take John Carter to Mars nearly two centuries later, this anonymous Space-traveller met with a Philosopher who turned the tables on De Foe by at once describing a machine called a 'Representative Consolidator' by which the people of the Moon visited the Earth—their Moon.

This 'proper *Engine*' was 'made up of Materials sent up to the King's Palaces', and 'the Outsides of which have five hundred and thirteen Knotches, to receive the same Number of Catches of the Moon's Attraction; whereby it is, with the Persons placed in it, circularly drawn by a spring Screw into the Lunar World [i.e. the Earth]. For by the Catches of the Moon's Attraction we are loosened from the Gravity we otherwise owe to our own Globe, and so are transmitted, in a regular Motion, from our own more refined Atmosphere into yours, without any Damages of Want of Air by the Way for Support and Breathing which are manifest Hinderances to your journeying hither after the same Manner'.

Later on the Lunar Philosopher describes this flying chariot in almost exactly De Foe's words. It is made of the best boards from the wood of the 'Collective Tree', instead of feathers, and the form of the engine is a huge chariot with wheels. But the hollows and cavities in the spokes of the wheels, as well as the body of the engine, 'must be well lin'd with the best *Lunar Earth*, through which no Air can pass; then the Cavities must be filled with a circumambient Flame, which must feed on a certain Spirit deposited in a proper Quantity to last out the Voyage', which puts the 'Engine in a Motion proportioned to the Rowling of the Moon's Rotation [once again referring to the Earth as the Moon], that its Attraction may fix on the Superficies of its Catches, by its Number of Knotches prepar'd to lay hold on the Spokes of the Chariot Wheels, whereby the Body of the Engine, or Chariot, is kept in a most regular and uniform Motion, with the Body always ascendant'.

The rest of this curious pamphlet consists of a history of the previous hundred years in the Moon as narrated by the Philosopher—which is actually a satirical account of English history, from the martyrdom of Charles I to the reign of George I, with several very shallow Lunar substitutes for the Earthly names.

At the end of this long and interesting discussion 'my Philosopher bad me look thro' the Window to the Eastern *Horizon*, where I might see the *Moon*, or the World I came from, advancing as the Sun declined; and behold! I saw a vast Body, half-illuminated, in the Figure of the

Moon at first Quarter, which appear'd twenty-six Times as big as the Moon with us, and this, my Philosopher told me, was the *World* I was come from'.

It would be tedious to dig any more such satirical imitations out of their well-merited oblivion, charming though this one example may be. We can confidently leave such a Moon-voyage as that concocted by the minor playwright and Shakespearean editor Francis Gentleman (1728–84), which was published in two volumes, at York in 1764, as *A Trip to the Moon. Containing an Account of the Island of Noibla, Its Inhabitants, Religious and Political Customs &c. By Sir Humphrey Lunatic, Bart.* That Moon-struck worthy fell asleep on a hill-side in the baleful rays of our satellite, and woke to find himself in another world where 'a Person of Venerable Aspect addressed me as follows: "Thou art now within the Limits of the LUNAR WORLD; the imperceptible Method of thy Conveyance I cannot explain to thy Comprehension; let it suffice to say that some Rays of Attraction, sent down from the Mount of Observation, a Spot which from Earth appears to be the Nose of the MAN in the MOON, drew thee from the Place where thou lay'st asleep; which powerful Operation was not a little facilitated by some sympathetic Pamphlets thou hadst in thy Pockets, Pieces originally planned in a certain Province of the LUNAR WORLD, and thence inspired into the *Moon-struck* Authors of them" . . .' And so Sir Humphrey proceeds with his guide round a world designed purely for purposes of political and literary satire of a dull and dated nature.

But we need follow this scion of the Lunaticks no further, nor go even as far with William Thomson's purely political *Man in the Moon* who carried off Charles James Fox into the satellite in 1784 for an object lesson in the art of government; nor trouble at all about another political *Voyage to the Moon* by 'Aratus' in 1793.

But there were a few simple adventurers among this crowd of political visitors, and one of the pleasantest was Mr. John Daniel whose series of surprising adventures 'Taken from his own Mouth by Mr. Ralph Morris' and published in 1751 included 'A Description of a most surprising Engine, invented by his son Jacob, on which he flew to the Moon, with some Account of its Inhabitants'.

This entertaining book is largely a ship-wreck and desert-island story which may have suggested many ideas to the ingenious author of *The Swiss Family Robinson*. John Daniel was wrecked on an island with but one companion, who turned out to be a woman in disguise; they married and peopled the island with their children, obtaining nearly as much in the way of useful supplies from the wrecked ship as the Swiss Family. When the eldest son Jacob grew up, he built a flying machine, all his own invention, which consisted of a square wooden platform (reached by a trap-door), with a pump in the middle and calico wings on thin iron ribs three yards long extending continuously all round it.

When the whole apparatus was completed, and anchored on four uprights sunk into the ground, 'my son opened his trapdoor', says John Daniel, 'and ascending through it, mounted his floor, fixed the handle, and began to play his wings, to see that all was right; (but very gently, for fear of rising off his poles till he was quite prepared). I then observed that when the pump handle was pressed downwards, as in pumping, that raising the sucker, the pendant iron raised the end of the ballances next to it, when the other extremities of the ballances hooked to the several ribs, necessarily descending, drew their corresponding ribs downwards; and that the uplifting of the handle consequently gave the ribs liberty, through their springiness to return to their horizontal position again; so that they were raised and deprest, proportionably to the motion and force of the handle, and exactly answered the use and play of wings in birds'.

While experimenting on this machine John and Jacob went too far from their mountain, found themselves over the sea, and could do nothing but work the pump-handles to keep themselves in the air. For sustenance they had the leaves of a certain plant which Jacob discovered to be a perfect substitute for food and drink, and a source of considerable energy.

Darkness fell, and they continued on their way faster and faster, higher and higher, until it seemed that the Sun was about to rise, and, says John, 'I was in hopes, by the Sun, to guess to what part of the compass we were steering; but to my prodigious surprise all around us seemed equally luminous, nor could we by any of the usual characters of the morning read in what place the Sun would shine first. . . . What puzzled me was that we were in bright daylight, and then immediately saw the sun all at once dart upon us very piercingly from the serenest sky that ever we beheld; and though we pumped ever so strong, we could not discern whether we moved upwards, downwards, or sideways'. Presently it became dark again and 'we saw a vast Moon beyond us, and at the same time the eagle [i.e. their flying-machine] wavering about quite surprised us and struck us into such terror', that they let go of the pump handles, and the machine swung about, turning over and over, as they clung on desperately, until it righted itself and they came down at length 'just as the Sun set, upon a prodigious high and craggy hill, with vast precipices on each side of us'.

They were on the Moon, but had no idea of the fact until after their return to Earth, and during all their stay in this 'strange country' failed to realise the obvious truth.

The first curiosity was the length of the night whose continuance they could not account for in any way. After waiting in vain for sunrise, they decided to explore, for 'it was not so dark but we could see the shapes and faces of each other by star-light and a vast moon that we saw'. So they descended the prodigious mountain, and wandered about the plain for the space of several days, until at last the Sun appeared.

'It gave us from the mountain we afterwards climbed up a prospect of the most romantick country I had ever beheld; there were prodigious mountains, extensive plains, and immense lakes, interspersed with the vastest plantations of trees that can be imagined to lie within the compass of the eye at once. And then the air was so serene, thin and transparent that we could see distinctly to a distance beyond comparison to what we ever could before.

'We entered the groves of trees and began to see several people and divers sorts of cattle, beasts and birds, but far different in make, shape and actions from what I had ever seen before. The people seemed of a bright copper colour all over, and had hair so thick and long as when it was justly distributed all round their head would almost cover the whole body. Some of these we saw just upon the approach of light, but all that presented after the Sun appeared had their hairs tied up in a great knot behind, when, their bodies being disencumbered from it, they shone like gold.'

The Daniels managed to catch one of these strange men, who proved quite friendly, though unintelligible, 'for his sounds were not articulate, being mostly short and broken aspirates'. This Lunarian took them to his home, which he shared with the whole tribe, in the bottom of a deep valley: it 'seemed just like the bottom of a well', and had caves and passages opening out of it on every side—as in the case of Wells's Selenites in 1901.

The Daniels remained with these friendly people for a Lunar day and night, but made few observations. During the long day they saw the harvest gathered in, a crop 'like our small rushes: these blades are filled with a pulp which, when so dry as to be crisp and brittle, they roll between two stones and then sifting it, it produces the lightest flour I ever saw; this they mix with water and dry great quantities of it in the sun, in lumps of a pound, or thereabouts, each; and when they want it they give it a stroke with their hand and it falls down into crumbles which they eat by handfuls.'

When the Sun began to set, all the Lunarians went out, and 'wringing their hands they set up such a howling, crying and shrieking as made the whole plain ring', since they were never certain that the Sun would return. When it did rise again a fortnight later they greeted its appearance with the wildest rejoicings.

Daylight having returned, John and Jacob Daniel mounted their 'eagle' once more and set out for home, still not realising that they had been to the Moon even when they found themselves out of sight of any earth or clouds and flying towards the sun; or even when suddenly 'the eagle pitched quite over and proceeded without ever once wagging more. We wondered at it, and especially that in the turn we did not seem the least likely to fall; and though we were sure we flew upon our heads, in respect to our former position, yet both Jacob stood and I sat, as little liable to fall as ever we did, and seemed to be still with our heads upwards'.

So they came back to Earth, and it was only the frog-footed sea-monster-man, the next strange creature they met, who told them where they had been.

After so many pseudo-scientific flying machines it is strange to find the hero of the Rev. Miles Wilson's *The History of Israel Jobson, the Wandering Jew* (1757) enjoying an 'Assumption thro' the Starry Regions, conducted by a Guardian Angel, exhibiting in a curious Manner the Shapes, Lives, and Customs of the Inhabitants of the Moon and Planets'.

The celestial visitant of this rare and interesting pamphlet took Jobson on his instructive tour as a holiday from his endless terrestrial wanderings, and taught him on the way a good deal of fairly reliable astronomy.

The Moon, however, they found to be inhabited by the ancestors of Baum's Tin-Man. They were, in fact, made of 'Pan Metal'. 'If an Hole be made either in the Head or Body to let out the Vital Heat, which their Life consists of, they immediately die.' They have 'no occasion for Meat, Drink or Cloaths', but constant warfare over trifles

keeps the Copper Smiths busy patching them up. The female Lunarians, made of 'Burnish'd Brass', 'use all Arts to inveigle and ensnare un-
wary Youth, but they only Flourish a while, for sometimes they
Scour their Copper Noses plain with their Faces, or their Bodies so thin
that the vital Heat evaporates'. The more amorous melt quickly owing to the heat of their embraces; and when asleep their snores resemble
'so many Organ Pipes or Brazen Trumpeters'.

On Mars, Jobson was shown nine million inhabitants, whose only
function is to glorify God. They are 'of the Neuter Gender, that is,
they are of no Sex: they never remove from their station, and are as
fix'd as Trees, and so will remain till the End of Time'. They are,
indeed, little more than stone images, but they have two sets of eyes:
with one set they can sleep, and with the other gaze with rapture on the
beauties of Creation.

The giants of Jupiter are merely cribbed from Gulliver's second
voyage, but the great Saturnians dwell on the edge of Paradise which
itself is on a star in the Milky Way. Having seen which, the Angel
restores Jobson to Earth with several pages of pious exhortation—and
omits to show him Venus or Mercury.

However seriously we are meant to take *The History of Israel
Jobson*, Wilson was also able to laugh at serious Space-flight, as he did
in a pamphlet called *The Man in the Moon* whose hero ascended to the
satellite by means of a ladder made of rope and wood. On reaching
the Moon, he found that the inhabitants fed only on common clay—
so he hastily descended for a good north-country high-tea of bacon
and eggs.

Another light-hearted Space traveller towards the end of the century
was Baron Munchausen, the earliest and most original of whose
adventures were published in 1785 by the German emigrant Rudolph
Erich Raspe.

On one occasion, so the Baron tells us, he was sold as a slave to the
Turks; but 'in that state of humiliation my daily task was not very hard
and laborious, but rather singular and irksome. It was to drive the
Sultan's bees every morning to their pasture-grounds, to attend them
all the day long, and against night to drive them back to their hives.
One evening I missed a bee, and soon observed that two bears had
fallen upon her, to tear her to pieces for the honey she carried. I had
nothing like an offensive weapon in my hands but the silver hatchet
which is the badge of the Sultan's gardeners and farmers. I threw it at
the robbers, with an intention to frighten them away, and set the poor

bee at liberty; but, by an unlucky turn of my arm, it flew upwards, and continued rising till it reached the Moon. How should I recover it? How fetch it down again? I recollected that turkey-beans grow very quick, and run up to an astonishing height. I planted one immedi-- ately; it grew, and actually fastened itself to one of the Moon's horns. I had no more to do now but to climb up by it into the Moon, where I safely arrived, and had a troublesome piece of business before I could find my silver hatchet in a place where everything has the brightness of silver; at last, however, I found it in a heap of chaff and chopped straw. I was now for returning, but alas! the heat of the Sun had dried up my bean: it was totally useless for my descent; so I fell to work, and twisted me a rope out of that chopped straw, as long and as well as I could make it. This I fastened to one of the Moon's horns, and slid down to the end of it. Here I held myself fast with the left hand, and with the hatchet in my right I cut the long, now useless, end of the upper part, which, when tied to the lower end, brought me a good deal lower. This repeated splicing and tying of the rope did not improve its quality, or bring me down to the Sultan's farms. I was four or five miles from the earth at least when it broke. I fell to the ground with such amazing violence that I found myself stunned, and in a hole nine fathoms deep at least, made by the weight of my body falling from so great a height'.

On which defiant note of Wonderland logic we may leave the Age of Reason.

CHAPTER SIX

UNPARALLELED ADVENTURES ON THE MOON

WITH the dawning of the nineteenth century the days of the fanciful Moon-voyage seemed to be numbered. William Herschel, discoverer of Uranus, had shown that gravity continued throughout the Solar System and did not end a few miles above earth; his son, Sir John Herschel, and many other astronomers were scanning the heavens with larger and larger telescopes—and they at least were convinced that the Moon was airless, waterless, and uninhabited.

The old dream of the Moon as a peopled world died hard, however; and fictional visits continued to be made, though they tended to grow more scientific, while the satiric intention grew less marked.

It was still there, however, when 'Mr. Nicholas Lunatic, F.R.S.' made *A Voyage to the Moon* the chief of his *Satiric Tales* published in 1808. His pseudonym seems never to have been pierced, nor his tales reprinted: but the disarming naïveté of his voyage and of the satire on contemporary London life which his Lunar world affords make him well worth rescuing from oblivion.

'I had always a most exalted opinion of the power of aerostatic machines,' he tells us, and so he determined to put this to practical proof and, 'should I succeed, not to confine my voyages to this Globe, but to endeavour to explore the unknown regions of the Moon!

'In order to prosecute my plan as privately as possible, I took a woodcutter's cabin in the centre of a forest in Warwickshire; laid in a small stock of provisions, and, unseen by mortal eyes, commenced my operations.

'I first made an immense bag of silk, of spherical form, more than twice the size of any balloon I had ever seen: this I strengthened by a coat of varnish, and covered it with a strong network; then I filled the silk with inflammable air.

'When I had done that, my fears were greatly excited by the astonishing propensity it had to ascend; and so great were its exertions, that it absolutely loosened two trees to which I fastened it; and had I not at that very moment succeeded in attaching it to double the number, my intended vehicle would most certainly have departed without me.

'As I did not know how long I might be on my journey, I determined to take with me sufficient provision for a week; and having fastened a long kind of vehicle resembling a boat, to the ends of the netting that was round the balloon, I put in it whatever I might have occasion for, and also made two pairs of oars to guide its course. Thus, everything being prepared, I fixed on the approaching night to commence my journey.'

After some trepidation, 'I jumped into the boat, cut some of the ropes which fastened the balloon to the trees, the struggles of which tore up entirely those it had before loosened, and, swifter than the ball from the cannon's mouth, I ascended into the regions of air.

'The rapidity of my ascension (being wholly unaccustomed to it, for I had never been in a balloon before) at first made me find great difficulty in breathing: but that, however, I soon conquered; and, after I had continued rising about three or four hours, I collected sufficient resolution to quit my convulsed hold of the sides of the boat, and thinking that the progress of the balloon was impeded by the trees, which hung to the ropes, I took my hatchet and cut them. The noise they made in their descent was awful, somewhat similar to the rushing of a vast cataract over irregular rocks. . . .

'The Earth was far distant beneath, and appeared but faintly irradiated with the lumen of the Moon; whilst to me her lucid beams seemed brighter than the Sun in his meridian glory . . . I soon beheld the clouds floating below me, which totally obscured the earth from my sight. The scene was awful—each star increased in size as I ascended, and many of the nearest appeared as large as the Moon does to you. . . .

'After having ascended some time, I found it necessary to make use of my oars, in order to keep the balloon as near to the Moon's course (whose rapid motion I could as plainly discover) as possible. The wind favoured my exertions, and my doubts of being able to attain the object of my journey almost vanished.'

Mr. Lunatic presently fell asleep, and when he woke he found that 'the Moon was not so luminous as it had before appeared to be; and I seemed as if I was descending on it, rather than ascending to it. This circumstance at first greatly astonished me; but my surprise ceased because I could account for that circumstance by having got within its attraction.

'Above me appeared an infinity of planets; some larger than others by reason of my proximity to them; the nearest to me, which I concluded must be our Earth, seemed nearly as luminous as the Moon, from whence I concluded that the Earth, in its turn, afforded light to that planet. . . . As I rapidly approached, I perceived that the view I had of the scenes below were similar, taken collectively, to the appearance we observe on the Moon's surface, but which was, as I then plainly saw, an immense continent, abounding with high mountains, large vallies, deep cavities, and even volcanos, the smoke of one of which, high as I was, I could distinguish.

'I now became rather anxious about my descent, for the continent was bounded by immense seas, on which I was as likely to alight as on the land. Whilst I was surveying the objects beneath me, to my horror I found that the balloon was approaching the volcano, which appeared to be much larger than Aetna. It was to no purpose that I endeavoured to use my oars to avoid the danger I was in, for the flames and the roaring of the volcano had the same effect to lull the wind as I have observed in engagements a constant discharge of ordnance has on the sea; and I descended rapidly towards the flaming mountain, already rendered uncomfortable by the heat and smoke, and expecting every moment to experience the fate of Empedocles.'

As the balloon continued to descend, Mr. Lunatic threw out everything in the boat, and finally cut loose even that when a stone from the volcano fell into it: 'Both instantly fell into the sea, and thus lightened the balloon swiftly ascended, and passed over a part of the continent', till it came down a little distance from the shore of another sea beyond it, where he was soon picked up by a Lunarian in a small boat.

With the rest of his adventures we need not concern ourselves. The inhabitants of the Moon turned out to be guilty of all the follies and vices of the age—which the author ingeniously credits to them alone, pointing out with fine irony that such things could never happen in England. At the end of the book he is still in the Moon, lamenting that he is 'condemned to reside amongst a people whose consummate folly is the least of their defects, for they are entirely destitute of those virtues which adorn my dear countrymen. Good Heavens! what could induce me to be so desirous of an empty fame, as to leave such an enlightened nation to herd with madmen!'

The volcanoes on the Moon were still active in 1827 when the first American astronaut (also concealed by an impenetrable pseudonym), Mr. Joseph Atterley, visited the satellite in company with a Burmese Brahmin, as described in *A Voyage to the Moon: With some account of the Manners and Customs, Science and Philosophy, of the People of Morosufia and other Lunarians.* The 'manners and customs', were once again purely satirical, in the Gulliver style, and are well forgotten. But the method of transport, though it may bear some of De Foe's suggestion of the 'Lunar earth', inaugurate the method of a 'new substance' for propulsion, which reached its most famous climax in H. G. Wells's 'Cavorite'.

'There is a principle of repulsion as well as gravitation in the earth', declared Atterley. 'It causes fire to rise upwards. It is exhibited in electricity. It occasions water-spouts, volcanoes, and earthquakes. After much labour and research this principle has been found embodied in a metallic substance. . . . This metal, when separated and purified, has as great a tendency to fly off from the earth, as a piece of gold or lead has to approach it. . . . In the course of our experiments we found that this same metal, which was repelled from the earth, was in the same degree attracted towards the Moon. . . .

'The machine in which we proposed to embark was a copper vessel that would have been an exact cube of six feet if the corners and edges had not been rounded off. It had an opening large enough to receive our bodies, which was closed by double sliding pannels, with quilted cloth between them. When these were properly adjusted the machine was perfectly air-tight, and strong enough by means of iron bars running inside and out, to resist the pressure of the atmosphere, when the machine should be exhausted of its air, as we took the precaution to prove by means of an air pump. On top of the copper chest and on the outside we had as much of the lunar metal (which I shall henceforth call *Lunarium*) as we found by calculation and experiment would overcome the weight of the machine as well as its contents, and take us to the Moon on the third day.'

These intrepid voyagers took with them a supply of air condensed in a small globular vessel 'made partly of iron and partly of lunarium to take off its weight'; they could break the fall onto the Moon by releasing lumps of lunarium which were held in place by screws operated from within the space-ship—and lumps of lead served the same purpose on the return journey.

So Atterley and the Brahmin sealed themselves into the Space-coffin, cut the mooring-ropes, and rose comfortably from the earth, releasing lumps of lead once the atmosphere was passed, and so increasing their speed considerably.

'A small circular window, made of a single piece of thick, clear glass, was neatly fitted on each of the six sides,' and the two Space-travellers had a fine view of the Earth growing speedily smaller and smaller beneath them until it seemed like a great moon which was suddenly above them instead of being below. For at the moment when the gravity changed the top of their machine became its bottom without the machine itself turning over or seeming to move at all: it was the whole firmament which appeared to swing round as they began to descend upon the new world of the Moon.

As they drew near, manipulating their lumps of lead and lunarium to break the fall, they found the physical features of the Moon to be much the same as those on Earth, with seas, rivers and lakes, fertile hills and valleys, and high, active volcanoes such as those which Nicholas Lunatic had encountered.

On leaving their Space-coffin they found themselves in 'a less extensive and more transparent atmosphere than upon the Earth. . . . The difference is so great that some astronomical observers have been induced to think she [the Moon] has none. If that, however, had been the case, our voyage would have been impracticable.'

On this the very verge of the desperately scientific, it is pleasant to hark back to more fanciful days and record the last visit to the Moon by the aid of birds: neither the severed wings of Icaro-Mennipus nor the flight of gansas which conveyed Domingo Gonsales, but a single mighty eagle, the only equivalent of the 'Roc' suggested by Wilkins as a means of reaching the Moon which seems to have been tried by Space-travellers.

This eagle conveyed an Irish gamekeeper named Daniel O'Rourke on a very drunken trip (according to Thomas Crofton Croker who collected the legend in 1829), when he had been foolish enough to take a rest under the haunted walls of Carrigapooka in 'the kingdom of Kerry'.

'Down it came with a pounce, and looked at me full in the face; and what was it but an eagle?'

It offered to give Daniel a lift home, 'though it is very improper for you to get drunk on Lady Day', and Daniel accepted gladly. 'I therefore mounted upon the back of the eagle, and held him tight enough by the throat, and up he flew in the air like a lark. Little I knew the trick he was going to serve me. Up—up—up, God knows how far up he flew. . . . At last where should we come to, but to the Moon itself. Now you can't see it from this, but there is, or there was in my time, a reaping-hook sticking out of the side of the Moon.

' "Dan," said the eagle, "I'm tired with this long fly; I had no notion 'twas so far. . . . You must get off and sit down on the Moon until I rest myself. . . . You can catch fast hold of the reaping-hook that's sticking out of the side of the Moon, and 'twill keep you up."

'When he had me there fairly landed, he turned about on me and said: "Good morning to you, Daniel O'Rourke," said he; "I think I've nicked you fairly now. You robbed my nest last year, and in return you are freely welcome to cool your heels dangling upon the Moon like a cock throw."

'Away he went, and I never saw him from that day to this—sorrow fly away with him! You may be sure I was in a disconsolate condition, and kept roaring out for the bare grief, when all at once a door opened right in the middle of the Moon, creaking on its hinges as if it had not been opened for a month before, I suppose they never thought of greasing 'em, and out there walks—who do you think, but the Man in the Moon himself? I knew him by his bush.

' "Good morrow to you, Daniel O'Rourke," said he; "how do you do?" "Very well, thank your honour," said I. "I hope your honour's well." "What brought you here, Dan?" said he. So I told him how I was a little overtaken in liquor at the master's, and how I was cast on a *disolute* island, and how I lost my way in the bog, and how the thief of an eagle promised to fly me out of it, and how, instead of that, he had fled me up to the Moon.

' "Dan," said the Man in the Moon, taking a pinch of snuff when I was done, "you must not stay here. . . . So be off in less than no time. . . . You'd better let go the reaping-hook: you had better, Dan."

' "Why then, my little fellow," says I, taking the whole weight of him with my eye from head to foot, "there are two words to that bargain, and I'll not budge, but you may if you like." "We'll see how that is to be," says he; and back he went, giving the door such a great bang after him (for it was plain he was huffed) that I thought the Moon and all would fall down with it.

'Well, I was preparing myself to try my strength with him, when back again he comes, with the kitchen cleaver in his hand, and, without saying a word, he gives two bangs to the handle of the reaping-hook that was keeping me up, and *whap!* it came in two. "Good morning to you, Dan," says the spiteful little old blackguard, when he saw me cleanly falling down with a bit of the handle in my hand.

' "God help me!" says I, "but this is a pretty pickle for a decent man to be seen in at this time of night: I am now sold fairly." The word was not out of my mouth when whiz! what should fly by close to my ear but a flock of wild geese, all the way from my own bog of Bally-ashenogh, else how should they know me? The *ould* gander, who was their general, turning about his head, cried out to me, "Is that you, Dan? . . . Dan," said he, "I'll save you: put out your hand and catch me by the leg, and I'll fly you home." "Sweet is your hand in a pitcher of honey, my jewel," says I, though all the time I thought within my-self that I don't much trust you. . . .'

So Daniel O'Rourke continued on his adventurous way, and had been nearly to Arabia, had landed in the sea, and made the acquaintance of a whale, before he 'came to' beneath the haunted walls of the Pooka's tower.

When Edgar Allan Poe (1809–49), just beginning his career as a young journalist on *The Southern Literary Messenger* in 1835, decided to write a Moon-voyage, he could smile indulgently at Daniel O'Rourke as 'a *jeu d'esprit* not altogether contemptible', though he considered Cyrano as 'utterly meaningless', and condemned Joseph Atterley out of hand, commenting on 'the stupidity of the book', and finding 'the *means* of the voyage more deplorably ill-conceived than are even the *gansas* of our friend Signor Gonsales', whom he knew only in the French version of 1648, which he described as 'a singular and somewhat ingenious little book'.

Poe professed to take a deeply scientific interest in the possibilities of a voyage to the Moon: the subject was very much in the news in 1835, since Sir John Herschel was at the Cape of Good Hope, making observations with the biggest telescope yet employed; and indeed Poe's story, *The Unparalleled Adventure of One Hans Pfaall* appeared only three weeks before the famous 'Lunar Hoax' in *The New York Sun*.

'In these various *brochures*,' wrote Poe of the four Moon tales which he knew, 'the aim is always satirical, the theme being a description of Lunarian customs as compared with ours. In none is there any effort of *plausibility* in the details of the voyage itself. The writers seem in each instance to be utterly uninformed in respect to astronomy. In *Hans Pfaall* the design is original, in as much as regards an attempt at *verisimilitude*, in the application of scientific principles (so far as the whimsical nature of the subject would permit), to the actual passage between the Earth and the Moon.'

Hans Pfaall is perhaps a little spoiled by the whimsical prologue and epilogue; and of course the actual method employed in reaching the

Moon is no nearer to modern scientific credibility than was that of Gonsales. Nevertheless Poe's claim has some foundation, and just as he has been claimed as the literary ancestor of Sherlock Holmes and of *Treasure Island*, so he might well be called the originator of science-fiction. The method of the accumulation of scientific detail and the meticulous realism of the flight was merely elaborated by Jules Verne, who was indeed a professed admirer of Poe's works, and particularly of *Hans Pfaall*.

The story is of a Dutch bellows-mender fallen upon evil days and persecuted by his creditors who combines a new discovery in pneumatics with his interest in astronomy to set out for the Moon and destroy his worst enemies at the same time.

Disposing of many of his household goods, and borrowing money which he had no intention of repaying, Hans set to work: 'I proceeded to precure at intervals, cambric muslin, very fine, in pieces of twelve yards each; twine; a lot of the varnish of caoutchouc; a large and deep basket of wicker-work, made to order; and several other articles necessary in the construction and equipment of a balloon of extraordinary dimensions . . . I worked up the twine into net work of sufficient dimensions; rigged it with a hoop and the necessary cords; and made purchase of numerous instruments and materials for experiment in the upper regions of the upper atmosphere. I then took opportunities of conveying by night, to a retired situation east of Rotterdam, five iron-bound casks, to contain about fifty gallons each, and one of a larger size; six tin tubes, three inches in diameter, properly shaped, and ten feet in length; and a quantity of a *particular metallic substance, or semi-metal*, which I shall not name, and a dozen demi-johns of *a very common acid*. The gas to be formed from these latter materials is a gas never yet generated by any other person than myself—or at least never applied to any similar purpose. I can only venture to say here that it is *a constituent of azote*, so long considered irreducible, and that its density is about 37.4 times *less than that of hydrogen*.'

Hans arranged his barrels in a circle twenty-five feet in diameter, with the big one in the middle, and secretly placed charges of gunpowder under each of them, with a slow-match that could be lit as he entered the balloon-car.

The balloon 'would contain more than forty thousand cubic feet of gas; would take me up easily, I calculated, with all my implements, and if I managed rightly, with one hundred and seventy-five pounds of ballast into the bargain.' Hans persuaded his three enemies, the most avid of the creditors, to help him fill the balloon with gas preparatory to launching it, promising 'payment of all scores in full as soon as I could bring the present business to a termination.

'In about four hours and a half I found the balloon sufficiently inflated. I attached the car, therefore, and put all my implements in it—a telescope; a barometer, with some important modifications; a thermometer; an electrometer; a compass; a magnetic needle; a seconds watch; a bell; a speaking trumpet, etc., etc., etc.,—also a globe of glass, exhausted of air and carefully closed with a stopper—not forgetting the condensing apparatus, some unslacked lime, a stick of sealing wax, a copious supply of water, and a large quantity of provisions, such as pemmican, in which much nutriment is contained in comparatively little bulk. I also secured in the car a pair of pigeons and a cat.'

When all was ready and daylight approaching, Hans dropped a lighted cigar onto the slow-match and jumped into the car: 'I immediately cut the single cord which held me to the earth, and was pleased to find that I shot upwards with inconceivable rapidity, carrying with all ease one hundred and seventy-five pounds of leaden ballast, and able to have carried up as many more. . . . Scarcely, however, had I attained the height of fifty yards, when, roaring and rumbling up after me in the most tumultuous and terrible manner, came so dense a hurricane of fire, and gravel, and burning wood, and blazing metal, and mangled limbs, that my very heart sunk within me, and I fell down in the bottom of the car trembling with terror.'

The explosion of the gunpowder, while it knocked Hans Pfaall insensible, sent his balloon rushing aloft on the gust of hot air with as much impetuosity as Nicholas Lunatic's had shown. When he recovered, at six o'clock in the morning, 'I was still rapidly ascending, and the barometer gave a present altitude of three and three-quarter miles'. All was going according to plan, and Hans was convinced that he would reach the Moon—and that he would find air all the way: after all, the highest altitude attained by 1835 was twenty-five thousand feet, and after that 'all such reasoning and from such *data*, must of course be simply analogical. . . . This is a moderate altitude . . . and I could not help thinking that the subject admitted room for doubt, and great latitude for speculation'. In fact, Hans argued with the aid of plausibly-sounding scientific reasons, 'there was a chance—there was a strong probability—that at no epoch of my ascent I should reach a point where the united weights of my immense balloon, the inconceivably rare gas within it, the car, and its contents, should equal the weight of the mass of the surrounding atmosphere displaced; and this will be readily understood as the sole condition upon which my up-ward flight would be arrested'. Indeed the only thing which still troubled Hans Pfaall at all was the discomfort he was likely to feel at the most rarefied point in the atmosphere, where Terrestrial gravity gave way to Lunar.

All being well at five miles, except for some rather wetting clouds, Hans flung out a few small pieces of ballast, and soared up faster than ever—thus avoiding a thunderstorm, which might have proved fatal: 'such perils, although little considered, are perhaps the greatest danger which must be encountered in balloons'.

At nearly ten miles up, Hans began to suffer considerably from nose- and ear-bleeding, and shortness of breath, and on increasing his speed suffered so violently that, lying almost insensible on the floor of his car, he decided to practise phlebotomy, and a drastic operation left him clear-headed and 'freer from absolute *pain* of any kind than I had been during the last hour and a quarter of my ascension'.

At seventeen miles breathing became so difficult that Hans set his 'condenser' to work, and drew an air-tight bag all round the car, to prevent his artificial atmosphere from escaping. He was quite enclosed now, with valves for the escape of bad air, and with windows at sides and bottom—and could continue comfortably on his journey with no further suffering. When twenty-five miles was reached, the barometer ceased to function, and feathers thrown out fell like bullets: the balloon, however, continued to ascend, and indeed was gaining speed all the time. The Earth below seemed still to be cup-shaped, but a vast extent was visible.

By the eighth day Hans Pfaall was looking down at an undeniable planet, and indeed 'found a sensible diminution in the Earth's apparent diameter, besides a material alteration in its general colour and appear-ance. The whole visible area partook in different degrees of a tint of pale yellow, and in some portions had acquired a brilliancy even painful to the eye'.

Day by day the Earth became yellower and yellower, more bright to the eyes, and the landmarks harder to distinguish. In time the Moon became invisible, since the balloon itself hid it from the occupant of the car, and the terrestrial globe shrank beneath him until 'not even the outlines of continents and seas could now be traced upon the Earth with distinctness'.

Several times Hans was alarmed by 'a loud, cracking and terrific sound for which I could in no manner account. It was of very brief duration, but, while it lasted, resembled nothing in the world of which I had any previous experience'. At length on the fifteenth day the sound came again, and 'gathered intensity as it continued'.

Terrified, Hans clung to the side of his car which 'vibrated with excessive violence, and a gigantic and flaming mass of some material which I could not distinguish came with a voice of a thousand thunders, roaring and booming by the balloon'. This meteorite Hans assumed to be 'some mighty volcanic fragment ejected from that world to which I was so rapidly approaching'.

On the seventeenth morning when Hans Pfaall woke from a short sleep it was to find the surface beneath him 'suddenly and wonderfully *augmented* in volume. I was thunderstruck! No words can give any adequate idea of the extreme, the absolute horror and astonishment, with which I was seized. . . . The balloon had positively burst! I was falling—falling with the most impetuous, the most unparalleled velocity!' But he did not seem to be moving very fast, and when he recovered from his fright he realised what had happened: 'in fact, amazement must have fairly deprived me of my senses, when I could not see the vast difference, in appearance, between the surface below me and the surface of my mother Earth. The latter was indeed over my head and completely hidden by the balloon, while the Moon— the Moon itself in all its glory—lay beneath me and at my feet!

'It lay beneath me like a chart. . . . The entire absence of ocean or sea, and indeed of any lake or river, or body of water whatsoever, struck me at the first glance as the most extraordinary feature in its geological condition. Yet, strange to say, I beheld vast level regions of a character decidedly alluvial, although by far the greater portion of the hemisphere in sight was covered with innumerable volcanic mountains, conical in shape. . . . The greater part of them were in a state of evident eruption, and gave me fearfully to understand their fury and their power, by repeated thunders of the miscalled meteoric stones, which now rushed upwards by the balloon with a frequency more and more appalling.'

On the nineteenth day of his voyage, Hans drew so near to the Moon that at length he came within atmosphere which he could breathe without too great a discomfort, and was able to dispense with his 'condenser' and airtight envelope or 'gum-elastic chamber'.

But all was not yet well: the atmosphere was not dense enough to support the weight beneath the balloon. 'I was now close upon the planet, and coming down with the most terrible impetuosity. I lost not a moment, accordingly, in throwing overboard first my ballast, then my water-kegs, then my condensing apparatus, and gum-elastic chamber, and finally every article within the car. But it was all to no purpose. I still fell with horrible rapidity, and was now not more than half a mile from the surface. As a last resource, therefore, having got rid of my coat, hat and boots, I cut loose from the balloon the *car itself*, which was of no inconsiderable weight, and thus, clinging with both hands to the net work, I had barely time to observe that the whole country, as far as the eye could reach, was thickly interspersed with diminutive habitations, ere I tumbled headlong into the very heart of a fantastical-looking city, and into the middle of a vast crowd of ugly little people, who none of them uttered a single syllable, or gave themselves the least trouble to render me assistance, but stood like a parcel of idiots, grinning in a ludicrous manner, and eyeing me and my balloon askant, with their arms set akimbo. I turned from them in contempt, and, gazing upwards at the Earth so lately left, and left perhaps for ever, beheld it like a huge, dull, copper shield, about two degrees in diameter, fixed immovably in the heavens overhead, and tipped on one of its edges with a crescent border of the most brilliant gold. No traces of land or water could be discovered, and the whole was clouded with variable spots, and belted with tropical and equatorial zones.'

And so Hans Pfaall ended the account of his unparalleled adventure, which he wrote out and sent back to Rotterdam by the hands of a Lunar inhabitant. The letter contained a request for a full pardon for the murder of the three creditors, in return for which he would impart all that he had learnt during his five years on the Moon.

'I have much to say of the climate of the planet; of its wonderful alterations of heat and cold; of unmitigated and burning sunshine for one fortnight, and more than polar frigidity for the next; of a constant transfer of moisture, by distillation like that *in vacuo*, from the point beneath the Sun to the point farthest from it; of a variable zone of running water; of the people themselves; of their manners, customs, and political institutions; of their peculiar physical construction; of their ugliness; of their want of ears, those useless appendages in an atmosphere so peculiarly modified; of their consequent ignorance of the use and properties of speech; of their substitute for speech in a singular method of inter-communication; and above all of those dark and hideous mysteries which lie in the outer regions of the Moon,—regions which owing to the almost miraculous accordance of the satellite's rotation on its own axis with its sidereal revolution about the Earth, have never yet been turned and, by God's mercy, never shall be turned to the scrutiny of the telescopes of man. . . .'

But that, as Kipling would have said, is another story—which Edgar Allan Poe did not choose to write.

Chapter Seven

THE GREAT LUNAR HOAX

L ESS than a fortnight after 'The Unparalleled Adventure of One Hans Pfaall' made its first appearance in *The Southern Literary Messenger*, the readers of *The New York Sun* were filled with an excitement that speedily became world-wide at the news of Sir John Herschel's astronomical discoveries recently made by means of his giant telescope at the Cape of Good Hope.

The reports, which were published daily for a week in September 1835, claimed to be reprinted from the Supplement to the *Edinburgh Journal of Science*:

'In this unusual addition to our journal, we have the happiness of making known to the British public, and thence to the whole civilized world, recent discoveries in astronomy which will build an imperishable monument to the age in which we live, and confer upon the present generation of the human race a proud distinction through all future time.'

So the first article began, and in this high strain the author continued, justifying his contribution to so learned a journal by the confident mass of scientific detail with which he seasoned his narrative.

To begin with, the telescope was described—such a telescope as had never yet been made. 'To render our enthusiasm intelligible, we will state at once, that by means of a telescope, of vast dimensions and an entirely new principle, the younger Herschel, at his observatory in the Southern Hemisphere, has already made the most extraordinary discoveries in every planet of our solar system; has discovered planets in other solar systems; has obtained a distinct view of objects in the Moon, fully equal to that which the unaided eye commands of terrestrial objects at a hundred yards; has affirmatively settled the question whether this planet be inhabited, and by what order of beings. . . .

'For our early and almost exclusive information concerning these facts, we are indebted to the devoted friendship of Dr. Andrew Grant, the pupil of the elder, and for several years past the inseparable coadjutor of the younger Herschel. The amanuensis of the latter at the Cape of Good Hope, and the indefatigable superintendent of his telescope during the whole period of its construction and operation, Dr.

Grant has been enabled to supply us with intelligence equal, in general interest at least, to that which Dr. Herschel himself has transmitted to the Royal Society.'

Whereupon the author proceeded to describe the telescope with its prodigious lens weighing 14,826 pounds, or nearly seven tons, after being polished; which had a magnifying power of forty-two thousand times, and would thus reveal objects on the Moon of eighteen inches in diameter. But even this was to be only 'a second magnifier'—he hoped in time even 'to study the entomology of the Moon, in case she contained insects upon her surface'.

At last the telescope was set up, with detailed mechanisms to move it in time with whatever heavenly body was focused on the lens— since otherwise the Moon would move too fast for the smaller objects to be seen.

At nine-thirty on the night of January 10th, 'the whole immense power of his telescope was applied, and to its focal image about one half of the power of his microscope. On removing the screen of the latter, the field of view was covered throughout its entire area with a beautifully distinct, and even vivid representation of *basaltic rock*.' This precipitous shelf was profusely covered with a dark red flower, 'precisely similar', says Dr. Grant, 'to the *papaver rhoeas*, or rose-poppy of our sublunary cornfield; and this was the first organic production of nature, in a foreign world, ever revealed to the eyes of men'. . . . The specimen of lunar vegetation '. . . demonstrated that the Moon has an atmosphere constituted similarly to our own, and capable of sustaining organized, and therefore, most probably, animal life'.

After this, trees were seen rather like English yews, in 'a mountainous district of a highly diversified and romantic character', and then a lake, or inland sea, which turned out to be the Sea of Clouds. 'Fairer shores never angel coasted on a tour of pleasure. A beach of brilliant white sand, girt with wild castellated rocks, apparently of green marble, varied by chasms, occurring every two or three hundred feet, with grotesque blocks of chalk or gypsum, and feathered and festooned at the summits with the clustering foliage of unknown trees, moved along the bright wall of our apartment until we were speechless with admiration. The water, whenever we obtained a view of it, was nearly as blue as that of the deep ocean, and broke in large white billows upon the strand.'

Next they saw some strange 'obelisk-shaped or very slender pyramids, standing in irregular groups, each composed of about thirty or

forty spires, every one of which was perfectly square. . . . They were
monstrous amethysts, of a diluted claret colour, glowing in the intensest
light of the sun! They varied in height from sixty to ninety feet,
though we saw several of a still more incredible altitude'. These were
situated in a valley half a mile from the Sea of Fruitfulness—a most
inappropriate name, for 'the sea-board was entirely composed of chalk
and flint, and not a vestige of vegetation could be discovered with our
strongest glasses'.

Over the next chain of mountains, however, were forests of mighty
trees resembling oaks but with broad glossy leaves 'and tresses of yellow
flowers which hung, in the open glades, from the branches to the
ground. These mountains passed, we arrived at a region which filled
us with utter astonishment. It was an oval valley, surrounded, except at
a narrow opening towards the south, by hills, as red as the purest
vermilion, and evidently crystallized; for whenever a precipitous
chasm appeared—and these chasms were very frequent and of immense
depth—the perpendicular sections presented conglomerated masses of
polygon crystals, evenly fitted to each other, and arranged in deep
strata, which grew darker in colour as they descended to the foundations
of the precipices. Innumerable cascades were bursting forth from the
breasts of every one of these cliffs, and some so near their summits,
and with such great force, as to form arches many yards in diameter.

'At the foot of this boundary of hills was a perfect zone of hills
surrounding the whole valley, which was about eighteen or twenty
miles wide, at its greatest breadth, and about thirty in length. Small
collections of trees, of every imaginable kind, were scattered about the
whole luxuriant area, and here our magnifiers blest our panting hopes
with specimens of conscious existence. In the shade of the woods, on
the south-eastern side, we beheld continuous herds of brown quadrupeds, having all the external characteristics of the bison, but more
diminutive than any species of the bos genus in our natural history. . . .
It had, however, one widely distinctive feature, which we afterwards
found common to nearly every species of lunar quadruped we have
discovered; namely, a remarkable fleshy appendage over the eyes,
crossing the whole breadth of the forehead and united to the ears. . . .
It immediately occurred to the acute mind of Dr. Herschel, that this
was a providential contrivance to protect the eyes of the animal from
the great extremes of light and darkness to which all the inhabitants of
our side of the Moon are periodically subjected.

'The next animal perceived would be classed on Earth as a monster.

It was of bluish lead-colour, about the size of a goat, with a head and beard like him, and a *single horn*, slightly inclined forward from the perpendicular. The female was destitute of the horn and beard, but had a much longer tail. It was gregarious, and chiefly abounded on the acclivitous glades of the woods. In elegance of symmetry it rivalled the antelope, and like him it seemed an agile sprightly creature running with great speed, and springing from the green turf with all the unaccountable antics of a young lamb or kitten.

'On examining the centre of this delightful valley, we found a large branching river, abounding with lovely islands, and water-birds of numerous kinds. A species of gray pelican was the most numerous; but a black and white crane with unreasonably long legs and bill, was also quite common. . . . Near the upper extremity of one of these islands, we obtained a glimpse of a strange amphibious creature of a spherical form, which rolled with great velocity across the pebbly beach, and was lost sight of in the strong current which set off from the angle of the island. We were compelled, however, to leave this prolific valley unexplored, on account of clouds which were evidently accumulating in the lunar atmosphere, our own being perfectly translucent. But this was itself an interesting discovery, for more distant observers had questioned or denied the existence of any humid atmosphere in this planet.'

After discovering 'the Valley of the Unicorn', midway between the Sea of Fruitfulness and the Sea of Nectar, Herschel's observations were interrupted for two nights by cloudy weather; but on the 13th the great telescope with its magnifying appendages was once again trained upon the Moon—with startling results.

The western portion was selected, in the neighbourhood of Endymion and Petavius, and they were soon aware of 'an oval-shaped mountain, inclosing a valley of an immense area, and having, on its western ridge, a volcano in a state of terrific eruption. . . . We carefully explored the Endymion [which] we found . . . rich . . . in every imaginable production of a bounteous soil. Dr. Herschel has classified not less than thirty-eight species of forest trees, and nearly twice this number of plants, found in this tract alone, which are widely different from those found in more equatorial latitudes. Of animals, he classified nine species of mammilia, and five of oviparia. Among the former is a small kind of reindeer, the elk, the moose, the horned bear, and the biped beaver. The last resembles the beaver of the Earth in every other respect than in its destitution of a tail, and its invariable habit of walking upon two feet. It carries its young in its arms like a human being, and moves with an easy gliding motion'.

On islands in a great lake nearby they first discovered lunar palm-trees, with great crimson flowers, and prolific growths of tree-melons. 'Of animals we saw only an elegant striped quadruped about three feet high, like a miniature zebra; and two or three kinds of long-tailed birds, which we judged to be golden and blue pheasants. On the shores, however, we saw countless multitudes˙ of univalve shell-fish, and among them some huge flat ones.'

Turning next to the Langrenus region they found a narrow valley opening onto a lake. 'Imagination, borne on the wings of poetry, could alone gather similes to portray the wild sublimity of this land-scape, where dark behemoth crags stood over the brows of lofty precipices, as if a rampart in the sky; and forests seemed suspended in mid-air. On the eastern side there was one soaring crag, crested with trees, which hung over in a curve like three-fourths of a Gothic arch, and being of a rich crimson colour, its effect was most strange upon minds unaccustomed to the association of such grandeur with such beauty. But whilst gazing upon them in a perspective of about half a mile, we were thrilled with astonishment to perceive four successive flocks of large winged creatures wholly unlike any kind of birds, des-cend with a slow even motion from the cliffs on the western side, and alight upon the plain. They were first noticed by Dr. Herschel, who exclaimed, "Now, gentlemen, my theories against your proofs, which you have often found a pretty even bet, we have here something worth looking at: I was confident that if ever we found beings in human shape, it would be in this longitude, and that they would be provided by their Creator with some extraordinary powers of locomotion: first exchange for my number D." This lens being soon introduced, gave us a fine half-mile distance; and we counted three parties of these creatures, of twelve, nine and fifteen in each, walking erect towards a small wood near the base of the eastern precipices. Certainly they *were* like human beings, for their wings had now disappeared, and their attitude in walking was both erect and dignified. Having observed them at this distance for some minutes, we introduced lens H.Z., which brought them to the apparent proximity of eighty yards: the highest clear magnitude we possessed until the latter end of March, when we effected an improvement in the gas-burners. About half of the first party had passed beyond our canvas; but of all the others we had a perfectly distinct and deliberate view. They averaged four feet in height, were covered, except on the face, with short and glossy copper-coloured hair, and had wings composed of a thin membrane, without hair, lying snugly upon their backs, from the top of the shoulders to the calves of the legs. The face, which was of a yellowish flesh-colour, was a slight improvement upon that of a large orang-outang, being more open and intelligent in its expression, and having a much greater expansion of forehead. The mouth, however, was very prominent, though somewhat relieved by a thick beard on the lower jaw, and by lips far more human than any species of the simia genus.

'Whilst passing across the canvas, and whenever we afterwards saw them, these creatures were evidently engaged in conversation; their gesticulation, more particularly the varied action of their hands and arms, appeared impassioned, and emphatic. We hence inferred that they were rational beings, and, although not perhaps of so high an order as others which we discovered the next month on the shores of the Bay of Rainbows, that they were capable of producing works of art and contrivance. The next view we obtained of them was still more favourable. It was on the borders of a little lake or expanded stream, which we then for the first time perceived running down the valley to a large lake, and having on its eastern margin a small wood. Some of these creatures had crossed this water, and were lying like spread eagles on the skirts of the wood. We could then perceive that their wings possessed great expansion, and were similar in construction to those of the bat, being a semi-transparent membrane, expanded in curvilineal divisions by means of straight radii, united at the back by the dorsal integuments. But what astonished us very much was the circumstance of this membrane being continued from the shoulders to the legs, united all the way down, though gradually decreasing in width. The wings seemed completely under the command of volition, for those of the creatures whom we saw bathing in the water, spread them instantly to their full width, waved them as ducks do theirs to shake off the water, and then as instantly closed them again in a compact form. Our further observation of the habits of these creatures, who were of both sexes, led to results so very remarkable, that I prefer they should first be laid before the public in Dr. Herschel's own work, where I have reason to know they are fully and faithfully stated, however incredulously they may be received. The three families then almost simultaneously spread their wings, and were lost in the dark confines of the canvas before we had time to breathe from our paralyzing astonishment. We scientifically denominated them the Vespertilio-homo, or man-bat; and they are doubtless innocent and happy creatures, notwithstanding some of their amusements would but ill comport with some of the terrestrial notions of decorum.'

On the following night the telescope brought the region near the active volcano of Bullialdus into view, and Dr. Herschel felt that its proximity 'must be so great a local convenience to dwellers in this valley during the long periodical absence of solar light, as to render it a place of popular resort for the inhabitants of all the adjacent regions. We therefore applied our full power to explore it, and rich indeed was our reward.

'The very first object in this valley that appeared upon our canvas was a magnificent work of art! It was a temple—a fane of devotion, or of science, which, when consecrated to the Creator, *is* devotion of the loftiest order. . . . It was an equi-triangular temple, built of polished sapphire, or of some resplendent blue stone, which, like it, displayed a myriad points of golden light twinkling and scintillating in the sun-beams. . . . The roof was composed of some yellow metal, and divided into three compartments, which were not triangular planes inclining to the centre, but subdivided, curved and separated, so as to represent a mass of violently agitated flames rising from a common source of conflagration, and terminating in wildly waving points. . . . It was open on each side, and seemed to contain neither seats, altars, nor offerings; but it was a light and airy structure nearly a hundred feet high from its white glistening floor to its glowing roof, and it stood upon a round green eminence on the eastern side of the valley.

'We had not far to seek for inhabitants of this "Vale of the Triads". Immediately on the outer border of the wood which surrounded, at the distance of half a mile, the eminence on which the first of these temples stood, we saw several detached assemblies of beings whom we instantly recognised to be of the same species as our winged friends of the Lake Langrenus. Having adjusted the instrument for a minute examination, we found that nearly all the individuals in these groups were of a larger stature than the former specimens, less dark in colour, and in *every respect* an improved variety of the race. They were chiefly engaged in eating a large yellow fruit like a gourd, sections of which they dextrously divided with their fingers, and ate with rather uncouth voracity, throwing away the rind. . . . They seemed to be eminently happy, and even polite, for we saw, in many instances, individuals sitting nearest these piles of fruit, select the largest and brightest speci-mens, and throw them archwise across the circle to some opposite friend or associate who had extracted the nutriment from those scattered round him, which were frequently not a few. While thus engaged in their rural banquets, or in social converse, they were always seated with their knees flat upon the turf, and their feet brought evenly together in the form of a triangle. And for some mysterious reason or other this figure seemed to be an especial favourite among them; for we found that every group or social circle arranged itself in this shape before it dispersed, which was generally done at the signal of an individual who stepped into the centre and brought his hands over his head in an acute angle. At this signal each member of the company extended his arms forward so as to form an acute horizontal angle with the extremity of the fingers. But this was not the only proof we had that they were creatures of order and subordination.

'We had no opportunity of seeing them actually engaged in any work of industry or art; and, so far as we could judge, they spent their happy hours in collecting various fruits in the woods, in eating, flying, bathing, and loitering about upon the summits of precipices.

'But, although evidently the highest order of animals in this rich valley, they were not its only occupants. Most of the other animals which we had discovered elsewhere, in very distant regions, were collected here: and also at least eight or nine new species of quadrupeds. The most attractive of these was a tall white stag, with lofty spreading antlers, black as ebony. We several times saw this elegant creature trot up to the parties of the semi-human beings I have described, and browse the herbage close beside them, without the least manifestation of fear on its part, or of notice on theirs. The universal state of amity among all classes of lunar creatures, and the apparent absence of every carnivorous or ferocious species, gave us the most refined pleasure, and doubly endeared to us this lovely nocturnal companion of our larger, but less favoured world. Ever again when I "eye the blue vault and bless the *useful* light", shall I recall the scenes of beauty, grandeur, and felicity I have beheld upon her surface, not "as *through* a glass darkly", but face to face; and never shall I think of that line of our thrice noble poet,

> Meek Diana's crest
> Sails through the azure air, an island of the blest,

without exulting in my knowledge of its truth.'

This virtually ended Herschel's observations as reported in *The New York Sun* from the Edinburgh article. Not until the end of March were the lunar observations recommenced, and of them Dr. Grant merely concludes that in 'The Valley of Rainbows' on Mount Atlas 'we found the very superior species of the Vespertilio-homo. In stature they did not excel those last described, but they were of infinitely greater personal beauty, and appeared, in our eyes, scarcely less lovely than the general representation of angels by the more imaginative school of painters. Their social economy seemed to be regulated by laws or ceremonies exactly like those prevailing in the Vale of the Triads, but their works of art were more numerous, and displayed a proficiency of skill quite incredible to all except actual observers. I shall, therefore, let the first detailed account of them appear in Dr. Herschel's authenticated natural history of this planet'.

The effect of the publication of *Great Astronomical Discoveries* was astounding. It was received with complete credence throughout America—a credence only equalled in its unexpectedness by the Orson Welles broadcast of *The Invasion from Mars* in 1938. The office of *The Sun* was besieged day by day, by larger and larger crowds, 'not a copy of the paper could be procured at any price' the day after issue, and 'the utmost capacity of the steam cylinder-press failed to afford an adequate supply'.

At the end of the week the article was issued in the form of an illustrated pamphlet, and twenty thousand copies were sold on the day of publication. The startling news of the Moon's inhabitants crossed the Atlantic, was translated into various European languages, and although not received so hysterically, and very soon disproved, it was still believed in central Europe twenty years later.

During its appearance in New York, while a crowd was besieging the offices of *The Sun*, an elderly Quaker 'completely dispelled the undecided opinions of the listening crowd around him, by asserting in the calmest, coolest, and most unquestioning manner, that he was fortunately engaged on commercial business at the East India Docks in London when the vast lens, of seven tons weight, and the whole gigantic apparatus of the telescope as described in the story, was taken on board an East India Ship, for erection at the Cape of Good Hope, and that he himself saw it craned on board', with various other corroboratory details.

'The then unknown author of the story was among the immediate listeners to this venerable witness's testimony to the truth of his conscious fiction.' The author was the popular and successful journalist

Richard Adams Locke (1800–1871), who had already achieved one successful 'scoop' for the new paper whose fortune was made by the Great Lunar Hoax.

Locke seems to have been the last writer to people the Moon until H. G. Wells invented his loathsome insect-like Selenites in 1900, and the charming 'Bat-men' fleeting the time as in the age of innocence about the lovely lunar lakes and islands make the pleasantest picture in the fiction of the Moon.

With the explosion of the Lunar Hoax died the last belief in a 'world in the Moon', though even in 1838 that pious astronomer and populariser Thomas Dick in his factual work *Celestial Scenery*, still felt that the Moon must have inhabitants, since otherwise one must believe that the works of the Creator were wasted. He maintained, however, that we could never see them, even if they existed—but that there were no seas or even clouds on the Moon, and that he was at a loss to imagine what the inhabitants could be like.

The Moon Hoax, however, he castigated unsparingly as an impious deception, and pointed out (as Poe had already done) that a little thought would have revealed its absurdity: for even if a telescope could be constructed with such an amazing power of magnification, and even 'supposing any beings resembling man to exist on that orb, we could only perceive the diameter of their heads, as an aeronaut does when he surveys the crowds beneath him from an elevated balloon'.

CHAPTER EIGHT

ROUND THE MOON WITH JULES VERNE

ELIEF in 'The Great Lunar Hoax' died hard, and even Sir John
B Herschel's real findings (the full text was published in 1847 as
*Results of Astronomical Observations made during the Years 1834–8 at the
Cape of Good Hope*) did not quite extinguish the popular belief in a
habitable, or even inhabited Moon.

Even as late as the eighteen-fifties a German scientist and astronomer
called Von Littrow seriously proposed describing enormous luminous
geometric figures on the Steppes of Siberia to be recognised by the
Selenites who would then presumably make their presence known by
similar means.

Herschel was certain that there were no Lunar inhabitants, but he
was prepared to believe that the Moon was egg-shaped, and that on
the end turned always away from the Earth there might be air and
water: 'It by no means follows,' he declared, 'from the absence of
visible indications of water or air on this side of the Moon, that the
other is equally destitute of them, and equally unfitted for maintaining
animal or vegetable life.'

Even as late as 1872 in his book *The Moon,* the astronomer Richard
Anthony Proctor, felt that 'the conclusion to which we seem forced
by all the evidence obtainable, is that either the Moon has no atmosphere
at all (which scarcely seems possible), or that her atmosphere is of such
extreme tenuity as not to be perceptible by any means of observation
we can apply'. However, he found himself unable to accept Herschel's
theory of possible oceans on the moon's further side, and was not
convinced that the Moon was egg-shaped.

It was at this point in the development of scientific and popular
knowledge that Jules Verne launched his famous projectile for its trip
round the Moon—and with it one of the few classics of Space-
literature, one that has still its readers who prefer it to any of today's
streamlined and highly coloured narratives which we may well live
to see translated into fact.

Jules Verne (1828–1905) needs no introduction: *Twenty Thousand
Leagues Under the Sea* and *Around the World in Eighty Days* are still
'familiar in our mouths as household words', even if better known on

the screen than between their old thick green covers and with their delightfully preposterous pseudo-Doré illustrations.

Verne, after a dozen years as a minor man of letters, after plays, stories and studies of which the very names are forgotten, struck gold suddenly in 1863 with the first of his great series of *Voyages Extraordinaires*—the logical literary development of the hoax—*Cinq semaines en ballon*.

This imaginary story, with the complete apparatus of reality, reached, with Verne, a high, almost a prophetic level. His model was Poe, particularly the Poe of 'Hans Pfaall', 'William Wilson' and the detective stories; but his concentration on scientific and geographic reality made his art a thing in itself: the basis of fact was so firm, indeed, that Verne is often hailed as the inventor of the submarine or of the airship. 'For the last twenty years,' Marshall Lyautey once remarked, 'the advance of the peoples is merely living the novels of Jules Verne.'

Five Weeks in a Balloon might have been a real record by David Livingstone, but Verne's next scientific romance, *Voyage au centre de la Terre* (1864) still waits, we might say, for confirmation. Speliographers of the future have still to discover the sea in the Earth's interior, and the surviving prehistoric monsters (whom Conan Doyle borrowed with much else nearly fifty years later for his *Lost World*), but once again the scientific background was so accurate and so detailed that the book convinced—and convinces even now.

So did *Les Aventures du Captaine Hatteras* (*The English at the North Pole*) next written, and serialised, though only published in book form in 1866: but the subsequent discovery of a Pole rather different from the volcanic island of Verne's forecast has cast this story into obscurity.

Having crossed unknown Africa in a balloon, discovered the North Pole half a century before Peary, and penetrated to the Earth's very core, Jules Verne was ready for new worlds to conquer: and with Poe as his literary hero, it was inevitable that the Moon should present the next challenge to a genius so peculiarly suited to the task.

De La Terre à la Lune which appeared in 1865, tells of the great experiment made by the Gun Club of Baltimore, a group of artillery men at a loose end owing to the close of the American Civil War, who 'conceived the idea of putting themselves in communication with the Moon, by sending to her a projectile'.

After raising over a million pounds by public subscription, the experts of the Gun Club chose a site in Florida, and constructed a gun of the Columbiad type nine hundred feet long run perpendicularly into the earth and pointing towards the zenith so that, if fired at the right moment, its projectile would strike the Moon at her nearest to the Earth—a mere 238,833 miles.

The plan was to discharge a spherical aluminium shell a hundred and eight inches in diameter made of aluminium twelve·inches thick and weighing 19,250 pounds, by means of a charge of four hundred thousand pounds of gun-cotton which would give it the initial velocity of at least twelve thousand yards in the first second—the speed necessary for it to escape from the Earth's gravity and cross into that of the Moon.

A monster telescope was constructed on an American mountain peak, powerful enough to follow the projectile's flight and witness its landing on the Moon.

All was prepared, except for the shell itself, when a cryptic telegram arrived from one of Verne's superbly nonchalant French adventurers named Michel Ardan: 'Substitute for your spherical shell a cylindro-conical projectile. I shall go inside.'

And not only did Ardan insist on having his way, but he persuaded Barbicane the president of the Gun Club to accompany him, and they took as third Captain Nicholl the original enemy of the scheme who had betted thousands of dollars on its failure: they were both, needless to say, won over and completely captivated by this irresistibly charming and vivacious Frenchman—direct descendant, in a more civilized and refined age, of Cyrano and D'Artagnan.

In consequence of this change of plans the projectile was altered in form and made into a comfortable little room for the intrepid Space-travellers: 'The upper part of the walls were lined with a thick padding of leather, fastened upon springs of the best steel'; the middle section of the padded walls consisted of the doors of cupboards; and the lower part, of a seat which ran all round the inside. 'The entrance into this metallic tower was by a narrow aperture contrived in the walls of the cone. This was hermetically closed by a plate of aluminium, fastened internally by powerful screw-pressure. The travellers could therefore quit their prison at pleasure, as soon as they should reach the Moon.

'Light and view were given by means of four thick lenticular glass scuttles, two pierced in the circular wall itself, the third in the bottom, the fourth in the top. These scuttles then were protected against the shock of departure by plates let into solid grooves, which could easily be opened outwards by unscrewing them from the inside. Reservoirs firmly fixed contained water and the necessary provisions; and fire and light were procurable by means of gas, contained in a special reservoir under a pressure of several atmospheres.'

Air was supplied by chemical means, enough to last the three travellers and their two dogs for twenty-six days. The projectile was also stored with scientific instruments, tools, weapons, Lunar charts, seeds and cuttings of shrubs, and compressed food to last a year. 'They were also supplied with brandy, and took water enough for two months, being confident from astronomical observations that there was no lack of water on the Moon's surface.'

So the great moment arrived. Countless multitudes gathered around the base of the hill into which the Columbiad was sunk. The three intrepid adventurers entered the projectile and screwed down the plate which covered the entrance aperture.

'A terrible silence weighed upon the entire scene! Not a breath of wind upon the earth! Not a sound of breathing from the countless chests of the spectators! Their hearts seemed afraid to beat! All eyes were fixed upon the yawning mouth of the Columbiad.'

As the fateful moment drew near, Murchison the Scotch engineer counted the last seconds, his finger on the switch: ' . . . -thirty-nine, forty! FIRE!!!'

'Instantly Murchison pressed with his finger the key of the electric battery, restored the current of the fluid, and discharged the spark into the breach of the Columbiad.

'An appalling, unearthly report followed instantly, such as can be compared to nothing whatever known, not even to the roar of thunder, or the blast of volcanic explosions! No words can convey the slightest idea of the terrific sound! An immense spout of fire shot up from the bowels of the earth as from a crater. The earth heaved up, and with great difficulty some few spectators obtained a momentary glimpse of the projectile victoriously cleaving the air in the midst of the fiery vapours!'

The atmospheric confusion caused by the explosion was so great that clouds and bad weather obscured the Moon for twelve nights—until long after the projectile should have arrived, since the journey was calculated to take ninety-seven hours and twenty minutes. When at last the projectile was sighted on the twelfth day, 'the startling news so impatiently awaited, burst like a thunderbolt . . . "This projectile has not arrived at its destination. It has passed by the side [of the Moon], but sufficiently near to be retained by the lunar attraction . . . It is now pursuing an elliptical orbit round the Moon of which it has become a true satellite." '

On this note of thrilling suspense Verne ended his book; nor did he publish the eagerly awaited sequel *Autour de la Lune* until 1870 (though it appeared a little earlier in serial form). Neither book was translated into English until 1873, when they appeared in a single volume, with the original illustrations, as *From the Earth to the Moon and a Trip Round it*. This, the official version, which is quoted here, was made by Louis Mercier and Eleanor E. King, and its very clumsiness and the awkwardness of its fidelity to the French seems to become a part of the atmosphere and glamour which remain with so many of us who were brought up on the stories of Jules Verne.

Before following Michel Ardan and his companions into Space it is worth pausing to ask whether Verne, who prided himself on his scientific accuracy, really considered the wild impossibilities of his Moon Voyage. 'People believed in it,' as Verne's biographer Kenneth Allott says of the Lunar Hoax, 'because they wished to believe,' and Verne's Moon stories 'are an amazing piece of virtuosity'. The accumulation of accurate mathematical formulae and calculations seems to have bridged the gaps in probability just as the complete realism of all but the initial impossibility does in the stories of F. Anstey and E. Nesbit.

Verne's most glaring absurdity is the assumption that his three Space-travellers could survive the initial shock of the discharge of the Columbiad. One moment they were stationary, the next they were moving at a speed of more than seven miles a second. Swallow that, and one hardly pauses to consider that such velocity in passing through the atmosphere would have reduced the projectile to incandescence in a moment of inconceivable friction; or that a few rockets could not have broken its fall on to the surface of the Moon.

Against this must, of course, be set today's vast increase of scientific knowledge. A schoolboy, brought up on such books as *The Conquest of Space*, would tell you that a human being cannot stand an increasing velocity of motion greater than thirty-two feet per second per second —but that, if built up at this rate of 'foot-seconds' he can perfectly well endure the speed of seven miles a second which, as Verne knew, is necessary for a Space-ship to attain before it can escape from terrestrial gravity.

Neither Verne nor his readers knew of this ratio: both, on the other hand, were aware of the shock of a sudden start. And Verne does not blink this difficulty—though he keeps the emphasis well off it with the aid of soluble problems presented as of much greater, and more vital interest.

'But, unhappy man, the dreadful recoil will smash you to pieces at your starting,' was one of Captain Nicholl's objections.

To it, however, Michel Ardan replied with his usual superb confidence: 'My dear contradictor, you have just put your finger upon the true and only difficulty; nevertheless, I have too good an opinion of the industrial genius of the Americans not to believe that they will succeed in overcoming it.'

'But the heat developed by the rapidity of the projectile in crossing the strata of air?' was Nicholl's next query.

'Oh! The walls are thick, and I shall soon have crossed the atmosphere.' Michel Ardan's reply is about all we hear on this subject: but the initial shock came in for maturer consideration—and was duly overcome by 'the industrial genius' of the American artillery expert Barbicane, who instead of fighting his duel with Nicholl, sat down and worked out that 'water, simply water will act as a spring!'

Accordingly, as soon as the projectile was cast, it 'had now to be filled to a depth of three feet with a bed of water, intended to support a watertight wooden disc, which worked easily within the walls of the projectile. It was upon this kind of raft that the travellers were to take their place. This body of water was divided by horizontal partitions, which the shock of the departure would have to break in succession. Then each sheet of the water, from the lowest to the highest, running off into escape tubes towards the top of the projectile, constituted a kind of spring; and the wooden disc, supplied with extremely powerful plugs, could not strike the lowest plate except after breaking successively the different partitions. Undoubtedly the travellers would still have to encounter a violent *recoil* after the complete escapement of the water; but the first shock would be almost entirely destroyed by this powerful spring'.

A detail like this, slipped in among so many indisputable facts, carried the book to as near a credence as the astounding charge of gun-cotton did the projectile itself till it seemed to miss its mark only by a hair's breadth.

Doubtless, none of the readers of *From the Earth to the Moon* were in any doubt that Ardan, Nicholl and Barbicane had survived the initial shock, however eagerly they may have snatched up *A Trip Round the Moon* to see in what extraordinary fashion the three Space-travellers had sent news of their adventures back to Earth.

Inside the projectile everything had gone almost to plan. A little while before the explosion the three lay down calmly on specially prepared beds on the floor. 'Suddenly a dreadful shock was felt, and the projectile, under the force of six billions of litres of gas, developed by the combustion of the pyroxyle, mounted in Space.

'What had happened? What effect had this frightful shock produced? Had the ingenuity of the constructors of the projectile obtained any happy result? Had the shock been deadened, thanks to the springs, the four plugs, the water cushions, and the partition-breaks? Had they been able to subdue the frightful pressure of the initiatory speed of more than 11,000 yards in a second . . .?'

All was well, however. They recovered consciousness after a few minutes, and only the dog Satellite had a fractured skull and died shortly afterwards—to be cast, rather improbably, into outer Space, there to become a satellite indeed, revolving round the projectile itself.

' "Yes," exclaimed Barbicane in triumph, "we are moving! This stifling heat, penetrating through the partitions of the projectile, is produced by its friction on the atmospheric strata. It will soon diminish, because we are already floating in Space, and after having been nearly stifled, we shall have to suffer intense cold. . . . If our initiatory speed has not been checked by the friction, six seconds would be enough for us to pass through the forty miles of atmosphere which surrounds the globe. . . .

' "I should not be surprised," Barbicane went so far as to admit, "if [our projectile] did not look like a meteor on fire to the eyes of the spectators in Florida."

' "But then Joseph T. Marston will think we are roasted!" objected Ardan.

' "I feared it," said Nicholl simply.

' "And you never mentioned it, my sublime captain," exclaimed Michel Ardan, clasping his friend's hand.'

Having effectively settled this question, and deciding that they heard no sound of the initial explosion because they travelled faster than sound, the three adventurers uncovered the window at the bottom of the projectile and looked down at the Earth.

'It was in its octant, and showed a crescent finely traced on the dark background of the sky. Its light, rendered bluish by the thick strata of the atmosphere, was less intense than that of the crescent Moon, but it was of considerable dimensions, and looked like an enormous arch stretched across the firmament. Some parts brilliantly lighted, especially on its concave part, showed the presence of high mountains, often disappearing behind thick spots, which are never seen on the lunar disc. They were rings of clouds placed concentrically round the terrestrial globe.'

At the distance of 4,650 miles from the Earth, the projectile encountered its most serious, and least expected, danger. Suddenly the travellers' 'attention was attracted by the approach of a brilliant object. It was an enormous disc, whose colossal dimension could not be estimated. Its face, which was turned to the Earth, was very bright. One might have thought it a small moon reflecting the light of the larger one. She advanced with great speed, and seemed to describe an orbit round the Earth, which would intersect the passage of the projectile. This body revolved upon its axis, and exhibited the phenomena of all celestial bodies abandoned in Space. . . . A collision was possible, and might be attended with deplorable results; either the projectile would deviate from its path, or a shock, breaking its impetus, might precipitate it to the earth; or, lastly, it might be irresistibly drawn away by the powerful asteroid'.

It passed, however, several hundred yards from the projectile, and Barbicane was able to identify it as 'a simple meteorite, but an enormous one, which the attraction of the Earth has retained as a satellite'. This novel fact in astronomy Verne fathers hastily onto 'a French astronomer, M. Petit', according to whose observations 'this meteorite will accomplish its revolution round the Earth in three hours and twenty minutes', but 'this second moon is so small, and its speed so great, that the inhabitants of the Earth cannot see it'—M. Petit merely determined its existence by 'noticing disturbances', and its presence is not generally admitted by astronomers.

The pseudo-satellite turned out to be one of the most important characters in Verne's story, for its unexpected visit drew the projectile sufficiently far from its course to make it miss the Moon and circle round it instead.

Meanwhile they sped on through Space, taking full advantage of the heavenly view laid out before them: 'the whole extent of the celestial sphere swarmed with stars and constellations of wonderful purity, enough to drive an astronomer out of his mind! On one side the Sun, like the mouth of a lighted oven, a dazzling disc without a halo, standing out on the dark background of the sky! On the other, the Moon returning its fire by reflection, and apparently motionless in the midst of the starry world. Then, a large spot seemingly nailed to the firmament, bordered by a silvery cord: it was the Earth!'

At 78,514 leagues came 'the point of equal attraction' when the projectile turned slowly and imperceptibly over so that the heavier base now pointed to the Moon. At the same time the travellers experienced the extraordinary sensation of the absence of weight: 'Nicholl, having accidentally let a glass slip from his hand, the glass, instead of falling, remained suspended in the air. . . . Diana too, placed in space by Michel, did not seem to know that she was floating in air. The three adventurous companions . . . felt that *weight* was really wanting to their bodies. If they stretched out their arms, they did not attempt to fall. Their heads shook on their shoulders. Their feet no longer clung to the floor of the projectile. . . . Michel, taking a spring, left the floor and remained suspended in the air. . . .'

But this state of things 'scarcely lasted an hour; the travellers felt themselves insensibly drawn towards the floor', and the long fall towards the Moon was beginning.

As they drew nearer, preparations were made to break the force of the fall—a ticklish business, however much smaller was the attraction of the Moon than the Earth. 'The projectile would smash like glass,' Nicholl had maintained, to which Ardan's reply was 'that he would break their fall by means of rockets properly placed'.

The idea was that 'powerful fireworks, taking their starting-point from the base and bursting outside, could, by producing a recoil, check to a certain degree the projectile's speed. These rockets were to burn in Space, it is true; but oxygen would not fail them, for they could supply themselves with it, like the lunar volcanoes, the burning of which has never yet been stopped by the want of atmosphere round the Moon.

'Barbicane had accordingly supplied himself with these fireworks, enclosed in little steel guns, which could be screwed on to the base of the projectile. Inside, these guns were flush with the bottom; outside, they protruded about eighteen inches. There were twenty of them. An opening left in the disc [the wooden floor, now replaced on its steel springs] allowed them to light the match with which each was provided. All the effect was felt outside.'

Here Verne, as Cyrano had done, and as his own contemporary Achille Eyraud did, touched by chance on rocket propulsion; and Verne knew that rockets would fire effectively in Space—but failed quite to see that here was the one probable means of Space-flight, which fifty years later, was to be put forward by scientists in sober earnest.

Meanwhile Barbicane and his companions were preparing to break the fall of their projectile on to the Moon by means of rocket-guns: but their belief in their efficacy was not to be put to the test.

'The Moon had grown so large in their eyes that it filled half the firmament. . . . At that moment Barbicane thought he could estimate the distance which separated them from their aim at no more than 700 leagues. . . . The projectile was evidently *nearing* the Moon, but it was also evident that it would never *reach* her. As to the nearest distance at which it would pass her, that must be the result of the two forces, attraction and repulsion, affecting its motion.'

As the projectile continued on its unknown way—to become the Moon's satellite, or to wander for ever in trackless Space, for ought they knew—Barbicane voiced the eager philosophy of the nineteenth century which underlies all Verne's desperate ventures and *voyages extraordinaires*: 'My friends, I do not know whither we are going; I do not know if we shall ever see the terrestrial globe again. Nevertheless, let us proceed as if our work would one day be of use to our fellow-men. Let us keep our minds free from every other consideration. We are astronomers; and this projectile is a room in the Cambridge Observatory, carried into Space. Let us make our observations!'

So they sped round the Moon, drawing ever nearer, seeing the well-known features of the lunar geography from a new and novel angle, their eyes dazzled by the vivid black and white of a world without atmosphere. Their glasses brought them to within two miles as they sped over the dark crater of Plato and approached Mount Gioja—the Moon's north pole as seen from the Earth—which they crossed at a distance of less than twenty-five miles from the surface.

'It seemed as if the Moon might be touched by hand!' and the glasses reduced the distance to a quarter of a mile. Then 'suddenly the projectile passed the line of demarcation between intense light and absolute darkness, and was plunged in profound night! . . . The transition was so sudden, without shade, without gradation of light, without attenuation of the luminous waves, that the orb seemed to have been extinguished by a powerful blow. . . . The darkness was complete, and rendered even more so by the rays from the stars. It was "that blackness" in which the lunar nights are insteeped, which last three hundred and four hours and a half at each point of the disc'.

Feeling, perhaps, that his reputation for scientific veracity was at stake, Verne did not let his travellers see or describe the side of the Moon which is for ever invisible from the Earth. Nor did he commit himself to any positive statement about the possibility of air, or even life, behind the Moon.

Once, as they sped on their way through the darkness, they saw 'a luminous brightness . . . a reddish incandescence' which they decided must be an active volcano—which might mean the presence of air, though Barbicane would not admit that it must do so. Yet, 'where heat exists, who can affirm that the vegetable kingdom, nay, even the animal kingdom itself, has not up to this time resisted all destructive influences?'

Then again, a burning meteor exploded suddenly quite near to them, 'and through a luminous emanation, which lasted some seconds, the whole three caught a glimpse of that mysterious disc which the eye of man now saw for the first time. What could they distinguish at a distance which they could not estimate? Some lengthened bands along the disc, real clouds formed in the midst of a very confined atmosphere, from which emerged not only mountains, but also projections of less importance; its circles, its yawning craters, as capriciously placed as on the visible surface. Then immense spaces, no longer arid plains but real seas, oceans, widely distributed, reflecting on their liquid surface all the dazzling magic of the fires of space; and, lastly, on the surface of the continents, large dark masses, looking like immense forests under the rapid illumination of a brilliance.

'Was it an illusion, a mistake, an optical illusion? Could they give a scientific assent to an observation so superficially obtained? Dared they pronounce upon the question of its habitability after so slight a glimpse of the invisible disc?'

The voyage continued prosaicly, however, after this moment of wishful thinking, and presently, as they neared the south pole they 'sighted towards the southern border of the Moon, and in the direction followed by the projectile, some bright points cut upon the dark shield of the sky': it was, in fact, the Sun 'lighting up the summit of the mountains situated on the southern borders of the Moon'.

They sped over Mount Doerfel a little to the east of the pole, and there decided that the dazzling white sheets noted on this range must be deeply frozen snow.

'Cooled lava would never give out such intense reflection,' declared Barbicane. 'There must then be water, there must be air on the Moon. As little as you please, but the fact can no longer be contested.'

Nevertheless, as they sped further and further from the Moon's surface their reasoned conclusion was: 'The Moon is not habitable.'

For, argued Barbicane, 'if there exist representatives of the animal kingdom on the Moon, they must have fled to those unfathomable cavities which the eye cannot reach; which I cannot admit, for they must have left traces of their passages on those plains which the atmosphere must cover, however slightly raised it may be. These traces are nowhere visible'.

So the great trip round the Moon ended. As the projectile drew further and further away, a last attempt was made to land, by discharging the rockets fixed to the base which was now pointing directly towards the Earth.

'The projectile sustained a certain shock, which was sensibly felt in the interior. . . .

'At this moment, Barbicane, quitting the scuttle, turned to his two companions. He was frightfully pale, his forehead wrinkled, and his lips contracted.

' "We are falling!" said he.

' "Ah!" cried Michel Ardan, "on to the Moon?"

' "On to the Earth!"

'And now this fearful fall had begun,' at the end of which they must strike the Earth at the speed of twelve thousand yards a second: ' "We are lost!" said Michel coolly.

But they were not lost. By supreme good fortune the projectile landed in the deepest part of the Pacific Ocean—to the amazement of Lieut. Bronsfield of the U.S. Corvette *Susquehanna*, whose attention, as he stood with his watch, 'was attracted by a distant hissing noise . . . produced in the highest regions of the air. They had not time to question each other before the hissing became frightfully intense, and suddenly there appeared to their dazzled eyes an enormous meteor, ignited by the rapidity of its course and its friction through the atmospheric strata. This fiery mass grew larger to their eyes, and fell, with the noise of thunder, upon the bowsprit, which it smashed close to the stem, and buried itself in the waves with a deafening roar!'—to rise to the surface and float comfortably when its plunge was accomplished.

'And the midshipman, making himself as it were the echo of the body, cried: "Commander, it is 'they' come back again!" '

Chapter Nine

THE CONQUEST OF MARS

WHATEVER its faults, Jules Verne's Moon voyage effectively superseded all the stories of Space-flight, all journeys into other worlds that came before it. Until his day, Gonsales and his gansas were still remembered: Verne mentions them in the course of his book, just as Poe does in the note to *Hans Pfaall*. But Godwin and Poe, and Cyrano too, dropped right out of the popular ken after the launching of Verne's projectile.

Looking forward also, Verne's book seemed the be-all and end-all of Lunar exploration. It could only be imitated: the Moon, as everyone now knew, was uninhabitable—and even Wells in 1900 was forced to rely once more on satire, aided by his rather macabre strain of fantasy, to effect one more memorable expedition.

The Moon was virtually a closed chapter when Verne's double volume arrived in England in 1873 to begin its career here as a minor classic. But just at the right time the planets began taking shape in readers' imaginations—the shape of habitable worlds; and the last quarter of the century came suddenly and spectacularly under the influence of Mars.

From the time of Herschel's observations earlier in the century the interest in Mars had begun, and astronomers were already mapping the planet. It was easily observed that the poles showed white, and snow was deduced: there was no cloud-envelope to hide the surface as in the case of Venus; Mars had an inclination of axis similar to the Earth's, with a day and night of a reasonable length.

Here indeed was a new world of exciting possibilities, and as telescopes grew, maps of the surface became more and more detailed. By the end of the century a popular astronomer such as Garrett P. Serviss in his handbook to *Other Worlds* (New York, 1901) was able to tell his readers confidently:

'To watch one of [the polar caps] apparently melting, becoming perceptibly smaller week after week, while the general surface of the corresponding hemisphere of the planet deepens in colour, and displays a constantly increasing wealth of details as summer advances across it, is an experience of the most memorable kind, whose effect upon the mind of the observer is indescribable.

'Two principal colours exist on the disc of Mars—dark, bluish grey or greenish grey, characterising areas which have generally been regarded as seas, and light yellowish red, overspreading broad regions looked upon as continents. It was early observed that if the dark regions really are seas, the proportion of water to land upon Mars is much smaller than upon the Earth. . . . Mars has generally been regarded as an older or more advanced planet than the Earth.'

This in itself was enough to raise Mars to the place in the imagination so long held by the Moon: but more spectacular discoveries were to come.

In 1877, and again in 1879, Mars was in the exceptionally favourable oppositions which occur about once every seventy years. The great red planet was a conspicuous object in the night sky even to the naked eye: but the Italian astronomer Schiaparelli trained his telescope across the thirty-five million miles then separating the two planets—and announced the most astounding discovery in the whole history of astronomy:

'There are on this planet,' he wrote, 'traversing the continents, long dark lines which may be designated as *canals*, although we do not yet know what they are. These lines run from one to another of the sombre spots that are regarded as seas, and form, over the lighter, or continental, regions a well-defined network. Their arrangement appears to be invariable and permanent. . . . They cross one another obliquely, or at right angles. They have a breadth of [seventy-four miles], and several extend over a length of [nearly three thousand miles]. Their tint is very nearly the same as that of the seas, usually a little lighter. Every canal terminates at both its extremities in a sea, or in another canal; there is not a single example of one coming to an end in the midst of dry land.'

Schiaparelli never maintained that his 'canals' were man-made, and indeed the Italian word is more accurately translated as 'channels'. But interest, particularly in America, was fomented by Percival Lowell who devoted most of his career to the observing and mapping of the canals, which he at least believed to be of human construction. He discovered that the Martian 'seas' were more or less dry (marshes rather than lakes) and that the canals represented stretches of vegetation: but this only strengthened the conviction that they were constructed—for it meant that a canal itself might be only of reasonable width, irrigating the land on either side, and not the water-ways over seventy miles wide which would have taxed the skill of even the most super-

Martians of invention. Lowell's two books, *Mars* (1896) and *Mars and Its Canals* (1911) had considerable effect on the stories concerning the planet: the first, for example, gives the factual background used by Wells in 'The Crystal Egg' and *The War of the Worlds*, while the second gave Edgar Rice Burroughs what little scientific help he needed for *A Princess of Mars* and its sequels.

Who can boast the honour of having made the first voyage to Mars (setting aside the spiritual excursions of Kircher or 'Israel Jobson') is uncertain: it may well have been that unnamed adventurer whose expedition *Across the Zodiac* was given to the world by the novelist Percy Greg (1836–89) in the year 1880. Greg's work ranged from domestic novels like *Ivy: Cousin and Bride* or *The Devil's Advocate*, to his great *History of the United States* published shortly before his death.

Across the Zodiac, his only venture into other worlds, tells in two fat volumes of a solitary voyage to Mars in the year 1830. The hero, who never gives his name, travelled in one of the largest Space-ships in fiction, with metal walls three feet thick: 'My Astronaut somewhat resembled the form of an antique Dutch East-Indiaman, being widest and longest in a plane equidistant from floor and ceiling, the sides and ends sloping outwards from the floor and again inwards towards the roof. The deck and keel, however, were absolutely flat, and each one hundred feet in length and fifty in breadth, the height of the vessel being about twenty feet.' There were crystal lenses in floor and roof to act as telescopes, and more ordinary windows in the sides and ends.

'I carpeted the floor with several alternate layers of cork and cloth. At one end I placed my couch, table, bookshelves, and other necessary furniture, with all the stores needed for my voyage, and with a further weight sufficient to preserve equilibrium. At the other I made a garden with soil three feet deep and five feet in width, divided into two parts so as to permit access to the windows. I filled each garden closely with shrubs and flowering plants of the greatest possible variety, partly to absorb animal waste, partly in the hope of naturalising them elsewhere.

'In the centre of the vessel was the machinery, occupying altogether a space of about thirty feet by twenty. The larger portion of this area was, of course, taken up by the generator, above which was the receptacle of the Apergy. From this descended right through the floor a conducting bar in an antapergic sheath, so divided that without separating it from the upper portion the lower might revolve in any direction through an angle of twenty minutes (20'). This, of course, was intended to direct the stream of the repulsive force against the Sun. . . .'

For 'Apergy' was the new discovery which enabled Greg's hero to carry his great Astronaut across the gulf of Space separating the Earth from Mars—the next development of Atterley's 'Lunarium'. Apergy, however, a 'curious secret of nature' was a 'repulsive force' only and not an attractive one as Lunarium had been. Its details are vague— partly due to the writer's anxiety to preserve his secret, and partly to the conveniently defective manuscript which narrates his experiences. Apergy 'acts through air or in a vacuum in a single straight line, without deflection, and seemingly without diminution', and all that was needed was to generate it and send it down a bar contained in an impervious or 'antapergic' sheath. 'By cutting across this conductor, and causing the further part to rotate upon the nearer, I could divert the current through any required angle. Thus I could turn the repulsion upon the resistant body (Sun or planet), and so propel the vessel in any direction I pleased.'

The vessel constructed and ready to set out at the date of the opposition, Greg's phlegmatic hero calmly entered it alone, sealed up the entrance-window, and set the generator to work, applying the force of the Apergy directly against the ground beneath him.

Glancing out of a window as he started, he 'saw the Earth falling from me so fast that, within five minutes after my departure, objects like trees and even houses had become almost indistinguishable to the naked eye'. In twenty minutes, the speed increasing steadily, he was thirty-five miles up, and the Earth appeared like a vast saucer. 'But my speed was constantly increasing, very much as the speed of an object falling to the Earth from a great height increases; and before ten more minutes had elapsed, I found myself surrounded by a blackness nearly absolute.'

So he went on his prosaic way with the Earth and the Sun directly behind him, and experienced the usual surprises of Space-travellers, though never without having anticipated them. Thus, for example, 'weight had become almost nonexistent. My twelve stone had dwindled to the weight of a small fowl, and hooking my little finger into the loop of a string hung from a peg fixed near the top of the stern wall, I found myself able thus to support my weight without any sense of fatigue for a quarter of an hour or more', and upsetting his coffee, was able to catch most of it before it touched the floor, since it fell 'as slowly as feathers in the immediate vicinity of the Earth'.

A meteor was met and avoided without any difficulty; various astronomical observations were made and recorded, and 'on the thirty-ninth morning of my voyage . . . I was within about 1,900,000 miles' of Mars. With a telescope he could already see clouds, land-locked seas, broad bands of water, and then the two moons of Mars, Deimos and Phobos—which had only been discovered in 1877 by the American astronomer Asaph Hall, though the savants of Laputa, according to Gulliver, had 'discovered two lesser Stars, or Satellites, which revolve about Mars', and had given them roughly their right distances from the planet and periods of revolution a hundred and fifty years earlier.

Soon the Astronaut turned over and began to fall onto Mars, slowed down and finally steered by the repulsive force of the Apergy. Presently 'I was within 8,000 miles of the surface, and could observe Mars distinctly as a world, and no longer as a star. The colour, so remarkable a feature in his celestial appearance, was almost equally perceptible at this moderate elevation. The seas are not so much blue as grey. Masses of land reflected a light between yellow and orange, indicating, as I thought, that orange must be as much the predominant colour of vegetation as green upon Earth. As I came still lower only parts of the disc were visible at once . . . I perceived at last a point which appeared peculiarly suitable for my descent . . . an isolated mountain of peculiar form. . . . Before I had satisfied myself whether the planet was or was not inhabited, I found myself in a position from which its general surface was veiled by the evening mist, and directly over the mountain in question, within some twelve miles of its summit. This distance I descended in the course of a quarter of an hour, and landed without a shock about half an hour after the Sun had disappeared below the horizon.'

Having landed after dark on a mountain where he was not likely to be surprised, the careful explorer took a good night's sleep, and next morning, having tested the air (which he found wholesome and of 'a pressure equal to that which prevails at a height of 16,000 feet on Earth'), he stepped out onto the new planet.

'Gravity on the surface of Mars is less than half what it is on Earth', but he found no difficulty in walking, and the birds he had brought with him flew easily and happily in this new world.

'The scene I now contemplated was exceedingly novel and striking. The sky, instead of the brilliant azure of a similar latitude on Earth, presented to my eye a vault of pale green. . . . The lower slopes were entirely clothed with yellow or reddish foliage. . . . Whatever foliage

I saw consisted distinctly of leaves analogous to those of our deciduous trees, chiefly of three shapes: a sort of square rounded at the angles, with short projecting fingers; an oval, slightly pointed where it joined the stalk; and lanceolate or sword-like blades of every size, from two inches to four feet in length. Nearly all were of a dull yellow or copper-red tinge. . . . I caught sight of a Martian animal: a little creature, not much bigger than a rabbit, itself a sort of sandy-yellow colour, bounded from among some yellow herbage by my feet, and hopped or sprang in the manner of a kangaroo down the steep slope.

'About twenty miles from where I stood, a deep arm of the sea ran up into the land, and upon the shores of this lay what was unquestionably a city. It had nothing that looked like fortifications, and even at this distance I could discern that its streets were of remarkable width, with few or no buildings so high as mosques, churches, state-offices or palaces in Tellurian cities. Their colours were most various and brilliant, as if reflected from metallic surfaces; and on the waters of the bay itself rode what I could not doubt to be ships. . . .'

There is no space to follow Greg's hero further through the six hundred pages of conscientious and carefully detailed narrative. The book reads like the account of an observant visitor to a little-known country, and scarcely a page lacks interest.

To some extent satire creeps into this new world. Mars, being so much older than Earth, has progressed hundreds of centuries beyond the civilization of Greg's day. Democracy has led to Communism and Communism to sheer anarchy, the dregs of civilization being rescued at length after devastating wars by a scientific intelligentsia (such as Wells imagined over half a century later in *The Shape of Things to Come*) who set up monarchical rule, but run the planet on scientific and utilitarian lines. Ages of machine-made ease produce an insipid, unambitious race, who, with the necessity for labour, have lost the enjoyment of leisure. With scientific proof as the be-all and end-all, religion has long been 'disproved' and forbidden; State Nurseries, the abolition of marriage, and the inevitable reduction of women from the equals to the chattels of their polygamous lords have stamped out all the better feelings—love, honour, loyalty, kindness, self-sacrifice—leaving only complete selfishness, and complete apathy.

This state of things is only stirred by the Unknown: a fanatic intolerance and antagonism is aroused at the suggestion that there is anything which cannot be proved and explained by science. The visitor from Earth arouses this antagonism of fear, and is about to be torn to pieces by the mob, when he is rescued by the powerful member of an Underground Movement—'The Children of Light'—who, in secret, believe in an Almighty Maker of the Universe, in a life after death, and in loyalty and affection at least amongst themselves, and who try to observe the sanctity and affection of family life.

The visitor's preserver, Esmo, the descendant of its Founder, is one of the leaders of this movement, and his daughter Eveena presently becomes the Earth-man's wife. The strangely assorted couple are summoned by the Campta, or Autocrat of Mars, and journey by sea— sometimes on the surface, sometimes deep beneath the waves—by canal, and by under-ground waterway to the Martian capital.

Finding favour in the Campta's sight, the hero is given a 'household', which includes several additional wives, and one of these turns out to be the tool of a plot to destroy the Children of Light. The Campta is also to be a victim of the plot, which the hero uncovers; but both Esmo and Eveena are killed (the latter giving her life for her husband) before the Campta can strike at the rebels and give immunity and recognition to the Children of Light.

Broken-hearted, the hero sets out for Earth in his Astronaut—and here the book ends. But the opening chapters suggest that he crashed on a South Sea Island on his return, leaving a manuscript account of his adventures to be decoded and edited by Greg.

As an account of a visit to another planet, *Across the Zodiac* possesses a good deal of the imagination which can inspire belief and call up pictures, or create a sensation of distance and wonder. But its real place, and that a considerable one, is with those forecasts and warnings of our future on this Earth; and the name of Percy Greg should hold an honourable place with those of Wells and Huxley and Orwell. Some of the predictions of this book published over seventy-five years ago have already been fulfilled, or show alarming signs of fulfilment in the world of today; and the psychological foresight is also much in advance of the book's period.

Mechanical prophecy is more obvious and easy, and Jules Verne had already predicted the submarine, although Greg's Martian aeroplanes preceded his 'Clipper of the Clouds' by six years. Martian inventions in *Across the Zodiac* included radio (though not without the use of wires) and sound-films, both well and carefully described.

Another forgotten book of the period, which scarcely deserves a mention here, the anonymous skit *Politics and Life in Mars* (1883), goes so far as to invent for its Martians (who live underwater) radio-receiving and transmitting sets carried on the wrist, and tanks which run over dry land by means of electricity. The book is otherwise of little interest, being mainly a political satire on the Irish question in the manner of *The Consolidator*, and there is no account of a journey to this new world, nor any attempt to describe the world itself.

Hugh MacColl in *Mr. Stranger's Sealed Packet* (1889) gave his Martians tape-recorders which could be read as books as well as repeating the voice, but otherwise they were very much behind the Earth as far as inventions were concerned. They had good electric lighting, and electric carriages like those described by Greg; and they had excellent food and drink made by chemical means: but there were no flying machines, and no weapons of war more progressive than a rather advanced form of cross-bow.

Mr. Stranger used a form of Apergy, though without naming it, to propel his Space-ship, the 'Shooting Star'. He discovered that 'the attracting force residing in every particle of matter . . . is capable of conversion into a repelling force'; that 'there is a certain remarkable metallic compound harder than steel or even diamond, and, unlike other metallic compounds, perfectly transparent, which possesses this capability of conversion to an enormous extent'; that 'the main agent of this conversion is electricity', and that 'the resultant repelling and attracting tendencies of a machine constructed of the metallic compound before mentioned can be turned in a moment in any direction' and increased or decreased to any velocity required.

Sufficient money, a detailed training in science and mechanics, and this remarkable discovery enabled Stranger to construct his Shooting Star in the space of five years on an out of the way island off the Scottish coast. 'My flying machine was only twenty feet long. The body was shaped somewhat like a cigar; while it had a curved head or prow, sharpened to a fine edge . . . for purposes of attack and defence, if I should meet with enemies on my arrival in another planet.' The whole machine was as transparent as glass, and 'in whatever position it might be placed, the attracting and repelling forces were so regulated that all objects inside were drawn towards the floor', and the whole machine itself could be made as attractive as a magnet enabling it to pick up any object.

With concentrated food and devices for heat and air, Mr. Stranger set off gaily for Mars, which he reached in about ten days. On the way he found 'the whole scene most impressive. All around, above, below, before, behind a sky of almost pitchy darkness, which threw into strong relief the light proceeding from the stars, the Earth, the Moon: and above all the dazzling splendour of the Sun'. Soon Mars began to draw near: 'from the bright red star with which we are familiar, it slowly increased until its round disc became plainly perceptible to the naked eye', and grew at a great speed until Mr. Stranger came safely to his journey's end.

He found Mars very much like the Earth, with large seas and wild mountains. The redness was in the atmosphere, low and dense, and not in the vegetation which was of the usual Tellurian green. The animals and birds differed comparatively little, though the first he encountered was a huge green monster with a body like a crocodile, a head and trunk like an elephant, and wings of over thirty feet from tip to tip.

So far as he or they knew, the only human inhabitants were the pale blue, civilized, people of the City of Grensum, and the wild Dergdunin with the colour and temperament of Red Indians who were their enemies. And both tribes were held to have come from Earth in the Stone Age when a wandering star drew the two planets out of their orbits so that they almost touched in passing.

'I found to my surprise,' says Stranger of the civilized Martians, 'that they now lived very happily under a form of socialism; but a socialism very different from what we commonly hear advocated, and which will only be possible upon Earth when science has learnt to place the means of subsistence and comfort within the reach of all. These conditions existed upon this planet. Here there was no struggle for existence. There was no necessity for the sowing of corn or the slaughter of animals for the support of human life. Their science, if behind ours in some respects, was far in advance of it in others. Food was almost as free and plentiful among them as the air which they breathed, because they had learnt to manufacture it from its chemical elements, oxygen, hydrogen, carbon, and nitrogen, which exist in abundance on their planet and on ours.'

Unlike Greg's hero, Mr. Stranger was welcomed by the Martians, but like him he soon married his hosts' daughter. Mr. Stranger's adventures are trivial compared with those in *Across the Zodiac*, just as the account of the new civilization is superficial, and the scientific background hazy in the extreme: but the story is pleasant, however slight. Mr. Stranger rushes about Mars in his Shooting Star, defeating the Dergdunin and having a variety of minor adventures; he takes his fiancée Ree with her mother and brothers on a casual trip into Space and back again, during which they land on Phobos, the nearer moon, but do not leave their air-tight ship. 'A desolate little world this satellite looked; a mere mass of grey rock with patches and streaks of brown-coloured moss here and there in small indentations which, in proportion to the size of the satellite [seven miles in diameter] might be dignified with the name of valleys. If we give the name of mountains to the range of hillocks which rose here and there on its surface, no mountain appeared to be more than fifty feet in height. . . . Nowhere could we see the smallest stream or rivulet; but down in its little valleys we could see winding lines of moss, which made me suspect that such streams had formerly flowed upon this tiny world.'

After his marriage, Mr. Stranger takes Ree to Earth for a honeymoon, promising not to land with her. He breaks the promise, however, and they have various small adventures before setting out on their ten-day trip across Space. But the visit proves fatal: Ree contracts an Earthly disease and dies in delirium on the way back to Mars. Mr. Stranger arrives in time to defeat the Dergdunin decisively, and then, heartbroken, sets out again for Earth to take the recipe for the chemical food. He too develops the disease which killed Ree, but after drifting in Space for a while he recovers sufficiently to reach Earth, and land in his own garden—where he leaves the Shooting Star open as he staggers up to bed for a night's rest. Hearing screams, he rushes out, only in time to see the Shooting Star rising slowly, its door wide open, and the terrified faces of his landlady and her daughter looking out at him: 'In a few seconds their shrieks, already faint, were no longer audible. A few seconds more and the machine dwindled into a small, glittering speck, which rapidly grew smaller and smaller, and finally disappeared. From that day to this I have never seen or heard of it more, and I know I never shall again. The frozen bodies of Mrs. Ridger and her daughter are at this moment travelling in the silent, starry wilderness of Space, and will probably do so for countless ages.'

After this, Mr. Stranger was ill with brain-fever, was declared mad, clapped into an asylum, and lost all his property. He escaped, and wandered away to make another machine and fly back to Mars.

Hugh MacColl seems to have been a one-book man, but Robert Cromie (1856–1907) who a year later published *A Plunge into Space* (1890), followed his one Martian voyage with a variety of sensational stories such as *The Crack of Doom* and *The New Messiah*.

His scientist, Henry Barnett, discovered 'the origin of *force*', how 'the law of gravitation may be diverted, directed, or destroyed' by obscure electrical means. Acting upon this discovery he constructed his version of the Shooting Star, a Steel Globe—'a jet black globe of steel fifty feet in diameter. . . . It was almost a perfect sphere, with only a certain flattening at the top and bottom—like the polar depressions of the Earth in miniature. . . A spiral staircase wound round the interior circumference of the globe. This staircase, or rather sloping path, had one very curious feature. The handrail was duplicated, so that one could walk on the under side of the spiral as conveniently as on its upper surface. In fact, so far as appearance went, there was neither upper nor underside, the one being a perfect duplicate of the other. Again, the roof and the floor of the globe were identically fitted. Below, there were comfortable armchairs, luxurious couches, writing-tables and bookcases. Exact duplicates of these hung from above, head-downwards, so to speak.

'Across the centre of the Steel Globe a commodious platform hung like a ship's lamp. On this a very large telescope was fixed, and the platform was literally packed with astronomical instruments.' There were numerous windows with triple plates of glass; tanks for compressed air; a plentiful store of provisions, and so on.

When the explorers were sealed into the Steel Globe (built secretly in the mountains of Alaska), Barnett had merely to turn a small switch and the gravitation of Earth ceased to exist. At once the starry sky seemed to be below instead of above:

'The effect is easily explained. It is caused by the fact that the attraction of Mars exceeded that of the Earth the moment that Barnett turned that screw. Our feet naturally point now towards the planet which has the strongest pull on us'—and Mars was in opposition.

Through the atmosphere the Steel Globe dropped until it reached its verge at the rate of 500 feet a second, when Barnett gave his screw a complete turn, and they were really off: 'Down from the sheltering surface of the Earth! Down at a rate of fifty thousand miles a minute! Down into space! The journey was begun. The silence of it! The awful and appalling silence! The thousands of constellations! The millions of stars!'

So they plunged sensationally into Space—within the Steel Globe, owing to its atmosphere there was 'a sunny summer's day; without, a universe in solemn night'—and crossed it in a little more than twelve hours. 'Sometimes the dead silence of the journey was broken by a startling crash as the Steel Globe plunged through a rush of meteors', and soon 'the planet Mars became perceptibly brighter to the naked eye. The Earth was but a brilliant star'.

As Mars drew nearer Barnett turned his screw once more: 'the attraction of Mars is now shut off, and that of the Earth full on': and the Steel Globe sank gently to the surface of the planet 'and rested upon it with a shock no greater than that of a shunting train'.

Martian air was breathable, and the adventurers disembarked—but to an unexpected and disappointing world: 'A boundless plain of fine red sand stretched round them as far as the horizon on every side. In this dead waste there was neither hill nor dale, mountain nor lake, bird nor beast. Neither was there any living thing whatsoever, animal or vegetable; not a shrub, not a leaf, nor even a blade of humblest herbage upon it, and over it all a dull red sky hung gloomily.'

They retreated hastily to the Steel Globe, which was already sinking into the sand, raised it to half a mile where Barnett 'succeeded in exactly balancing the attraction and repulsion of Mars', and waited for the great wind which presently carried them away to the south, as a terrible sand storm raged beneath. 'I am convinced,' was Barnett's comment, 'that the canals which Schiaparelli observed from Milan in '77 are in reality simoons crossing the great central continents of Mars.'

But all of Mars was not desert: on the Lagrange peninsula sticking out into the Maraldi sea they came upon a perfect paradise of 'plains covered with luxuriant vegetation, sweeping, flower-decked hills, terraces of swelling green, brilliant with myriads of gaudy blossoms, beautiful trees, waving feathery foliage over countless swarms of happy song-birds', and then a great city built of marble. But Barnett prophecied truly: 'I tell you, the planet Mars is old. Rude and hardy vegetation has everywhere, as you see, been supplanted by delicate growths. Those pretty animals are delicately shaped, but see how sensitive they are—a thousand of them would not face a tiger. The inhabitants that we shall find will be creatures far surpassing ourselves in every attribute of mind and body. They will have developed social, moral, and physical conditions such as we cannot imagine. They are at the pinnacle of their perfection. Before them is no further progress. Their only change must be towards decay.'

Mars had reached a state of civilized perfection more acute (though far less realistic, owing to the poverty of the author's imagination) than in *Across the Zodiac*. The Martians 'only work two hours a day. The population is stationary, or slightly decreasing, so there is no emigration. The whole planet is one nation, speaking one language, so they have no foreign complications. They are governed by one set of unchanging laws, so they have no politicians'.

Their science was ages in advance of the Earth's: having discovered the secret of 'animal electricism', they could float and fly in the air; but they travelled any distance by a supersonic 'aerial car going at a rate of a thousand miles an hour', and they could communicate with each other and broadcast plays by both radio and television. Their brainpower was so highly developed that the family with whom Barnett and his friends settled learnt English perfectly in a few days.

During their stay in this Martian paradise the Earthly visitors found that 'the bound giant' of Electricity (still almost a magic word at the end of the nineteenth century) was responsible for making 'the land more beautiful than even Nature had shaped it, and the lives of men upon it more blessed than prophecy had foretold. He manufactured rich cloths and carried them by underground tubes to customers at short distances, by air-ships to distant lands. He arranged the weather to your liking. He lighted and heated your house, cooked your food and served it. . . . He was everywhere and did everything—a silent, but momentous witness that the sorrowful days of human toil were passed away, that man on Mars had mastered force'.

But in spite of the excellent 'build-up', *A Plunge into Space* quickly degenerates into cheap sensationalism. The greatness of the Martian attainments does not prevent the Earth-men from unsettling them to such an extent that they are soon asked to leave, the crisis coming when Durand the novelist falls in love with the Martian girl whom they call Mignonette, and she with him.

So they depart, but Mignonette accompanies them as an unexpected stowaway. While hiding in the Steel Globe she has damaged the oxygen tank; the air runs short during the journey, and she jumps into outer space to relieve them of the extra pair of lungs. They reach Earth just in time, but Durand has gone mad, and blows up the Steel Globe with Barnett in it—and so the wonderful discovery is lost—and another trip to Mars remains the only one of its kind.

CHAPTER TEN

MARS IN OPPOSITION

During his sojourn on Mars the hero of *Across the Zodiac* steadfastly refused to give away the secret of Apergy, fearing lest the Martians should make use of it to invade the Earth. While Greg's Martians (other than the Children of Light) might have proved inimical to our civilization, and could certainly have conquered our armies, these were ordinary human beings, and his hero left them at a moment when the highest ideals of religion and morality showed signs of triumphing over the spiritual degradation produced by ages of applied science.

Taking their cue from the Astronomers, most writers of Martian fiction pictured the planet as far older than Earth, and all found variations there in animal and plant life. But though the inhabitants themselves might be as short as Esmo or as blue as Ree, these differences were purely superficial.

At the end of the nineteenth century, however, the macabre and rather unpleasant imagination of H. G. Wells—the most popular writer of his day—blotted the fair surface of the Red Planet with the fiendish and reptilian 'things from Outer Space' which still haunt the pages of today's 'Scientifiction'.

On its own level of sensational invention *The War of the Worlds* (1898) is a brilliant piece of work. Wells, as always, had an axe to grind, and he ground it in this case until the edge cut like a razor: his text was the smug security of mankind in the fancied stability of their civilization on the threshold of the new century.

'At most, terrestrial man fancied there might be other men upon Mars, perhaps inferior to themselves and ready to welcome a missionary enterprise. Yet across the gulf of space, minds that are to our minds as ours are to those of the beasts that perish, intellects vast and cool and unsympathetic, regarded this Earth with envious eyes, and slowly and surely drew their plans against us. And early in the twentieth century came the great disillusionment.'

Strictly speaking *The War of the Worlds* is outside the scope of this book, and it is certainly too well-known (if only in its recent, Americanised, film-version) to need re-telling. For Wells's idea of Mars itself we need to turn to his short-story 'The Crystal Egg' included in *Tales of Space and Time* (1899) in which by some strange and undefined scientific means the Martians, spying upon us, become visible in their own world for brief moments to Mr. Cave the antique dealer who had chanced upon the crystal which was the eye-piece of a kind of inter-planetary radio-periscope.

'The view, as Mr. Cave described it, was invariably of an extensive plain, and he seemed always to be looking at it from a considerable height, as if from a tower or a mast. To the east and to the west the plain was bounded at a remote distance by vast reddish cliffs. . . . These cliffs passed north and south—he could tell the points of the compass by the stars that were visible of a night—receding in an almost illimi-table perspective and fading into the mists of the distance before they met. He was nearer the eastern set of cliffs; on the occasion of his first vision the Sun was rising over them, and black against the sunlight and pale against their shadow appeared a multitude of soaring forms that Mr. Cave regarded as birds. A vast range of buildings spread below him. . . . There were also trees curious in shape, and in colouring, a deep mossy green and an exquisite grey, beside a wide and shining canal. . . . In front of the façade [of the great range of buildings] was a terrace of massive proportions and extraordinary length. . . . The terrace overhung a thicket of the most luxuriant and graceful vege-tation, and beyond this was a wide grassy lawn on which certain broad creatures, in form like beetles but enormously larger, reposed. Beyond this again was a richly decorated causeway of pinkish stone; and beyond that, and lined with dense *red* weeds, and passing up the valley exactly parallel with the distant cliffs, was a broad and mirror-like expanse of water. The air seemed full of squadrons of great birds, manoeuvring in stately curves; and across the river was a multitude of splendid buildings, richly coloured and glittering with metallic tracery and facets, among a forest of moss-like and lichenous trees.'

At length Mr. Cave came to the conclusion that the winged creatures were the Martians, and that the wings were flying-machines of great complexity: 'The body was small, but fitted with two bunches of prehensile organs, like long tentacles immediately under the mouth.' Martians without their wings 'were visible, hopping busily upon their hand-like tangle of tentacles' on the causeways and terraces. But the wings were in general use, since the buildings 'had no doors, but the great circular windows, which opened freely, gave the creatures egress and entrance'. Mr. Cave 'several times saw certain clumsy bipeds, dimly suggestive of apes, white and partially translucent, feeding among certain of the lichenous trees, and once some of these fled before one of the hopping, round-headed Martians. The latter caught one in its tentacles, and then the picture faded suddenly.' Had it not done so, Mr. Cave would have seen that the Martians fed by sucking this creature's blood—as they were to feed on human victims during their invasion of the Earth.

'On another occasion a vast thing that Mr. Cave thought at first was some gigantic insect, appeared advancing along the causeway beside the canal with extraordinary rapidity. As it drew nearer Mr. Cave perceived that it was a mechanism of shining metals and of extraordinary complexity.'

From Mr. Cave's various observations of the stars, his friend Mr. Wace decided that it was indeed Mars onto which he was looking, and particularly so because 'there were two small moons, like our Moon but smaller, and quite differently marked, one of which moved so rapidly that its motion was clearly visible as one regarded it. These moons were never high in the sky, but vanished as they rose: that is, every time they revolved they were eclipsed because they were so near their primary planet'.

By means of these 'crystal eggs' on top of the masts, the Martians spied out our Earth before sending their expeditionary force to over-run and devastate England, in preparation for a full-scale emigration from their dying planet—as described in *The War of the Worlds*.

'During the opposition of 1894 a great light was seen on the illuminated part of the disc [of Mars]. . . . I am inclined to think that this blaze may have been the casting of the huge gun, in the vast pit sunk into their planet, from which their shots were fired at us.' For the Martians came in monster projectiles like Jules Verne's, though we are not told how they managed to survive the shock.

On Earth, the Martians found the increased gravity trying, but it did not take them long to construct their fighting-machines from which they could burn up all before them with a 'Heat-Ray', or gas all living creatures with their 'Black Smoke': they proceeded to devastate Surrey, and to clear London of its inhabitants.

As for the Martians themselves, 'they were the most unearthly creatures it is possible to conceive. They were huge round bodies—or, rather, heads—about four feet in diameter, each body having in front of it a face. This face had no nostrils—indeed, the Martians do not seem to have had any sense of smell, but it had a pair of very large dark-coloured eyes, and just beneath this a kind of fleshy beak. In the back of this head or body—I scarcely know how to speak of it—was the single tight tympanic surface, since known to be anatomically an ear, though it must have been almost useless in our denser air. In a group round the mouth were sixteen slender, almost whiplike tentacles, arranged in two bunches of eight each. . . . The greater part of the structure was the brain, sending enormous nerves to the eyes, ear and tactile tentacles. Besides this were the bulky lungs, into which the mouth opened, and the heart and its vessels. . . . And this was the sum of the Martian organs. . . . They were heads—merely heads. Entrails they had none. They did not eat, much less digest. Instead, they took the fresh, living blood of other creatures, and *injected* it into their own veins . . . blood obtained from a still living animal, in most cases from a human being, was run directly by means of a little pipette into the recipient canal.'

It was by means of this fiendish form of blood-transfusion as well as by the Earthly germs of which they knew nothing, that the invading Martians all came to their end, just as they were about to launch a great flying-machine to augment their ruthless work of conquest and annihilation They died, just as Ree had died in *Mr. Stranger's Sealed Packet*—an unexpected, but a very right and obvious fate, and an excellent denouement to such a convincing horror story as *The War of the Worlds*.

Popular though his Martian phantasmagoria proved to be, Wells did not make immediate converts among the Space-travellers at the beginning of this century. An unexpected glimpse of Mars in the following year certainly deprives the planet of human beings, but its only originality is to make Mars startlingly volcanic. This occurs in a pedestrian epic of over ten thousand lines by a certain Horatio Hunt, called *Nero; or the Trials, Battles, and Adventures of the Sixth Emperor of Rome in Darkest Hades*. In this most serious work the disembodied Emperor pays an unexpected visit to Mars, and returns to describe what he has seen:

> '*Tis full of huge volcanoes, and contains*
> *More water than the Earth. The forms of life*
> *Inhabiting this planet chiefly are*
> *Of an amphibious kind, of monstrous size.*
> *All sorts of saurian reptiles crawl about*
> *Upon its banks; whilst here and there I saw*
> *A huge rhinoceros or wingéd beast*

With several heads; but human creatures there
Were none; nor any form akin to man.
The heat was most intense; and though I was
Not clothed with flesh, yet I distinctly felt
Th' oppression of the sultry atmosphere.
A flight of vultures now and then would soar
Above our heads, and then on some remote
And lofty cliff would perch. The thundering sound,
Caused by the terrible volcanic fires,
Was louder than the everlasting roar
Of Vulcan's furnace: while the constant streams
Of lava, which the mountains belched, one half
The globe did darken! This accounts for that
Peculiar reddish colour which doth make
The planet Mars conspicuous.

From this preposterously banal epic of Hades it is a relief to turn to one of the freshest and slightest of Martian romances, *Lieut. Gullivar Jones: His Vacation*, given to an unresponsive world in 1905 by Edwin Lester Arnold, son of the Orientalist poet, and speedily forgotten.

Edwin Lester Arnold (1857–1935), traveller and ornithologist, is best known for his romance of historical reincarnation *Phra the Phoenician* (1891), one of the minor classics which only disappeared from the bookshops after the holocaust of 1940. Type-cast in the school of Weyman, he failed of recognition for his best book, the farcical romance of *Lepidus the Centurion: A Roman of Today* (1901), and upon the similar rejection of his Martian fantasy he gave up writing altogether.

Lieut. Gullivar Jones is a gay, fay dream-story with the slightest and least memorable of plots and the sketchiest of scientific backgrounds: but it is the most haunting and convincing picture of the immeasurably ancient world of Mars, before the discovery of Malacandra.

In defiance of all the Space-ships of fiction, Gullivar Jones, the despondent lieutenant in the American Navy, went to Mars by magic-carpet, wafted suddenly across the forty-eight million miles of void by an imprudent wish—and naturally took a little while to believe in what had happened to him.

'And yet, and yet, it might be so! Everything about me was new and strange, the crisp, thin air I breathed was new; the lukewarm sunshine was new; the sleek, long, ivory faces of the people new! Yesterday—was it yesterday?—I was back there—away in a world that pines to know of other worlds, and one fantastic wish of mine, backed by a hideous, infernal chance, had swung back the doors of space and shot me—if that boy spoke true—into the outer void where never living man had been before: all my wits about me, all the horrible bathos of my earthly clothing on me, all my terrestrial hungers in my veins!'

So he set out for the Martian city, conducted by the boy-girl An (one of those Martians who, like the blue fairies in the Never-Never-Land, 'are not quite sure what they are'), and began to observe this strange new world: 'All the way from the plain where I had awoke to the walls of the city stood booths, drinking-places, and gardens divided by labyrinths of canals, and embowered in shrubberies that seemed coming into leaf and flower as we looked, so swift was the process of their growth. These water-ways were covered with skiffs being pushed and rowed in every direction; the cheerful rowers calling to each other through the leafy screens separating one lane from another till the place was full of their happy chirruping. Every booth and wayside halting-place was thronged with these delicate and sprightly people, so friendly, so gracious, and withal so purposeless.

'They were playing inconsequent games and breaking off in the middle of them like children looking for new pleasures. They were idling about the drinking booths, delicately stupid with quaint, thin wines, dealt out to all who asked; the maids were ready to chevy, or be chevied through the blossoming thickets by anyone who chanced upon them, the men slipped their arms round slender waists and wandered down the paths, scarce seeming to care whose waist it was they circled or into whose ear they whispered the remainder of the love-tale they had begun to some one else.'

These carefree Martians, dawdling in a golden age of pale and shadowy sunlight, were the last remnant of a civilization immeasurably old, living in the crumbling cities built by a lost civilization well in advance of any known on Earth. Everything about them was pale and evanescent: it was the second childhood of the race, and only the boy-girls who did what little work was needed knew any touch of care or sadness. They had a king, himself a mere shadow of authority, but the state was run, or ran itself, on vaguely communistic lines: 'Everything is his who will take it, without exception. What else is the good of a coherent society and a Government if it cannot provide you with so rudimentary a thing as a meal?' Nevertheless, though the race was worn out, the planet was not. Beyond the sea in the wild forests and hills a new race was fighting its way up from barbarism, a strong, savage tribe of young and vigorous Vikings who waited only an excuse to exterminate or enslave the outworn race. Once a year their shadow fell fearfully across the carefree life of the doomed lotus-eaters, when emissaries came to demand their tribute of goods and slave-girls.

'These new-comers were utterly unlike any others—a frightful vision of ugly strength amidst the lolling loveliness all about. Low of stature, broad of shoulder, hairy, deep-chested, with sharp, twinkling eyes, set far back under bushy eyebrows, retreating foreheads, and flat noses in faces tanned to a dusky copper hue by exposure to every kind of weather that racks the extreme Martian climate, they were so opposite to all about me, so gaunt and grim amongst those mild, fair-skinned folk, that at first I thought they were but a disordered creation of my fancy.'

Needless to say, Gullivar Jones was soon disabused. The lovely princess Heru, whom he had just won as wife in the annual lottery of girls (with the aid of a little sharp practice on her side), was chosen as slave-wife for the savage wood-king Ar-hap, and carried away in triumph. But the adventurous Lieutenant, failing to arouse even King Hath out of his lethargy, set out alone to rescue Heru—and many were his adventures in the Martian forests amidst the strange flora and fauna of the Red Planet. 'Everything in that forest was wonderful! There were plants which turned from colour to colour with the varying hours of the day, while others had a growth so swift it was dangerous to sit in their neighbourhood since the long, succulent tendrils clambering from the parent stem would weave you into a helpless tangle while you gazed, fascinated, upon them. There were plants that climbed and walked; sighing plants who called the winged things of the air to them with a noise so like a girl sobbing that again and again I stopped in the tangled path to listen. There were green bladder-mosses which swam about the surface of the still pools like gigantic frog-broods. There were on the ridges warrior trees burning in the vindictiveness of a long forgotten cause—a blaze of crimson scimitar thorns from root to topmost twig; and down again in the cool hollows were lady-bushes making twilight of the green gloom with their cloudy ivory blossoms and filling the shadows with such a heavy scent that the head and heart reeled with fatal pleasure as one pushed aside their branches.'

The fauna is not so minutely described: 'the shadows were still black, and strange things began to move in them—things we in our middle-aged world have never seen the likeness of: beasts half birds, birds half creeping things, and creeping things which it seemed to me passed through lesser creations down to the basest life that crawls, without interruption or division.' Gullivar Jones also was present at a midnight battle between 'two vast rat-like shadows, but as big as elephants, and bringing a most intolerable smell of sour slime with them', but it was too dark to see them properly.

So he made his way to the town of Ar-hap and, aided by a terrible drought caused by the near approach of a meteor, he rescued Heru and carried her back to Seth—'the city of a fallen magnificence, where the spent masters of a strange planet now lived on sufferance—the ghosts of their former selves.'

But Ar-hap and the 'Thither-folk' now had their excuse, and the time was ripe for their invasion: 'We who are *men*, not Peri-zad, not overstayed fairies,' as one of them told Gullivar Jones. 'We came but a few generations ago from where the golden curtains of the sun lie behind the westward pine-trees, and as we came we drove, year by year, those fays, those spent triflers, back before us. All this land was theirs once, and more and more towards our old home. You may still see traces of harbours dug and cities built thousands of years ago, when the Hither folk were living men and women—not their shadows. . . . But King Ar-hap has their pretty noses between his fingers—it will not be much excuse he will need to lick up the last of those triflers, those pretences of manhood.'

By rescuing Heru, Gullivar Jones brought about the end of the Hither folk; all were slain or enslaved in the great final invasion from which he only escaped back to Earth by stumbling upon his missing magic carpet as he fled into the depths of the burning palace pursued by Ar-hap and his fierce warriors.

From the compellingly vivid and highly coloured pages of Edwin Lester Arnold's delightful fantasy it is like stepping into a bath of cold water if we journey *To Mars via the Moon* through the prosaic pages of Mark Wicks's 'Astronomical Story' in 1911. His book, intended for younger readers, claims that 'the astronomical information is, in all cases scientific fact according to our present knowledge: the story itself, as well as the attempt to describe the physical and social conditions on Mars, is purely imaginative. It is not, however, merely random imagining', the Space-ship is pure fiction, 'but the other ideas are mainly logical deductions from known facts and scientific data, or legitimate inferences'.

As a whole the book, when not imparting knowledge, is an enthusiastic defence of the findings or suggestions of Percival Lowell the most whole-hearted of the followers of Schiaparelli and an ardent believer in the theory of man-made canals.

Briefly, the narrator William Poynders, an astronomer, his adopted son John Claxton, and the comic Scotch engineer, McAllister, build the 'Areonel', a ninety-five-foot Space-ship very like Hugh MacColl's 'Shooting Star'. It was constructed of 'a special metal—our joint invention—which we had named "martialum". . . . All the machinery was either electric or magnetic'.

They set out in a most casual fashion at a speed of 150 miles per hour, which increased to 83,000 when the atmosphere was passed, and circled the Moon on their way without making any discoveries, and raced for Mars.

Arrived at the planet, they descended over the great city of Sirapion, situated at the junction of several canals on the Sinus Titanum of the earthly Martographers. 'We had already examined our three machine-guns so that they might be in readiness for any emergency, if some of the ideas of which we had read as to the probable ferocity of the Martians should prove correct. . . . My own conception of the Martians was, however, a very different one.' And correctly so, for they soon found that 'those people are not the big, ugly giants nor the strange animals which some of our folk have imagined the inhabitants of Mars to be. They appear a bit tall, but they are a fairly good-looking lot'.

In fact they were far more civilized than the Earthmen, and startled the travellers by greeting them in English—a mystery explained by the young Martian called Merna who was a reincarnation of Poynders's dead son Mark. Moreover the Martians possessed such powers of thought-transference that they claimed to be responsible for bringing the expedition and even for 'inspiring' Poynders and Claxton with the invention of 'Martialum' and the method of building and propelling the Areonel.

On landing, the travellers expected and found considerable difficulty with the smaller gravitation (which Arnold, for example, had completely ignored). 'In spite of weighted boots which we had taken the precaution to wear, we had some difficulty in walking properly—we had an irresistible tendency to lift our feet much too high at every step.'

Once arrived and introduced, the three Earth-visitors had no adventures: Merna merely took them on sight-seeing excursions—mainly to examine the canals.

'Our seas and other bodies of water have long ceased to exist,' he told them, 'and we are therefore dependent upon the water arising from the dissolving snow of our polar snow-caps for the supply of that prime necessity of life. Our canal system is, therefore, the most supremely important work which we háve to maintain and develop so that every part of the planet may be supplied with water, and also keep in touch with the rest of the planet.'

The main canals were about sixty yards wide, but there were many smaller ones paralleling them and linked by patches of vegetation. 'We also observed many splendid wide motor-roads running between the single canals, as well as others running straight across the system, being carried across the canals by the most beautiful and fairy-like bridges that we had ever seen. They were all constructed of a metal identical with our "Martialum" which we had used in the construction of the Areonel.'

Besides ground vehicles the Martians used large airships, having passed to them from aeroplanes, via helicopters, on discovering the new power produced by 'natural forces emanating from the Sun and from their own planet'. But for pleasure they sailed on the smaller canals, shaded by lovely trees—rather as Arnold's Martians had done.

Wicks's Mars was, however, a complete Utopia: 'Everything upon Mars is honest, true and straightforward—open and above-board.' The Government was an Ideal Socialism with complete State Owner-ship and a six-hour day. There were no wars, largely because their folly was so apparent, besides the risk of endangering the canals. Per-fect birth control was practised so that the water would suffice for every Martian: as the water grew less, so the control would tighten, and in the end they would become extinct on purpose, having no fear of death since they knew that 'to die would be an awfully big adventure' followed by certain rebirth on some other planet.

Apart from the canals, there was no Martian scenery, and there is no suggestion of the wonder, strangeness or beauty of an alien world. 'Phobos appears rather larger than our Moon, because it is so near the planet,' besides being one of Wicks's few astronomical mistakes, is the only suggestion of the slightest difference between a Martian and a Terrestrial night.

Similarly dim is Siloni, the Martian girl with whom John Claxton falls in love. Their love is cut short with few pangs when it is decided that they must return to Earth without her—'our terrestrial microbes would probably prove fatal to a Martian', and anyhow she was seven feet tall! So Claxton and McAllister return alone, since Poynders remains on Mars with his re-born son Merna, and proceed to sing the praises of that great astronomer Percival Lowell whose observations had proved so demonstrably accurate.

Six years after Mark Wicks had launched his pleasant but uninspired 'day-excursion to Mars', the Red Planet was visited—and speedily conquered—by a compatriot of Lieut. Gullivar Jones, Captain John Carter of Virginia, lately in a cavalry regiment fighting for the Southern States in the American Civil War.

In March, 1866, John Carter, prospecting for gold, found himself in a mysterious cave in Arizona, pursued by Indians. And there, by some inexplicable power, he left his body lying stark and dead on the ground and yet stepped out into the night his own double, living and breathing—definitely in the body, and yet looking down 'at my lifeless clay there upon the floor of the cave. . . . There I lay clothed, and yet here I stood but naked as at the minute of my birth.

'As I stood thus meditating, I turned my gaze from the landscape to the heavens, where the myriad stars formed a gorgeous and fitting canopy for the wonders of the earthly scene. My attention was quickly riveted by a large red star close to the distant horizon. As I gazed upon it I felt a spell of overpowering fascination—it was Mars, the god of war, and for me, the fighting man, it had always held the power of irresistible enchantment. As I gazed at it on that far-gone night it seemed to call across the unthinkable void, to lure me to it, to draw me as the lodestone attracts a particle of iron. My longing was beyond the power of opposition; I closed my eyes, stretched out my arms towards the god of my vocation, and felt myself drawn with the suddenness of thought through the trackless immensity of Space. There was an instant of extreme cold and utter darkness.

'I opened my eyes upon a strange and weird landscape. I knew that I was on Mars; not once did I question either my sanity or my wakefulness. . . . I found myself lying prone upon a bed of yellowish, moss-like vegetation which stretched around me in all directions for interminable miles. . . . Springing to my feet I received my first Martian surprise, for the effort, which on Earth would have brought me standing upright, carried me into the Martian air to the height of about three yards. . . .'

Scarcely had John Carter time to observe the young Green Martians hatching out in their great incubator (all Martians, he was later to discover, were oviparous) when Tars Tarkas, afterwards Jeddak of Thark, was upon him—a great Green Martian fifteen feet high, with four arms, gleaming white tusks and eyes on short antennae—riding his mighty Thoat which 'towered ten feet at the shoulder; had four legs on either side, a broad flat tail, larger at the tip than at the root, and which it held straight out behind while running; a gaping mouth which split its head from its snout to its long, massive neck. Like its master, it was entirely devoid of hair, but was of a dark slate colour and exceedingly smooth and glossy. . . .'

A jump of thirty feet carried John Carter to the other side of the incubator, and so impressed Tars Tarkas that he at once made friends with him and carried him off to his chieftain, Lorquas Ptomel.

But we cannot follow John Carter through all the hair-raising adventures which at length raised him to the position of Warlord of all Mars, and husband of the beautiful Dejah Thoris, princess of Helium —whose inhabitants, though red and oviparous, did not otherwise differ from the inhabitants of Earth.

Edgar Rice Burroughs (1875–1950) is an author hard to criticise. In 1914, three years before *A Princess of Mars*, appeared his first book, *Tarzan of the Apes* in which he created a character whose adventures he was to continue in twenty-one sequels and who has 'won his way to the mythical'. John Carter is merely Tarzan without the apes: the strong fighting man of incredible courage and no subtlety. Adventure and excitement, with love as the prize, is all that goes to make up any book by Burroughs—coupled with a truly amazing power of invention which can stimulate the imagination, though he had little of that deeper quality himself.

Burroughs was purely a man of action. Like John Carter he had been a cavalry officer serving in Arizona; he had also been a gold-miner in Oregon, a cowboy in Indiana, a policeman in Saltlake City, and was a Militia Major in an infantry regiment for the last few months of the First World War. *Tarzan of the Apes* is said to have been written as a joke, to see how far the assumptions made by Kipling in *The Jungle Books* could be driven without exceeding the bounds of popular acceptance. He is probably the first author mentioned in this book whose works are almost unreadable by the adult who opens them for the first time; though his three earliest Martian romances, and *Moon Maid*, hold a higher place than anything else of his, not excepting the chronicles of Tarzan.

But to the schoolboy in his early teens, Burroughs can open magic casements with the best—on perilous seas at least, though hardly upon faery lands forlorn. I could still take high honours in an examination set on the first dozen Tarzans and half that number of Martians. Mars is indeed still largely the 'Barsoom' described by Burroughs: a recent cartoon in *Punch* (April 11th, 1956) proves that others have also come under his sway, and Shelob in *The Lord of the Rings* is so like the Siths of the Barsoomian caves that an unconscious borrowing seems probable.

In the background of the Martian romances is a dying world of dead sea-bottoms covered with red and yellow herbage and crossed by canals. Already the air has become too thin to support life, and an artificial atmosphere is manufactured by the Red Men, the most civilized of Barsoomians, in the great Atmosphere Factory—to which John Carter penetrated when the pumps had stopped and the Keepers had died, only just in time to save the lives of all on the planet, at the end of *A Princess of Mars*.

Over the dead sea-bottoms roam the wild bands of the Green Men, the warriors of Thark or Warhoon, mounted on their mighty Thoats, dealing death with their forty-foot spears, their swords, and the terrible Martian rifles which are accurate up to more than two miles. In cities dotted about the canals live the Red Men, in Helium or Zodanga, Gathol or Ptarth, highly civilized and cultured, but joying in battle like all the peoples of the Planet of War: they use rifles, but no heavy artillery or bombs, and they move about at a great speed in their fliers and airships, which are propelled and sustained in the air by the Eighth Ray, or Ray of Propulsion which is peculiar to Barsoom, as is also the Ninth Ray by means of which the atmosphere is maintained.

At the south of the planet is a deep valley, a hollow land most fertile, into which flows the one great river, Iss, through long subterranean caves. The people of Barsoom, who live for a thousand years, were accustomed to make their last pilgrimage down this river, believing that paradise lay at its end—until John Carter, returning to Mars after twenty years of exile (as narrated in *The Gods of Mars*) revealed that there lived the White Men of Mars, the evil Therns, and fed such of their victims as they did not enslave to the horrible Plant Men with mouths in the palms of their hands, who are born on trees like the Tree Men whom Cyrano met on the Sun.

The North Pole is protected by a great glass dome, and is unapproachable, since on the Magnetic North stands a mighty magnet which draws all fliers to their destruction—until John Carter turned off the current in the nick of time, shortly before he became *The Warlord of Mars*. Here at Okar, dwell the Yellow Men, who slay the wild Apts and Siths, and differ little except in colour from the Heliumites, though practising extreme cruelties under their evil Jeddak, Salensus Oll, until John Carter slew him to save both Dejah Thoris and the great air-fleet of Helium.

Besides these are many, many other races scattered upon the planet: there are the Black Men, the 'First Born', Pirates of Barsoom; the Fair Race of Lothar, with their phantom bowmen from whom Carthoris, John Carter's son, rescued *Thuvia, Maid of Mars*; the Headless Humans from whom Gahan of Gathol snatched Tara of Helium before they were captured by U-Thor, the Jed of Manatos, ruler of *The Chessmen of Mars*; the people of Jahar and Ghasta, the cannibals of U-Gor, and other strange beings met by Hadron of Hastor, *A Fightingman of Mars* —and so on, throughout the lesser and later books, from the immitative *Master Mind of Mars* which brings another Earthman, Ulysses Paxton, to Barsoom and the tender mercies of Ras Thavas, a kind of Martian Dr. Moreau, to the positively unpleasant *Synthetic Men of Mars* of 1940, which seems to borrow the horrors of Morbus from the ectoplasmic Martians of the remote future in Olaf Stapledon's *Last and First Men* (1930).

Among the later stories only *Swords of Mars* (1936) can claim a place with the best of the series. Here once again John Carter is the hero and Dejah Thoris the heroine—better always than the Martian principles, Carthoris and Thuvia, Gahan and Tara, Hadron and Tavia, and the rest—far better than that dreary counterfeit Ulysses Paxton. In this story many of the adventures happen on Thuria, the nearer moon of Mars (Phobos) where all visitors shrink in size to fit this tiny world.

Burroughs, whatever else he failed to do, made the Martian scene vivid for his readers, and the night scene in particular—even if astronomers deny the brilliant pageant of the two moons. Thuria goes 'hurtling through the Barsoomian heavens' like a meteor, lighting up strange, half-ruined cities with a truly unearthly radiance, the chasing shadows and moonbeams adding a spice of uncanniness as well as danger to the numerous nocturnal escapes and adventures. And through this wavering light move the vast, blurred shapes of fantastic beasts—Thoats and Zitidars, Banths and Apts, Calots and Soraks— described but not truly imagined so that the mind's eye calls up only approximations, just as the characters live only in two dimensions, a name and a place in an adventure—with perhaps a little more realization for John Carter and Dejah Thoris, and, oddly enough, for Tars Tarkas the great monstrosity of a Green Man, riding in his glittering harness across the red sea-bottoms of desolate Barsoom.

Those of us who read him at the right age owe a great debt of gratitude to Edgar Rice Burroughs, even though we must now revisit the Mars of John Carter, the Jungles of which Tarzan was lord, or Pellucidar the land at the Earth's core, only with the aid of memory, lest the old bright enchantment fade quite away into the mists of past experience.

Malacandra has blotted out Barsoom as the rising Sun does the Moon: yet sometimes we are tempted to believe that John Carter's planet still moves in the orbit of Mars—a duplicate planet behind the Sun such as Paul Capon was to plant in our own orbit.

CHAPTER ELEVEN

THE MOON ENDURETH

ALTHOUGH the discovery of the 'canals' brought Mars into the forefront of the imagination as a probable abode of human beings at much the same time that the Moon was recognised as essentially a dead world, our satellite, the nearest and clearest of heavenly bodies, never quite lost her place in fiction. She suffered, indeed, only a partial eclipse and of recent years has come into her own again as the promise of actual Space-flight makes her the obvious first goal of tomorrow's Astronauts.

After Jules Verne, however, Moon flights for forty years were few and fantastic; usually, in fact, they are to be found in the fairy stories for children which were such a notable feature of the period.

Thus in his fantasy *At the Back of the North Wind* (1871) George MacDonald brought down the Moon in a dream so that the child Nanny could enter it like a house and meet the little old man whom Daniel O'Rourke had encountered.

'The Moon itself, as big as a little house, and as round as a ball, shining like yellow silver. It stood on the grass, down on the very grass: I could see nothing else for the brightness of it. And as I stared and wondered, a door opened in the side of it, near the ground, and a curious little old man, with a crooked thing over his shoulder, looked out, and said: "Come along, Nanny, my lady wants you. We're come to fetch you." I wasn't a bit frightened. I went up to the beautiful bright thing, and the old man held down his hand, and I took hold of it, and gave a jump, and he gave me a lift, and I was inside the Moon. And what do you think it was like? It was such a pretty little house, with blue windows and white curtains! At one of the windows sat a beautiful lady, with her head leaning on her hand, looking out. . . . The little man closed the door, and began to pull at a rope which hung behind it'—and the Moon went up into the sky once more, like an old-fashioned lift.

The Man in the Moon had taken Nanny away with him to clean the windows, as he was growing too old: 'I did the best I could with the dusters,' she told Diamond, 'and crawled up to the top of the Moon. But what a grand sight it was! The stars were all over my head, so bright and so near that I could almost have laid hold of them. The round ball to which I clung went bobbing and floating away through the dark blue above and below and on every side. It was so beautiful that all fear left me and I set to work diligently.' But curiosity overcame her when she saw through one window the casket where the mysterious Lady kept her still more mystic Golden Bees which 'gather their honey from the Sun and the Stars', and like Pandora she opened it and let out some of its strange occupants—and so was sent back to Earth in disgrace.

A brief visit was paid also by Griselda in Mrs. Molesworth's most famous story *The Cuckoo Clock* (1877). In this charming fantasy the Cuckoo takes Griselda to the other side of the Moon and she finds herself on the shores of the Lunar sea: 'such a great, strange, silent sea, for there were no waves. Griselda was seated on the shore, close beside the water's edge, but it did not come lapping up to her feet in the pretty, coaxing way that *our* sea does when it is in a good humour. There were here and there faint ripples on the surface, caused by the slight breezes which now and then came softly round Griselda's face, but that was all.'

And so she set out on her dream-voyage over that strange, silent ocean—a Sea of Dreams such as Thomas Hood imagined:

> *A lake and a fairy boat*
> *To sail in the Moon-light there;*
> *And merrily we will float*
> *From the dragons that wait us here.*

To the Moon also went King Prigio of Pantouflia in Andrew Lang's fairy story *Prince Ricardo* (1893) to fetch thence a lump of Stupidity, the heaviest thing in the world, to drop upon the Earthquaker and so rescue Princess Jacqueline. Prigio, who was 'too clever by half', knew that Stupidity was kept on the Moon, whence it descended to Earth in the form of fine dust—for he was familiar with his Ariosto. Expert knowledge of *The Arabian Nights* told him where to find the famous Flying Horse of the King of Delhi, and up he flew until his head 'swam with the swiftness of the flight. Soon the Earth below him was no bigger than a top, spinning on its own axis, and as night fell Earth was only a great red moon.

'Through the dark rode King Prigio, into the silver dawn of the Moon. All now became clear and silvery; the coasts of the Moon came into sight, with white seas breaking on them; and at last the King reached the silver walls, and the gate of opal. Before the gate stood two beautiful ladies. One was fair, with yellow locks, the colour of the harvest moon. She had a crown of golden snakes and white water-lilies, and her dress now shone white, now red, now golden; and in her hand was the golden pitcher that sheds the dew, and a golden wand. The other lady was as dark as night—dark eyes, dark hair; her crown was of poppies. She held the ebony Wand of Sleep. Her dress was of the deepest blue, sewn with stars. The King knew that they were the maidens of the bright and the dark side of the Moon—of the side you see, and the side that no one has ever seen, except King Prigio.'

The Moon Maidens led Prigio to the volcano beneath which lay the Storehouse of Stupidity. 'There it all lay in masses—the Stupidity of bad sermons, of ignorant reviewers, of bad poems, of bad speeches, of dreary novels, of foolish statesmen, of ignorant mobs, of fine ladies, of idle, naughty boys and girls; and the king examined them all; and all were very, very heavy. But when he came to the Stupidity of the Learned—of dull, blind writers on Shakespeare, and Homer, and the Bible—then King Prigio saw that he had found the sort he wanted, and that a very little of it would go a long way.'

So Prigio, with the aid of a magic spell to lighten his load, set out on his Flying Horse towards 'the bright moon of Earth, shining far off in the heavens', and the mass of Stupidity proved sufficient to flatten the Earthquaker and save the princess for his son Prince Ricardo.

Lang might well have added to his Lunar store the Stupidity of bad writers of science-fiction had he read a book published a few years earlier, *Les Exiles de la Terre* (1888) by the voluminous jack-of-all-trades Paschal Grousset (1844–1909) who wrote under the name of André Laurie. His book, which was translated into English in 1889 as *The Conquest of the Moon*, is quite the most preposterous journey to another world of the century. Its literary progenitors seem to be Jules Verne, Victor Hugo and Henty: its characters consist of melodrama villains, caricatures—and the Hunchback of Notre Dame (disguised as the Black Dwarf) and now called Kaddour.

Early in the story the three villains form a fraudulent company to build a railway to the Moon in a steel tube, but their scheme is annihilated at their great meeting of share-holders in Australia by the young French scientist Norbert Mauny. It is impossible to go to the Moon, he declares, on account of the distance, the difficulty of transport, and the lack of a Lunar atmosphere.

'These considerations have forced upon me the conclusion,' he ends, 'that there is only one solution of the problem—we must endow the Moon with an atmosphere similar to our own, and we can only do this by *forcing the Moon to come down into our atmospheric zone*. . . . This would annihilate the distance between us, and do away at the same time with many other difficulties. Our satellite would henceforth be *at our mercy*. We could go there either in a balloon or by means of a tubular railway. We could turn to account all her resources, and, getting hold of her riches, bring them to Earth—unless, indeed, we might choose to settle down permanently in our lunar colony. . . . In fine, the whole question may be thus resolved: *We must not go to the Moon: we must force her to come to us*.'

This astounding scheme can be performed quite easily—did not the astronomer Secchi declare that all the heavenly bodies 'act and react upon each other *as if they were great magnets of immense power*'? Obviously, 'in order to bring the Moon within our grasp, and diminish the distance between us, *we have only to increase, by artificial means, the power of the earthly magnet*'.

And Mauny proceeded to do just this, with the aid of an incredible English nobleman called Sir Bucephalus Coghill with his still more incredible comic servant Tyrrel; Dr. Briet, his own servant Virgil—and the three villains. The most suitable site on Earth was in the Soudan: the Peak of Tehbali in the Bayouda was to be turned into a magnet, in spite of the fact that the whole country was occupied by the Mahdi's forces. Half the book is taken up with Hentyesque adventures with Arabs and dervishes at the time of Gordon's death, and the machinations of the terrible dwarf Kaddour isolate the adventures on the Peak of Tehbali, plus the heroine Gertrude Kersain and her servant Fatima.

But 'it was done. . . . The Peak of Tehbali—the enormous rock of bisulphate of iron—was isolated from the sandy subsoil by a sheet of glass. It was isolated from the terrestrial globe itself. There at length was the colossal magnet dreamed of by Norbert Mauny. It lay before them an inert mass seemingly, but yet full of power, that only wanted the stimulus of electricity to make it irresistible'.

The dervishes and the appointed day came together: 'It will take her six days, eight hours, twenty-one minutes, forty-six seconds to come down to us, if I have calculated rightly,' said Mauny as he turned the switch.

Down came the Moon, causing no damage beyond dense clouds and some stormy weather, and was about to rest gently on the Sahara Desert, when Tyrrel the comic servant switched off the current—and the Moon sprang back to her orbit.

But she did not go alone. The Peak of Tehbali was lifted off entire and undamaged, complete with the observatory and its inhabitants, and planted conveniently on top of the Crater of Rheticus in the Lunar Apennines, hard by the Sea of Vapours, now only a sandy plain. Conveniently, too, the crater was full of air at the time, and this was trapped and held by the flat-bottomed mountain: a shaft from the observatory made breathing conveniently easy, and exploration could be carried on with the aid of oxygen masks and containers.

So they remained on the Moon for a lunar month, having several adventures with the impossibly evil villains and the dwarf who had a feud to the death against the said rascals.

Exploration took them over the line into the dark of the Moon, where they found a tiny volcano still active, 'the orifice not ten yards across'. They also found magnificent ruins of incredible age which showed bas-reliefs of life on the Moon in the days when Earth was still incandescent, and the body of a Selenite cased in gold and thirty feet in length—'so we may conclude that the Moon was inhabited, and that the Selenites were giants'.

Return to Earth was comparatively simple, though shortage of oxygen, and other incredible misdoings by the villains added a flavour of doubt: at the right moment Mauny had merely to switch on the undamaged magnet, and Moon and Earth drew together once more.

As the Earth approached to within a few miles, 'it was darker than any night they had ever seen, for not only was there not the slightest gleam of starlight, but the sky itself was completely *gone*: its place was occupied by the terrestrial globe'.

Descent was to be made by means of a giant parachute, which was cut loose at the right moment, and the magnetism switched off to prevent a collision of Moon and Earth (leaving the dwarf and his three villainous victims to suffer the fate which he had planned for them on the airless satellite).

'The Moon, suddenly freed from her terrestrial attraction, sprang back to her own orbit amidst strange rumblings around that were an evidence of the catastrophe inevitable in such an upheaval of nature.'

Nevertheless the adventurers landed safely near Khartoum (where they failed to rescue Gordon): nobody on Earth appeared to have noticed the two near approaches of the Moon—and their story was not believed.

In spite of its absurdity, one turns from *The Conquest of the Moon* to *The First Men in the Moon* almost with reluctance. The extraordinary facility of Wells, suggestive even of insincerity, causes an unconquerable antipathy in some readers, just as does the insectile obsession which produced both his Martians and his Selenites.

The First Men in the Moon is, however, the classic Moon-voyage in English, and much of it certainly deserves its fame and popularity—nor does so widely read a book call for much quotation here.

With Jules Verne still so widely popular, Wells wisely gave little space or thought to the journey from the Earth to the Moon. He was content to borrow freely from his predecessors, inventing 'Cavorite', a substance similar to Lunarium or Apergy—or rather combining the two, since it neither attracts nor repels, but simply does away with gravity, like the unnamed power in *A Plunge into Space*. By opening the Cavorite blinds the sphere is attracted to whatever heavenly body is nearest on the side so exposed to normal gravity. The tiresome Mr. Bedford, who tells the story, by his complete ignorance of science and astronomy, saves Wells any necessity for building up a credible scientific background.

'The inner glass sphere can be air-tight, and, except for the manhole, continuous, and the steel sphere can be made in sections, each section capable of rolling up after the fashion of a roller blind. These can easily be worked by springs, and released and checked by electricity conveyed by platinum wires fused through the glass. All that is merely a question of detail. So you see, that except for the thickness of the blind rollers, the Cavorite exterior of the sphere will consist of windows or blinds, which ever you like to call them. Well, when all these windows or blinds are shut, no light, no heat, no gravitation, no radiant energy of any sort, will get at the inside of the sphere; it will fly on through Space in a straight line, as you say. But open a window, imagine one of the windows open. Then at once any heavy body that chances to be in that direction will attract us.'

It was just as simple as that. By the Spring of 1900 all was complete. Cavor and Bedford, with requisite luggage and additional oxygen, sealed themselves into the sphere which was placed on a furnace—'the last stage of Cavorite making, in which the paste is heated to a dull red glow in a stream of helium, would be accomplished when it was already on the sphere'—and when the right temperature was reached, Cavorite was made, and off they went. Cavorite removed the air in front of them, so no friction was to be feared; meteorites were conveniently absent; hunger hardly made itself felt: 'And so, sleeping, and sometimes talking and reading a little, and at times eating, though without any keenness of appetite, but for the most part in a sort of quiescence that was neither waking nor slumber, we fell through a space of time that had neither night nor day in it, silently, softly, and swiftly down towards the Moon.

'I remember how one day Cavor suddenly opened six of our shutters and blinded me so that I cried aloud at him. The whole area was Moon, a stupendous scimitar of white dawn with its edge hacked out by notches of darkness, the crescent shore of an ebbing tide of darkness, out of which peaks and pinnacles came climbing into the blaze of the sun. . . . Athwart this world we were flying scarcely a hundred miles above its crests and pinnacles. And now we could see, what no eye on Earth will ever see, that under the blaze of the day the harsh outlines of the rocks and ravines of the plains and crater floor grew grey and indistinct under a thickening haze, that the white of their lit surfaces broke into lumps and patches, and broke again and shrank and vanished, and that here and there strange tints of brown and olive grew and spread.'

Later, 'for a flash Cavor opened a window Moon-ward, and we saw that we were dropping towards a huge central crater with a number of minor craters grouped in a sort of cross about it', and a moment later the sphere was rolling down a hillside coated in frozen snow, into the darkness preceding the Lunar dawn.

'As we saw it first it was the wildest and most desolate of scenes. We were in an enormous amphitheatre, a vast circular plain, the floor of the giant crater. Its cliff-like walls closed us in on every side. From the westward the light of the unseen sun fell upon them, reaching to the very foot of the cliff, and showed a disordered escarpment of drab and greyish rock, lined here and there with banks and crevices of snow. . . . Whatever light was about us was reflected by the westward cliffs. It showed a huge undulating plain, cold and grey, a grey that deepened eastward into the absolute raven darkness of the cliff shadow. Innumerable rounded grey summits, ghostly hummocks, billows of snowy substance, stretching crest beyond crest into the remote obscurity, gave us our first inkling of the distance of the crater wall. These hummocks looked like snow. At the time I thought they were snow. But they were not—they were mounds and masses of frozen air!'

And so Bedford and Cavor land on the Moon; there is a small atmosphere which melts with the rising Sun, a shallow soil with fast-growing plants, and enough water to support life. The fauna—and the Selenites—live underground during the Lunar nights, just as Samuel Butler of *Hudibras* had suggested a couple of centuries before that they,

> *When the sun shines hot at noon,*
> *Inhabit cellars under ground,*
> *Of eight miles deep and eighty round.*

They set out to explore this amazing new world: 'About us the dream-like jungle, with the silent bayonet leaves darting overhead, and the silent, vivid, sun-splashed lichens under our hands and knees, waving with the vigour of their growth as a carpet waves when the wind gets beneath it. Ever and again one of the bladder fungi, bulging and distending under the sun, loomed upon us. Ever and again some novel shape in vivid colour obtruded. The very cells that built up these plants were as large as my thumb, like beads of coloured glass. And all these things were saturated in the unmitigated glare of the sun, were seen against a sky that was bluish black and spangled still, in spite of the sunlight, with a few surviving stars. Strange! the very forms and texture of the stones were strange. It was all strange, the feeling of one's body was unprecedented, every other movement ended in a surprise. The breath sucked thin in one's throat, the blood flowed through one's ears in a throbbing tide—thud, thud, thud, thud.

'And ever and again came gusts of turmoil, hammering, the clanging and throb of machinery, and presently—the bellowing of great beasts!'

It is in these descriptions of the lunar landscape, the vivid realisation of all that is strange and different upon another world, the compelling re-creation in the reader's mind of Mr. Bedford's experiences, that Wells excels all earlier writers and conquers the Moon once and for all. We may forget the story and the actors in it; the Selenites and their unpleasant civilization may leave no more than a slightly repellent after-taste: but scene after scene remains in the memory like moments in those dreams which come occasionally and leave a picture as clear as any born of actual experience.

Dawn on the Moon, the melting air and the growth of the cactus and fungus-like vegetation; the two-hundred-foot-long Moon-calves seen through the strange jungle; the stupendous cave going down to some sunless sea in the Moon's centre; the sudden change in the landscape when Cavor and Bedford escape to the surface again and find 'all sere and dry in the late autumn of the Lunar afternoon; the misty blueness of coming night stealing down the stupendous cliffs'—and most of all Mr. Bedford rushing with great leaps of his Earth-muscles to reach the sphere as the deathly shadow of the unutterable cold and darkness pursues him.

'Before me the pale serpent-girdled section of the Sun sank and sank, and the advancing shadow swept to seize the sphere before I could reach it. I was two miles away, a hundred leaps or more, and the air about me was thinning out as it thins under an air-pump, and the cold was gripping at my joints. But had I died I should have died leaping. Once, and then again my foot slipped on the gathering snow as I leapt, and shortened my leap; once I fell short into bushes that crashed and smashed into dusty chips and nothingness, and once I stumbled as I dropped, and rolled head over heels into a gully, and rose bruised and bleeding. . . . The frost gathered on my lips, icicles hung from my moustache, I was white with the freezing atmosphere. . . . Over me, around me, closing in on me, embracing me ever nearer, was . . . that enormous void in which all light and life and being is but the thin and vanishing splendour of a falling star, the cold, the stillness, the silence—the infinite and final Night of Space.'

And so Mr. Bedford reaches the sphere, manages to return to Earth meaning to bring help to the captive Cavor—and leaves the sphere on the beach at Littlestone, where a boy enters it, moves the Cavorite shutters, and flies off to be lost in Space precisely as Mr. Stranger's house-keeper was carried off in the Shooting Star.

There the story proper ends, Mr. Bedford decamps to Amalfi, changing his name to 'H. G. Wells, which seemed to me to be a thoroughly respectable sort of name', and writes his story, which began to appear in *The Strand Magazine* in November 1900. But two numbers were added at the end (July and August 1901) which consist of wireless messages from Cavor in the Moon, describing the Selenites who turn out to be super-intelligent 'brains' (like the Fourth Men or 'Great Brains' in *Last and First Men* thirty years later), and allow Wells to sketch one of his typical Utopias of scientific progress, and aim a few darts of satire at mankind.

Of particular interest is the idea that the Selenites live *inside* the Moon—'the whole of the Moon's substance for a hundred miles inward, indeed, is a mere sponge of rock. Partly this sponginess is natural, but very largely it is due to the enormous industry of the Selenites in the past. The enormous circular mounds of the excavated rock and earth it is that form these great circles about the tunnels known to Earthly astronomers (misled by a false analogy) as volcanoes'. Below these caverns and shafts is the Central Sea of phosphorescent water 'like luminous blue milk that is just on the boil'.

Wells may have derived this idea from some subterranean romance such as Verne's *Journey into the Interior of the Earth* or Lytton's *The Coming Race*, but he probably passed on the idea to Edgar Rice Burroughs who produced his most unusual book and only Lunar romance twenty-five years later as *The Moon Maid* (1926).

This is a romance of the Future. On June 10, 1967, the author is crossing the Atlantic on the one-night air-ferry, when he meets the mysterious Julian who can remember his own reincarnations: or, more correctly, *pre*-incarnations, since they are all in the future. The day of their meeting is 'Mars Day', that on which radio contact was first made with Barsoom, directly after the last World War (1959–67) has ended 'in the absolute domination of the Anglo-Saxon race over all the other races of the world', and victors and vanquished alike were celebrating the Peace and dumping all armaments into the oceans.

The main incarnation is that of Julian 5th, born in the year 2000 and a Captain in the International Peace Fleet (the only people on Earth allowed to possess fire-arms or even knives of more than six inches in length), who was one of the five men chosen to make the first trip to Mars.

Julian was in command of the Space-ship *Barsoom*, but its inventor and engineer was his hated rival Orthis—the most brilliant of Earthly scientists and the most evil of men. The flight (which was to be made at the speed of twelve hundred miles an hour) was made possible by the discovery of the Eighth Ray: 'powerful multiple-exhaust separators isolated the true Barsoomian Eighth Ray in great quantities, and, by exhausting it rapidly earthward, propelled the vessel toward Mars.'

All went well until they were a little past the Moon, on which they could discern 'weird fungus-like vegetation' similar to that described by Wells; but then Orthis, under the influence of drink and vindictiveness, wrecked the engines and the wireless apparatus, and the ship drifted helplessly down toward the Lunar mountains.

As they approached they became aware that 'there is an atmosphere surrounding the Moon. It is extremely tenuous, but yet it was recorded by our barometer at an altitude of about fifteen hundred feet above the highest peak we crossed. Doubtless in the valleys and deep ravines, where the vegetation thrived, it is denser, but that I do not know, since we never landed upon the surface of the Moon'.

Down went the *Barsoom* directly over a crater several miles wide, up and down which they drifted in an unaccountable fashion until they came to rest in mid air many miles below the Moon's surface. Each time they passed this point 'the ship had rolled completely over', and after passing it they noted a strange luminosity far below them.

There seemed to Julian only one 'single and rather preposterous hypothesis' possible: 'that the moon is a hollow sphere, with a solid crust some two hundred and fifty miles in thickness. Gravity is preventing us from rising above the point at which we now are, while centrifugal force keeps us from falling.'

Experiment showed that the air was equivalent to that on the Earth's surface, and as only the Space-engines were wrecked, Julian started the ordinary atmosphere motors, and they soon found themselves rising *up* into a world inside the Moon.

Unlike Pellucidar, the land At the Earth's Core, which David Innes had discovered shortly before in a couple of Burroughs's romances, this world was not lit by a central sun, but by the brilliant luminosity of the soil and rock itself: 'A soft, diffused light revealed to us in turn mountains, valleys and sea. The mountains were as rugged as those upon the surface of the satellite, and appeared equally as lofty. They were, however, clothed with verdure almost to their summits. And there were forests, too—strange forests, of strange trees, so unearthly in appearance as to suggest the wild phantasmagoria of a dream.

'Above us were banks of fleecy clouds, the under surfaces of which appeared to be lighted from beneath, while, through breaks in the cloud banks we could discern a luminous firmament beyond. . . . The clouds themselves cast no shadows upon the ground, nor, in fact, were there any well-defined shadows even surrounding the forest trees.

'Centrifugal force, in combination with the gravity of the Moon's crust, confined the internal lunar atmosphere to a blanket which we estimated at about fifty miles in thickness over the inner surface of this buried world. This atmosphere rarifies rapidly as one ascends the higher peaks, with the result that these are constantly covered with perpetual snow and ice, sending great glaciers down mighty gorges toward the central seas. . . . There are periodic wind-storms which occur with greater or less regularity once each sidereal month, due, I imagine, to the unequal distribution of crater openings through the crust of the Moon, a fact which must produce an unequal absorption of heat at various times and in certain localities. . . . There are never any dark, lowering days within the Moon, nor is there any night.

'Several miles from the ship rose foothills which climbed pictures-quely toward the cloudy heights of the loftier mountains behind them, and as we looked in the direction of these latter, and then out across the forest, there was appreciable to us a strangeness that at first we could not explain, but which we later discovered was due to the fact that there was no horizon, the distance that one could see being dependent solely upon one's power of vision. The general effect was of being in the bottom of a tremendous bowl, with sides so high that one might not see the top.

'The ground about us was covered with rank vegetation of pale hues—lavenders, violets, pinks and yellows predominating. Pink grasses which became distinctly flesh-coloured at maturity grew in abundance. . . . We already had seen evidences of life of a low order —toad-like creatures with the wings of bats, that flitted among the fleshy boughs of the forest, emitting plaintive cries; . . . a five-foot snake with four frog-like legs, and a flat head with a single eye in the centre of the forehead.'

Julian and Orthis (the latter injudiciously freed on parole) were speedily separated from their three companions and captured by the Va-gas—barbarous centaurs of little intelligence and cannabalistic habits, whose simple speech (common throughout the Moon) 'is more aptly described as song, the meaning of each syllable being governed by the note in which it is sung'. From these Julian escaped, rescuing Nah-ee-lah, the beautiful princess of the U-ga, the civilized human beings of the Moon, who was also a prisoner, from the undesirable attentions of Orthis who had curried favour with the Va-ga king by promising to make guns for his people.

Then they had many adventures in the usual Burroughs' style, every bit as good and compelling as any that John Carter experienced on Mars. In the end they escaped the Kalkars, the savage, evil people of the Moon who were fast overcoming the dwindling U-gas; but at length the Kalkars attacked and stormed the city of the Moon Maid's people, aided by the renegade Orthis who had already made mortars and hand grenades. When all was lost and Laythe in flames, Julian and his Moon princess escaped by means of the lunar flying suits—a buoyancy tank strapped to the shoulders, and artificial wings which functioned like the fans which Gonsales had found in use on the Moon three centuries earlier.

They reached the Space-ship *Barsoom* to find it repaired and about to set out for Earth, and safely home again, Julian married his Moon Maid.

But they did not live happily ever afterwards: Orthis was still in the Moon, and in 2050 he attacked the Earth with a thousand great Space-ships, each bearing a hundred Kalkars and a Va-ga, 'arms and ammunition and strange, new engines of destruction fashioned by the brilliant mind of the archvillain of the universe. No one but Orthis could have done it. No one but Orthis would have done it'.

Earth was utterly unprepared, in spite of Julian's repeated warnings, and suffered total conquest, followed by the swift end of civilization as more and more Kalkars poured in from the Moon. Julian killed Orthis and met his own death in the final battle, but was incarnated in the year 2100 as Julian 8th, and grew up in the ruins which had once been Chicago.

The second part of this extraordinary book tells of this incarnation, with mankind reduced to the status of domestic animals by the Kalkars; and the third part, set in the twenty-fifth century, tells through the mouth of Julian 20th of the gradual renaissance of tortured humanity who, by then, have reached the status of the early Red Indians and are slowly driving back and exterminating the degenerate Kalkars.

Altogether the whole book, and particularly the last section with its picture of the new civilization struggling upwards, clinging to uncomprehended remnants surviving from the old, is on a higher plane than any other book by Burroughs—and, perhaps on account of this very difference of scope and greater depth of thought, seems to have been one of his few failures from the popular point of view: it soon went out of print in America, and has never been published in England.

The Moon Maid is virtually the last of the pseudo-scientific romances of the Moon, and it looks back to the older type of story rather than forward to the new.

So, in its own way, does such a nursery classic as *Doctor Doolittle in the Moon*, published two years later, which needs little introduction here. Hugh Lofting's immortal physician journeyed to the Moon on the back of a giant Lunar Moth, in company with Chee-Chee the monkey, Polynesia the parrot, and his stowaway friend and biographer Tommy Stubbins. They crossed the 'Dead Belt' of airless Space easily enough with the aid of the oxygen contained in the Moon-flowers brought for them, and found themselves in a wonderful land of plants and trees which could converse by signs.

There they met the Man in the Moon himself, a person of enormous size (due to eating a certain lunar fruit—which also had its effect on the Doctor) called Otho Bludge who had accompanied the Moon when it was blown off the Earth in pre-historic times.

After several pleasant adventures, and many delightful descriptions of the wonderful scenery of the Moon, Doctor Doolittle returned to the trials and tribulations of this Earth—not the least, in his case, being his remarkable increase in size.

But the new age of Space-flight was already dawning: Fritz von Opel was demonstrating the use of rocket-propulsion, as a practical possibility, on the ground in 1928 and in the first 'jet-propelled' aircraft in 1929, and a few years later David Lasser, President of the American Interplanetary Society was writing, in *The Conquest of Space*: 'Among unprejudiced and far-sighted men of science there is agreement today that man has in the rocket an engine to carry him away from the Earth, across hundreds of thousands and millions of miles to the Moon, or Mars, or Venus. And pursuing the development of that rocket, scientists in half a dozen nations are now labouring with energy and enthusiasm.'

The same note was struck by Otto Willi Gail in the introduction to perhaps the first example of pure 'Scientification' of the modern kind, *By Rocket to the Moon*, in 1931:

'Can it be that Jules Verne's genial conception of a trip to the Moon has passed out of the boundless realm of fantasy and stands at the threshold of actual accomplishment? . . . The story of Hans Hardt's trip "By Rocket to the Moon" is not merely Utopian. To be sure, Hans Hardt's adventures may appear fantastic. They are, however, a logical consequence of initial accomplishments which can no longer be doubted, and are based on the results of the most recent experimentation in modern natural science.'

In this spirit Hans Hardt and his companions set out in a rocket-ship, dropping a step-rocket on the way as they emerged from the Earth's atmosphere at the scientifically correct speed to escape from gravity, after increasing it only at the pitch that the human organism can actually endure.

Their crossing of Space was as prosaically accurate as astronomical findings could make it, and they landed upon a Moon which the hundred-inch telescopes of Arizona had brought almost as near as

Locke fabled that Herschel's instrument had done a hundred years earlier.

Bare, cold rocks and empty valleys were explored in the Space-suits which the cinema and the comic-strip have since made so familiar, and only the tiniest breath of vapour was discovered, and a few 'thrilling regions of thick-ribbed ice'.

Only at the bottom of a deep, dark crater was fancy admitted: there they discovered a somewhat denser atmosphere, plants and a little animal life: 'These dark spots are plant life; broad, fern-like weeds, stunted in their development.' . . . The plants wavered. Almost immediately a gleaming grey streak came towards the observers from the obscurity. It was a snake, something with life. The Moon was not as dead as people thought. The strange, slimy reptile lay motionless for a time, very near the men. 'It is an amphibian, like a proteus,' whispered Dr. Hardt. 'It is almost colourless, and has no eyes, as is the case with the grotto proteus, which lives in perpetual darkness in the subterranean caves of the Dalmatian mountains. Such a large proteus does not exist in our realm, however. This animal is almost two yards long.' As Dr. Hardt bent nearer to examine the large, wormlike body, with short, fin-like legs which gave it a ludicrous appearance, the reptile lifted up the fore-part of its body, and with head waving from side to side, instinctively opened and closed its jaws. . . . Simultaneously the proteus clapped its strong, pointed tail to the ground, and gave a sudden leap upward. Its undulating body flew through the mist in broad, spiral curves, and finally disappeared from the astounded gaze of the explorers.'

And so, after a few more botanical and geological investigations, they re-entered their Space-ship and returned comfortably to Earth—and with them the Moon, stripped of her last vestiges of magic, passed into the cold keeping of science.

CHAPTER TWELVE

WORLDS BEYOND MARS

MEANWHILE, though the Moon was waning, and Mars becoming over-populated, there were other planets waiting to be conquered—even if the nearness of our satellite and the mystery of the Martian canals kept them relatively in the background.

In a vague way Voltaire peopled Saturn as early as 1750 in his short satirical tale *Micromegas*. The hero, who gives his name to the story, was 'a young gentleman . . . eight leagues in height', an inhabitant 'of one of the planets that revolve round the star known by the name of Sirius'. 'In his last voyage to this our little ant-hill', he visited Saturn on the way, where 'he could not for his life repress that supercilious and conceited smile which often escapes the wisest philosopher, when he perceived the smallness of that globe, and the diminutive size of its inhabitants: for really Saturn is but about nine hundred times larger than this our Earth, and the people of that country mere dwarfs, about a thousand fathoms high'.

Micromegas and the Saturnian 'dwarf' of six thousand feet set out together in the direction of Earth, 'and at one jump leaped upon the ring, which they found pretty flat . . .; from thence they easily slipped from moon to moon; and a comet chancing to pass near the last one they sprung upon it with all their servants and apparatus. Thus carried about one hundred and fifty millions of leagues, they met with the satellites of Jupiter, and arrived upon the body of the planet itself'. Leaving Jupiter (which is not described) they passed Mars without landing, since they thought it too small, and came to the Earth— which they found a very contemptible planet.

Seven years later when Israel Jobson, the Wandering Jew, touched at Saturn (in Miles Wilson's planetary tour), he found the Saturnians to be as large as Micromegas had done, but noted the grotesqueness of their appearance with one eye in front and another at the back.

A brief glimpse of Saturn was obtained by Herschel (on the fictitious authority of Locke in the Great Lunar Hoax), who 'clearly ascertained that these rings are composed of rocky strata, the skeletons of former globes, lying in a state of wild and ghastly confusion, but not devoid of mountains and seas. The belts across the body of Saturn he has discovered to be the smoke of a number of prodigious volcanoes, mingled with the tropical clouds, carried in these straight lines by the extreme velocity of the rotary motion'.

That not only Saturn but even its rings were inhabited was the ardent belief of such a theological scientist as Thomas Dick, who set out to prove in his *Celestial Scenery* (1838) that piety demanded a belief in a population for all the planets.

'These rings contain a surface of about *thirty millions* of square miles,' he cried. 'It is not likely that the Creator would leave a space equal to nearly six hundred times the habitable parts of our globe, as a desolate waste, without any tribes of either sensitive or intelligent existence. . . . It may perhaps be objected to the habitability of these rings that, while one side is enlightened during fifteen years without intermission, the other side remains in the dark during the same period. But the same thing happens with regard to extensive regions on the globe of Saturn; and doubtless arrangements are made for the enjoyment of the inhabitants in both cases, during this period. They enjoy in succession, and sometimes all at once, the light reflected from at least seven moons, and they behold occasionally the body of Saturn reflecting the solar rays.'

Doubtless Dr. Dick's readers pictured all planetary beings as ordinary humans, and he certainly did little to suggest that any other interpretation was permissible. But a more liberal view, and one of considerable imagination, had been put forward eight years earlier by Sir Humphry Davy, inventor of the miners' safety-lamp, in the first chapter of his *Consolations in Travel* (1830).

Sitting in the Colosseum, and dreaming of the splendours of Imperial Rome, Davy was visited by a Genius, who took him across the void of Space in an instant, saying:

'Prepare your mind and you shall at least catch a glimpse of those states which the highest intellectual beings that have belonged to the Earth enjoy after death, in their transition to new and more exalted natures. . . . There are creatures far superior to any your imagination can form in that part of the system now before you, comprehending Saturn, his moons and rings. . . .

'I saw below me a surface infinitely diversified, something like that of an immense glacier covered with columnar masses, which appeared as if formed of glass, and from which were suspended rounded forms of various sizes, which, if they had not been transparent, I might have supposed to be fruit. From what appeared to me to be analogous to masses of bright blue ice, streams of the richest tint of rose-colour or purple burst forth and flowed into basins, forming lakes or seas of the same colour. Looking through the atmosphere towards the heavens I saw brilliant opaque clouds of an azure colour that reflected the light of the sun, which had to my eyes an entirely new aspect, and appeared smaller, as if seen through a dense blue mist. I saw moving on the surface below me immense masses, the forms of which I find it impossible to describe; they had systems for locomotion similar to those of the morse or sea-horse, but I saw with great surprise that they moved from place to place by six extremely thin membranes which they used as wings. Their colours were varied and beautiful, but principally azure and rose-colour; I saw numerous convolutions of tubes, more analogous to the trunk of the elephant than to anything else I can imagine, occupying what I supposed to be the upper parts of the body, and my feeling of astonishment almost became one of disgust, from the peculiar character of the organs of these singular beings; and it was with a species of terror that I saw one of them mounting upwards apparently flying towards those opaque clouds I have before mentioned.'

But the Genius reassured him: 'Those beings who are before you, and who appear to you almost as imperfect in their functions as the zoophytes of the polar seas, to which they are not unlike in their apparent organization to your eyes, have a sphere of sensibility and intellectual enjoyment far superior to the inhabitants of your Earth; each of those tubes which appears like the trunk of an elephant, is an organ of peculiar motion or sensation. They have many modes of perception of which you are wholly ignorant, at the same time that their sphere of vision is infinitely more extended than yours, and their organs of touch far more perfect and exquisite. It would be useless for me to attempt to explain their organization, which you could never understand; but of their intellectual objects of pursuit I may perhaps give you some notion. They have used, modified and amplified the material world in a manner analogous to man; but with far superior powers they have gained superior results. Their atmosphere being much denser than yours and the specific gravity of their planet less, they have been able to determine the laws belonging to the solar system with far more accuracy than you can possibly conceive. . . . Their sources of pleasure are of the highest intellectual nature; with the magnificent spectacle of their own rings and moons revolving round them—with the various combinations required to understand and predict the relations of these wonderful phenomena, their minds are in unceasing activity, and this activity is a perpetual source of enjoyment.

'As I cannot describe to you the organs of these wonderful beings, so neither can I show to you their modes of life; but as their highest pleasures depend upon intellectual pursuits, so you may conclude that these modes of life bear the strictest analogy to that which on Earth you would call exalted virtue. I will tell you however that they have no wars, and that the objects of their ambition are entirely those of intellectual greatness. . . . If I were to show you the different parts of the surface of this planet, you would see marvellous results of the powers possessed by these intellectual beings and of the wonderful manner in which they have applied and modified matter. Those columnar masses, which seem to you as if arising out of a mass of ice below, are results of art, and processes are going on in them connected with the formation and perfection of their food. . . .'

And so the vision, or the Space-trip, ended, the Genius telling Davy before he left him to his contemplations in the Colosseum: 'The Universe is everywhere full of life, but the modes of this life are infinitely diversified, and yet every form of it must be enjoyed and known by every spiritual nature before the consummation of all things.'

Perhaps these Saturnians, with their six thin membranes and the trunk-like tubes, gave Wells the idea for his Martians: but Humphry Davy would have been horrified indeed could he have foreseen the hideous spawn of reptilian nightmare terrors which Wells's reduction of them to the merely sensational and horrific was to let loose on the imagination of the twentieth century.[1]

Compared with such flights of fancy, Jules Verne erred on the side of scientific safety when he kept Hector Servadac and his companions at little less than telescopic distance from Jupiter and Saturn.

Nevertheless *Hector Servadac, or The Career of a Comet* (1877—in English the following year) is one of his best stories, and has been unduly neglected. Impossible though the initial idea may be, Verne works it out with his habitual skill in verisimilitude, so that credulity is never strained, nor is the spell broken.

The book (one of 'André Laurie's' most obvious sources for *The Conquest of the Moon* ten years later) tells how the unrecorded and rather erratic comet Gallia grazed the Earth in passing and drew off

---

[1] This is no exaggeration or bias of opinion: having written the above I picked up today's *Times* (June 11, 1956) and found the reviewer of the latest Space-film declaring that: 'Outer Space would be unthinkable without its monsters.'

with it into Space a suitable quantity of atmosphere and several portions of the Earth's surface with all that was on them.

Quite unaware of what had happened, Hector Servadac and his
servant Ben Zoof recovered from the shock to find themselves still in
their familiar surroundings in Algeria. But they were quickly aware
that something cataclysmic had chanced. The sun was sinking in the
east; in jumping a ditch Ben Zoof soared to a height of forty feet and
landed unhurt—'What means all this,' muttered Servadac. 'Laws of
gravity disturbed! Points of the compass reversed! The length of the
day reduced one half! . . . Something has happened!'

'Another thing that now struck Servadac was the extraordinary
contraction of the horizon. Under ordinary circumstances, his elevated position would have allowed him a radius of vision at least five
and twenty miles in length; but the terrestrial sphere seemed, in the
course of the last few hours, to have become considerably reduced in
volume, and he could now see for a distance of only six miles in every
direction.'

Not yet realising where they were, Servadac did not recognise the
huge celestial body, which on the first night shone strangely behind
the clouds, as the Earth from which they were hastening towards the
Sun. 'For about an hour some luminous body, its disc evidently of
gigantic dimensions, shed its rays upon the upper strata of the clouds;
then, marvellous to relate, instead of obeying the ordinary laws of
celestial mechanism, and descending upon the opposite horizon, it
seemed to rise in a line perpendicular to the plane of the equator, and
vanished.'

When the Earth was visible again it was much smaller than the
Moon, and Servadac would have taken it for a planet, were it not that
he was just able to distinguish a single satellite near by: 'It was neither
Mercury nor Venus, because neither one nor the other has any satellite
at all!'

They were drawing near to Venus, however, though they could
see nothing of its surface but dense clouds, with several spots that were
perhaps seas. Mercury also was passed at a reasonable distance, and
they could make out 'its glacial and its torrid zones which, on account
of the great inclination of the axis, are scarcely separable; its equatorial
bands; its mountains eleven miles high'.

So the comet swung round the Sun, and raced for outer Space, while
Servadac, now joined by Count Timascheff on his yacht, explored
their new world without realising what it was until they found the

old astronomer Professor Rossette dying of cold in his observatory on what had been the peak of a Balearic island.

This, with the large piece of Algeria and a fragment of Gibraltar (complete with two English officers and a small garrison, very amusingly described) were almost all the fragments of Earth caught onto the comet. Gallia itself consisted of barren rock of tremendous density, and sea; its whole circumference at the equator being about fourteen hundred miles.

As it drew further and further into Space the cold became extreme, and the inhabitants were only able to bear it by the providential discovery of a volcano with caverns giving access to the molten lava.

'Throughout the day the pale rays of the Sun, apparently lessened in its magnitude cast only faint and somewhat uncertain shadows; but at night the stars shone with surpassing brilliancy. Of the planets, some, it was observed, seemed to be fading away in remote distance. This was the case with Mars, Venus, and that unknown orb which was moving in the orbit of the minor planets; but Jupiter, on the other hand, had assumed splendid proportions; Saturn was superb in its lustre, and Uranus, which hitherto had been imperceptible without a telescope, was . . . plainly visible to the naked eye.'

At the distance of twenty-two million leagues from the Sun, Gallia passed through the orbit of the asteroids, and 'captured for herself a satellite . . . Nerina, one of the asteroids most recently identified'.

The three dozen human beings on Gallia passed through many adventures of the desert-island type, always distinguished by the novelty of their unique position in Space. Verne describes with great vividness the lessening of the light as the comet passes further and further from the Sun, and the effect on his characters of their desperate struggle for life in the bowels of the volcano which itself becomes extinct before they have recrossed the more temperate orbits on their return journey.

The trials of that grim winter are mitigated by comic passages, in the usual Verne manner, his butts being the detestable German Jew (of fiction) Isaac Hakkabut, the intolerant temper of the Professor, and the humours of Ben Zoof the over-zealous French servant—with delightful incidents in Servadac's dealings with the English who insist on holding Gibraltar until relieved from London, refuse to believe that they are on a comet, and remain floating in Space when the comet splits shortly before crossing the orbit of Earth on the return journey.

During their two-year course Jupiter was passed at a distance of thirty-one million miles, and there was great fear lest the comet should be drawn into that gigantic orbit and become an additional Jovian moon. At this time Jupiter shed a most marvellous brilliancy upon Gallia, and the 'belts' with their strange colours were wonderfully visible; but 'the physiology of belts and spots alike were beyond the astronomer's power to ascertain', and Professor Rossette was unable 'to enlighten his brother *savants* to any great degree as to the mysteries that are associated with this, which must ever rank as one of the most magnificent amongst the heavenly orbs'. Nor did they pass Saturn near enough to solve any of its problems, or indeed to see it so clearly as an Earth-bound astronomer with his best telescope.

The trip of the comet Gallia ended happily. It passed Earth without striking it, but so near that its atmosphere was returned whence it came, gently but firmly. It took with it Hector Servadac and his companions, who had trusted themselves to a gigantic balloon in which they had a most thrilling approach to the Earth: 'It totally eclipsed an enormous portion of the firmament above, and approaching with an ever-increasing velocity, was now within half its average distance from the Moon. So close was it, that the two poles could not be embraced in one focus. Irregular patches of greater or less brilliancy alternated on its surface, the brighter betokening the continents, the more sombre indicating the oceans that absorbed the solar rays. Above, there were broad white bands, darkened on the side averted from the Sun, exhibiting a slow but intermittent movement; these were the vapours that pervaded the terrestrial atmosphere. But as the aeronauts were being hurried on at a speed of seventy miles a second, this vague aspect of the Earth soon developed itself into definite outlines. Mountains and plains were no longer confused, the distinction between sea and shore was more plainly identified, and instead of being, as it were, depicted on a map, the surface of the Earth appeared as though modelled in relief. . . .

'The growing expanse of the Earth's disc seemed like a vast funnel, yawning to receive the comet and its atmosphere, balloon and all, into its open mouth. . . . Every passenger in the quivering car involuntarily clung spasmodically to its sides, and as the two atmospheres amalgamated, clouds accumulated in heavy masses, involving all around in dense obscurity, while flashes of lurid flame threw a weird glimmer on the scene. In a mystery everyone found himself upon the Earth again . . . contrary to previous computation, the comet had merely grazed the Earth, and was traversing the regions of Space, again far away!'

Letting the 'I dare not' of scientific accuracy wait upon the 'I would' of the imagination, Jules Verne kept his comet at a respectful distance from the major planets; but John Jacob Astor (1864–1912), the American millionaire and inventor, cousin of the first Viscount Astor, had no such qualms, and in his one romance *A Journey in Other Worlds* (1894) he boldly landed his three adventurers on both Jupiter and Saturn.

The story is set in the year 2000, which gave Astor the chance of airing his love for mechanical inventions. Skimming delicately over the politics of the twentieth century with the remark that the European countries wasted away in the fruitless preparation of armaments, which were never used since no Great War broke out, he presents a world of Anglo-Saxon dominance, the United States having swallowed up the whole of both American continents, while Britain had apparently done the same for Africa. Transport has become power (as in Kipling's stories of the future a decade later), but transport is purely electric. In spite of writing in the early 'nineties, Astor prophesied neither radio transmission nor the internal combustion engine: broadcasting and television are both achieved by a superior telephone system, and cars, aeroplanes, airships and liners are all run by cunningly stored electricity. His most interesting forecast describes the roads of the future, with lanes for traffic of various speeds and phosphorescent 'cat's eyes' to mark them. Many of his smaller inventions, from the hollow masts of liners to the automatic door-answerer are amusing in a Heath Robinson manner: in real life Astor was the inventor of the bicycle brake and a 'pneumatic road improver'. It is a sad stroke of irony that after his careful description in *A Journey in Other Worlds* of the improved safety devices for ocean-going vessels he should have gone down in the *Titanic* disaster. From the point of view of the story, the most important recent discovery in A.D. 2000 is of 'Apergy' (borrowed shamelessly from *Across the Zodiac*) which is being used when the story opens to assist the straightening of the Earth's axis, in the interest of temperate weather—the theme of the unsuccessful attempt by the Gun Club in Jules Verne's story *The Purchase of the North Pole* (1889).

Apergy, we are told, is a force 'obtained by simply blending negative and positive electricity with electricity of the third element or state, and charging a body sufficiently with this fluid, gravitation is nullified or partly reversed, and the Earth repels the body with the same or greater power than that with which it still attracts or attracted it, so that it may be suspended or caused to move away into Space. *Sic itur ad astra*, we may say'.

With this power at their command, President Bearwarden and his two friends, Dr. Cortlandt and Richard Ayrault, feeling in need of holiday and adventure, turned their eyes toward the stars and decided to make the first voyage into Space.

'I have it!' exclaimed Ayrault, jumping up. 'Apergy will do it. We can build an air-tight projectile, hermetically seal ourselves within, and charge it in such a way that it will be repelled by the magnetism of the Earth, and it will be forced from it with equal or greater violence than that with which it is ordinarily attracted.'

This decided upon, 'Ayrault immediately advertised for bids for the construction of a glucinum cylinder twenty-five feet in diameter, fifteen feet high at the sides, with a domed roof, bringing up the total height to twenty-one feet, and with a small gutter about it to catch the rain on Jupiter or any other planet they might visit. The sides, roof and floor were to consist of two sheets, each one third of an inch thick and six inches apart, the space between to be filled with mineral wool, as a protection against the intense cold of Space. There were also to be several keels and supports underneath on which the car could rest. Large, toughened plate-glass windows were to be let into the roof and sides, and smaller ones in the floor, all to be furnished with thick shades and curtains. Ayrault also decided to have it divided into two stories, with ceilings six and a half and seven and a half feet high, respectively, with a sort of crow's nest or observatory at the top. . . . There were also a number of sixteen-candle-power incandescent lamps, so that when passing through the shadow of a planet, or at night after their arrival on Jupiter, their car would be brightly illuminated. They had also a good searchlight for examining the dark side of a satellite, or exploring the spaces in Saturn's rings.'

Thus equipped, with the addition of the usual stores, weapons, instruments and oxygen plant, they set gaily forth, and were soon traversing Space at the speed of a million miles an hour—keeping a good look out for meteors and asteroids which might damage their Space-ship, the 'Callisto'.

As for the choice of a destination, there had been no doubt: 'We know all about Mars; it is but one seventh the size of the Earth, and as its axis is inclined more than ours, it would be a more uncomfortable globe than this. . . . The axis of Venus is inclined to such a degree that it would be almost uninhabitable to us. . . . Neither Venus nor Mars would be a good place.'

But Jupiter was another matter altogether: its mean distance from the Sun was 480,000,000 miles, certainly, 'but its axis is so nearly straight that I think, with its internal warmth, there will be nothing to fear from cold. Though, on account of the planet's vast size, objects on its surface weigh more than twice as much as here, if I am able to reach it by means of apergy, the same force will enable me to regulate my weight.'

Soon the Earth, 'which at first had filled nearly half their sky, was rapidly growing smaller. . . . They were already moving at such speed that their momentum alone would carry them hundreds of thousands of miles into Space, and were then almost abreast of the Earth's satellite, which was but a few thousand miles away. The spectacle was magnificent. As they looked at it through their field glasses or with the unaided eye, the great cracks and craters showed with the utmost clearness, sweeping past them almost as the landscape flies past a railway train.'

Soon after this, with their colossal increase of speed, it was Mars that was holding their attention: 'They noticed red and brownish patches on the peaks that had that morning turned white, from which they concluded that the snow had begun to melt under the warm spring sun.' Obviously the climate was most changeable, and they were not tempted to land.

Apparently of more interest were the two moons of Mars. Deimos showed signs of volcanic action, with mountains as much as a hundred feet high, but no signs of air or water; Phobos seemed much the same, but 'the mountain ranges were considerably more conspicuous than on Deimos, and there were boulders and loose stones upon their slopes, which looked as if there might at some time have been frost and water on its surface; but it was all dry now, neither was there any air. . . . When abreast of it they were less than two miles distant, and they secured several instantaneous impressions, which they put aside to develop later'.

But then, 'applying the full apergetic force to Mars and the larger moon, they shot away like an arrow', and, overtaking and photographing a comet on their way, went dodging through the asteroids.

Pallas, one of the largest of these, they treated with scorn since it had obviously no atmosphere, though the mountains were of the height of fifteen miles. But to their amazement, when Hilda occulted Jupiter, 'the light was not instantly shut off, as when the Moon occults a star, but there was evident refraction. 'By George!' said Bearwarden, 'here is an asteroid that *has* an atmosphere!'

'There was no mistaking it. They soon discovered a small ice-cap at one pole, and then made out oceans and continents, with mountains, forests, rivers, and green fields. The sight lasted but a few moments before they swept by, but they secured several photographs, and carried a vivid impression in their minds. Hilda appeared to be about two hundred miles in diameter.'

Soon after this they were rushing upon Jupiter: but the speed was checked by the use of apergy, and with the aid of one of Jupiter's dead moons, Callisto (after which their Space-ship was named), they landed with ease. As they descended they observed 'two crescent-shaped continents, a speckled region and a number of islands', and when nearer 'the rocky tops of the great mountains shining like helmets' in the rays of the newly risen Sun, which revealed also the dense atmosphere which they had expected. 'Beneath them was a vast continent variegated by chains of lakes and rivers. . . . To the eastward were towering and massive mountains, and along the southern border of the continent smoking volcanoes, while toward the west they saw forests, gently rolling plains, and table-lands. . . .'

The air proved satisfactory for Earthly lungs, the double attraction of Jovian gravity equally supportable, and they set out at once to explore: 'The ground was rather soft and a warm vapour seemed to rise from it.' The first creature they found was a huge poisonous reptile which propelled itself by inflation; after shooting this so as to examine it more closely, they were surprised by the sudden fall of the tropic twilight and with it the strange song or music of the Jovian flowers: 'The large trumpet-shaped lilies, reeds, and heliotropes seemed fairly to throb as they raised their anthem to the sky and the setting Sun, while the air grew dark with clouds of birds', which carried the pollen from flower to flower as the bees do on Earth. The night was enlivened by will-o'-the-wisps 'as bright as sixteen-candle-power lamps' and fireflies 'the size of a small dog', and in the morning, after another chant from the flowers, they set out to explore, marvelling at the 'apparent flatness and wide range of vision', due to Jupiter's vast size.

Through all their adventures and explorations it is impossible to follow them in detail. Jupiter, they found, was in the Carboniferous Period, the huge, warm forests tenanted by 'prehistoric' beasts such as mammoths, mastodons, pterodactyls, gymnotuses, glyptodons, dinosaurs and the rest.

The more unusual flora of Jupiter included the great flowers with the sweetest song which enticed birds into their open petals and then seized and devoured them, a plant species which Edwin Lester Arnold transplanted to Mars some years later in *Lieut. Gullivar Jones*; while an exaggerated ant thirty feet long with razor-sharp pincers, the strangest of the fauna, was borrowed by Burroughs for *Pirates of Venus* in 1934. Except that there were no human beings, their experiences on Jupiter were much the same as those of Doyle's four heroes in that strangely derivative adventure story *The Lost World*.

After several weeks of exploration in this 'sportsman's paradise', the adventurers set out in the Callisto for Jupiter's north pole, mapping the oceans and continents as they went. The famous 'Red Spot' turned out to be a huge tract of forest where all the trees wore autumnal tints for several years in succession, and 'in the varying colours of the water' in the vastly preponderant oceans, 'they recognised what they had always heard described on Earth as the bands of Jupiter, encircling the planet with great belts, the colour varying with the latitude'.

Passing Ganymede, Jupiter's largest moon, five hundred miles greater in diameter than Mercury, and possessed of an atmosphere, they plunged still deeper into Space until they came to Saturn.

Having decided that the Rings, which they proved to consist of innumerable particles of stone ranging from the microscopic to the meteoric, were kept in position by means of natural apergy, they descended upon Saturn.

The atmosphere was cold, but not unbearably so, gravitation almost that of Earth, and the vegetation largely fungoid. 'The cold, distant-looking Sun, apparently about the size of an orange, was near the horizon.' Night fell rapidly, and 'six of the eight moons, each at a different phase, and with varied brightness, bathed the landscape in their pale, cold rays; while far above them, like a huge rainbow, stretched the great rings in effulgent sheets, reaching thousands of miles into Space, and flooding everything with their silvery light'.

Snow fell during the night without incommoding them, and when they woke 'the scene was indeed weird. The east, already streaked with the rays of the rising far-away Sun, and the pale moons nearing the horizon in the west, seemed connected by the huge bow of light. The snow on the dark evergreens produced a contrast of colour, while the other trees raised their almost bare and whitened branches against the sky, as though in supplication to the mysterious rings, which cast their light upon them and on the ground. As they gazed, however, the rings became grey, the moons disappeared, and another day began.'

Soon life became apparent in the form of small burrowing rodents, and then four-legged birds of all sizes, and flying lizards over twenty feet long and breathing poison. Then they came upon dragons twice the size of the lizards, a huge flock of them, busily engaged in eating the giant toadstools, and were only saved from them by a Providential earthquake which opened a chasm between them and let loose a curtain of scalding steam.

'Providential' proved the operative word, for on Saturn (taking, perhaps, a leaf out of Humphry Davy's book) Astor introduced his Space-travellers to the souls of the dead: 'It is sheol, the place of departed spirits,' the ghost of Violet Slade, a lost love, told Ayrault. 'Those whose consciences made them happy on Earth are in paradise here; while those good enough to reach Heaven at last, but in whom some dross remains, are further refined in spirit, and to them it is purgatory.'

The spirit of a dead Bishop, besides delivering several excellent and most edifying sermons, imparted to his listeners some interesting new facts about the planets.

'You can hardly realise,' he told them, 'the joy that a spirit in paradise experiences when, on reopening his eyes after passing death, which is but the portal, he finds himself endowed with sight that enables him to see such distances and with such distinctness. The solar system, with this ringed planet, its swarm of asteroids, and its intra-Mercurial planets—one of which, Vulcan, you have already discovered —is a beautiful sight. The planets nearest the Sun receive such burning rays that their surfaces are red-hot, and at the equator at perihelion are molten. These are not seen from the Earth, because, rising or setting almost simultaneously with the Sun, they are lost in its rays. The great planet beyond Neptune's orbit is perhaps the most interesting. This we call Cassandra because it would be a prophet of evil to any visitor from the stars who should judge the Solar system. This planet is nearly as large as Jupiter, being 80,000 miles in diameter. . . . It is about 9,500,000,000 [miles from the Sun][1]. . . . Cassandra takes, in round numbers, a thousand years to complete its orbit, and from it the Sun, though brighter, appears no larger than the Earth's evening or morning star. Cassandra has also three large moons: but these, when full, shine with a pale grey light. . . . The temperature at Cassandra's surface is

---

[1] Pluto, the planet beyond Neptune, was only discovered in 1930. Its size is barely that of Mars, and its mean distance from the Sun is about 3,675,500,000 miles, its revolution 248 years. 'Vulcan' was 'discovered' in 1859; a photograph in 1876 showed only a sunspot, and it is generally accepted as mythical.

but little above the cold of Space, and no water exists in the liquid state, it being as much a solid as aluminium or glass. There are rivers and lakes, but these consist of liquified hydrogen and other gasses. . . . Were there mortal inhabitants on Cassandra, they might build their houses of blocks of oxygen or chlorine, as you do of limestone or marble, and use ice that never melts in place of glass. . . . The brightness of even the highest noon is less than an Earthly twilight, and the stars never cease to shine. The dark base of the rocky cliffs is washed by the frigid tide, but there is scarcely a sound, for the pebbles cannot be moved by the weightless waves, and an occasional murmur is all that is heard. Great rocks of ice reflect the light of the grey moons, and never a leaf falls or a bird sings. With the exception of the mournful ripples, the planet is silent as the grave. The animal and plant kingdoms do not exist; only the mineral and spiritual worlds. I say spiritual because there are souls upon it; but it is the home of the condemned in hell. . . .'

Finally the ghostly Bishop told them of Cosmos, the central sun round which all the stars with their systems revolve, far too distant as yet to be seen from Earth by mortal eyes. Round Cosmos circles a Saturn-like ring of attracted stars—the real home of the blessed, 'beautiful and gently rolling slopes', spirit-lands to be 'inhabited only by spirits'. There 'are great phosphorescent areas, and the colour of the surface changes with every hour of the day, from the most brilliant crimson to the softest shade of blue, radiant with many colours that your eyes cannot now see. There are also myriads of scented streams, consisting of hundreds of different and multi-coloured liquids, each with a perfume sweeter than the most delicate flower, and pouring forth the most heavenly music as they go on their way.'

Fortified and encouraged by so direct a revelation of the life after death, the three travellers returned safely to Earth, nearer to the true Heaven for their trip through Space.

Altogether Astor's book is one of the most unusual and interesting, it fails chiefly from the literary point of view in its poverty of language, its lack of anything like a plot or any feeling of suspense, and the way in which it falls apart into its three sections: forecast of the future, trip to another world, and spiritual vision.

Nevertheless few Space-travellers have ventured so far, and in the Solar System only Olaf Stapledon went further, taking a division of his Last Men, remote aeons in the future, to their final home on Neptune.

Last and First Men (1930) belongs to the same class as *A Journey in Other Worlds*, though it is the work of a far maturer imagination. It is, nevertheless, a cold, unsatisfying book with a vivid interest—such an interest as we might find in a long-drawn-out study of the damned, and all the more soul-searing from the fact that its author does not seem to see that he is describing the cosmic tragedy of a race of megalomanic materialists.

'A mind without religious sentiment is like a star without atmosphere,' as Rider Haggard once observed, and vivid though his scientific nightmare may be, it has about it the coldness of outer Space while Astor, however blurred his vision, at least writes with humility and sees Man in his proper environment.

In the remote distance of the Future, according to Stapledon, Mankind, then living on Venus, discovers that a 'volume of non-luminous gas' will hit the Sun which will blaze up and destroy or render uninhabitable most of the planets. Neptune alone might be able to support life: 'Ether-vessels were able to reach that remote world and set up chemical changes for the improvement of the atmosphere. It was also possible, by means of the lately re-discovered process of automatic annihilation of matter, to produce a constant supply of energy for the warming of an area where life might hope to survive until the Sun should be rejuvenated. When at last the time for migration was approaching, a specially designed vegetation was shipped to Neptune and established in the warm area to fit it for man's use. Animals, it was decided, would be unnecessary. Subsequently a specially designed human species, the Ninth Men, were transported to man's new home. The giant Eighth Men could not themselves inhabit Neptune. The trouble was not merely that they could not support their own weight, let alone walk, but that the atmospheric pressure on Neptune was unendurable. For the great planet bore a gaseous envelope thousands of miles deep. . . . The Eighth Men, therefore, dared not emerge from their ether-ships to tread the surface of the planet save for brief spells in steel diving suits.'

So they perished on Venus when the 'dark stranger from Space' swept it into the Sun together with Saturn, Earth and the Asteroids: 'Henceforth the centre of the Solar System was a star nearly as wide as the old orbit of Mercury.'

And the new men on Neptune nearly perished also, were reduced to beasts, and after millions of years evolved once more through various stages of humanity until the Eighteenth Men appeared, the most highly civilized of any in the history of Mankind's progress through the Solar System, and Stapledon's idea of the glorious culmination of humanity.

But his Last Men too were doomed, since a cosmic poison was about to destroy the whole Solar System, and man's hope of burning the planets one by one and then moving Neptune to a new orbit round some younger star was prevented. But even so they would not learn humility, and Stapledon leaves them still rejoicing in their hideous pride and striving with the 'task of disseminating among the stars the seeds of a new humanity'.

CHAPTER THIRTEEN

THE VIGIL OF VENUS

'VENUS,' wrote Thomas Dick in 1838, 'although a small fraction smaller than the Earth, may hold a rank in the Solar System, and in the empire of the Almighty, in point of population and sublimity of scenery, far surpassing that of the world in which we dwell.'

The nearest planet to the Earth, and the most beautiful object in our night sky, after the Moon, it seems strange that Venus has played so small a part in the imagination which has peopled Mars so thickly and conducted so many journeys into other worlds.

Venus, as Flammarion the French astronomer pointed out in the sixties of last century, 'is surrounded by a transparent atmosphere in the midst of which are combined thousands of shades of light. Clouds rise from the stormy ocean, and transport into the sky snowy, silvery, golden and purple tints. At morning and evening when the dazzling orb of day, twice as large as it appears from the Earth, lifts its enormous disc at the east or inclines towards the west, the twilight unfolds its splendours and charms.'

The deep atmosphere, denser than on Earth, suggests abundant life and would make flying twice as easy as here; the close envelope of clouds, while it hides the surface of Venus from our eyes, seems to offer wide scope for the imagined world within. The nearness of the Sun promises eternal summer, while the density of the clouds suggests a fertile surface, perhaps largely consisting of ocean.

The angel Cosmiel brought Theodidactus to Venus in Kircher's *Extatic Journey*, but only to point out its guiding spirits, 'young people of ravishing beauty, living in the midst of perfect happiness'. Late in the eighteenth century Bernerdin de St. Pierre, author of *Paul et Virginie* described a terrestrial paradise and placed it in the planet Venus; but the first real journey thither from this world seems to have been in an obscure work in French by a contemporary of Jules Verne: '*Voyage à Venus* (1865) by Achille Eyraud. This may have been an attempt to steal Verne's market between the serial publication of *De la Terre à la Lune* in 1864 and its appearance in book form the following year.

Eyraud's only real importance rests in the fact that his Space-ship is the first in all fiction (setting aside Cyrano's short trip in his firework-car) to be propelled through Space by rocket propulsion. The book, nevertheless, seems to have fallen dead from the press, was never translated, and had no influence on later works of fiction.

Probably the first visit to Venus in English fiction (even the ubiquitous Israel Jobson did not come within the Earth's orbit) is that described by John Munro in *A Trip to Venus* (1897). Its author, an electrical engineer and later Professor of Mechanical Engineering at Bristol, wrote no other fiction but was responsible for several books on Electricity.

The story is very slight, and there are several rather tedious digressions of an instructive nature; but his picture of the Venerian world is completely delightful, fresh, spontaneous and never laboured.

The method of the flight is not divulged: Nasmyth Carmichael, discoverer of the 'new force', retains his secret. But after discussing the possibilities of a magnetic gun or a rocket-propelled projectile, Professor Gazen the astronomer and the unnamed narrator of the story, decide that these are only possibilities of the future and that the new invention must be trusted if the trip is to be made by them.

These are the three voyagers, with the important addition of Carmichael's daughter, the first female Space-traveller in fiction—since Gertrude Kersain in *The Conquest of the Moon* can hardly count, as the Moon came down to fetch her, and carried her off against her will, just as the Comet in *Hector Servadac* chanced to take the little Italian girl Nina as its only female captive.

The description of the Space-ship is designedly vague: 'in the darkness it might have been mistaken for a tubular boiler of a dumpy shape. It was built of aluminium steel, able to withstand the impact of a meteorite, and the interior was lined with caoutchouc, which is a non-conductor of heat, as well as air-proof. The foot or basement contained the driving mechanism, and a small cabin for Mr. Carmichael. The upper shell, or main body, of an oval contour, projected beyond the basement, and was surrounded by an observatory and conning tower. It was divided into several compartments, that in the middle being the saloon, or common chamber. At one end there was a berth for Miss Carmichael, and at the other one for Professor Gazen and myself, with a snug little smoking cell adjoining it. Every additional cubic inch was utilised for the storage of provisions, cooking utensils, arms, books, and scientific apparatus.

'The vessel was entered by a door in the middle, and a railed gallery or deck ran round it outside. The interior was lighted by ports or scuttles of stout glass; but electricity was also at our service. Air constantly evaporating from the liquid state would fill the rooms, and could escape through vent holes in the walls. This artificial atmosphere was supplemented by a reserve fund of pure oxygen gas compressed in steel cylinders, and a quantity of chemicals for purifying the air. . . .'

The ship rose so gradually from the ground that they nearly forgot to close the last scuttle when the atmosphere grew too thin to breathe. But once in open Space the speed was increased to a suitably meteoric figure.

'Gazen made numerous observations of the celestial bodies, more especially the Sun, which now appeared as a globe of lilac fire in the centre of a silvery lustre. . . . The Earth, with its ruddy and green continents, delineated as on a map, or veiled in belted clouds, was a magnificent object as it wheeled in the blue rays of the Sun.

'Venus, on the other hand, waxed more and more brilliant until it rivalled the Moon, and Mercury appeared as a rosy star not far from it. . . . Slowly and steadily the illuminated crescent of the planet grew in bulk and definition, until we could plainly distinguish all the features of her disc without the aid of glasses. For the most part she was wrapped in clouds, of a dazzling lustre at the equator, and duskier towards the poles. Here and there a gap in the vapour revealed the summit of a mountain range, or the dark surface of a plain or sea.

'By an illusion familiar in railway trains, it seemed to us that the car was stationary, and the planet rushing towards us. On it came like a great shield of silver and ebony, eclipsing the stars and growing vaster every moment. . . . The climax of magnificence was reached when the approaching surface came so close as to appear concave. . . . The sky suddenly became blue, the stars vanished from sight, the Sun changed to a golden lustre, and the broad day was all around us.'

Finding the atmosphere of Venus not merely breathable but invigorating, they opened the scuttles and descended slowly through the dense clouds. 'Lost in the vapours, our car seemed at rest; but although we saw nothing, we could hear a vague and distant murmur . . . the car shot into the clear air beneath the clouds. "The sea! The sea!" cried Miss Carmichael; and sure enough we were flying above a dark blue hemisphere which could only be the ocean.'

For a long time it seemed that Venus would turn out to be all water, but at last an island appeared in the distance, 'like a volcanic peak, and was evidently encircled with a barrier reef, as we could trace a line of snowy surf breaking on its outer verge. . . . The steep sides of the mountain, broken with precipices, and shaggy with vegetation, ascended from a multitude of spurs and buttresses, resembling billows of verdure, and towered into the clouds. . . . The entire forest was streaked like a rainbow with innumerable flowers, and the breeze which blew from it was laden with the most delightful perfume.'

The volcano, one of stupendous size, was not only extinct, but its crater of vast extent contained a great lake and a large fertile country, a paradise of eternal spring, of glorious flowers and trees and creatures. 'Butterflies with azure wings of a surprising spread and lustre, alighted on the flowers, and great birds of resplendent plumage flashed from grove to grove. A Sun, twice the diameter of ours, blazed in the northern sky, but the intensity of his rays was tempered by a thin veil of cloud. The atmosphere although warm and moist, was not oppressive.'

On the shores of the lake the travellers found a city of apparently friendly inhabitants and so came gently to rest as the evening drew in. 'The huge limb of the Sun, red and glowing, sank to rest in a bed of purple clouds on the summit of the rosy precipice, and filled all the green plain with a rich amber light. The fantastic towers and trees of the distant city by the lake shone in his mellow lustre; the solitary island swam in a flood of gold, and the quaint edifice which crowned it blazed with insufferable splendour.'

The question of day and night on Venus raises the probable reason why so few authors have felt inspired to send their voyagers to her clouded surface. At much the same time as he was discovering his 'canals' on Mars and turning the red planet into a probably inhabited and certainly provocative world for imaginative exploration, Schiaparelli was declaring his conviction that Venus 'takes as long to turn about her own axis as she does to go round the Sun, and that as a consequence she always presents the same side to the luminary'. This theory is still supported by many astronomers, and obviously a planet divided between endless day and endless night presented few attractions to writers who had the more manageable movements of Mars, or even the Moon, before them.

However, Professor Gazen discovered that, although Schiaparelli was right, the planet still had a strip at least of its surface with an alternate day and night of about fifteen hours each—caused, very plausibly, by a continual 'wobble' of Venus on her course round the Sun, just as a top wobbles when slowing down.

For the inhabitants of 'Womla', the beautiful land in the crater of the greater volcanic island, the Sun seemed always to rise and set in the same place, ascending only a little distance above the cliffs on the horizon, 'and in the evening dipping down behind them, leaving a twilight or gloaming, which continued throughout the night'; and they knew also that 'far away to the east and west of Womla there was a deserted land, covered with snow and ice, on which the Sun never shone'.

As for the people of Womla themselves, although they were not 'unfallen' in the theological sense, they lived almost sinless lives in a perpetual paradise—a believable one, and most simply and convincingly suggested. It is certainly a refreshing change to find a planetary world where science is of little importance and the arts take the foremost place in the ideal civilization which has as its background a direct belief in the love of God, in the immortality of the soul, and that 'the world around them is a divine work which they are to reverence and perfect'.

'The people, according to their tradition, came originally from a temperate land far across the ocean to the south-east, which is now a dark and frozen desert. They are a remarkably fine race, probably of mixed descent, for they found Womla inhabited, and their complexions vary from a dazzling blonde to an olive-green brunette. They are nearly all very handsome, both in face and figure, and I should say that many of them more than realise our ideals of beauty.' Their senses of sight and touch are keener than ours, of hearing and of heat rather blunter; they wear few clothes, and these 'of a simple and graceful order', largely in the nature of veils and made 'from silky fibres which grow on the trees, and tinged with beautiful dyes'. By temperament they are bright and ingenious, of a happy disposition, guileless and chaste, and almost free both from disease and from crime; consequently they have few laws and fewer punishments.

Beauty being so much a part of their lives as of their-religion, they love all Nature, cultivating gardens and making friends with the animal kingdom. They never kill, live solely on fruit and vegetable foods, and brew no alcoholic liquors: most of them cultivate more than enough for all their needs in their gardens, any surplus going to a general store which is open to all without payment.

'They rejoice when a child is born, and cherish it as the most holy gift.' Education is careful and restrained, 'their object is to train and form the pupil according to the intention of Nature without forcing him beyond his strength, or into an artificial mould. Studious to preserve the harmony and unity of mind, soul and body, they never foster one to the detriment of the others, but seek to develop the whole person. It is not so much words as things, not so much facts, dates and figures, as principles, ideas, and sentiments, which they endeavour to teach. . . . In the cultivation of the mind they give the first and foremost place to the imagination. The reason, they say, is mechanical, and cannot rise above the known; that is to say, the real; whereas the imagination is creative and attains to the unknown, the ideal. Its highest work is the creation of beauty. . . . The most important study of all is the art of living, in other words the art of leading a simple, noble, beautiful life.'

They do not live an idle life, however: 'They believe that labour like virtue is a necessity, and its own reward; but it is a moderate labour of the right sort, which is a blessing and not a curse. (Since an unfit employment is a mistake, and a source of unhappiness, everyone is free to choose the work that suits his nature). They are artists in all and above all. They hold that every beautiful thing has a use, and they never make a useful thing without beauty.' Their literature is of a very high order, embracing poetry, drama and fiction; they excel in their pictures and statuary, while 'they are clever architects and gardeners'.

'Some of their public buildings are magnificent; but most of their private houses are pretty one-storied cottages, each more or less isolated in a big garden, and beyond earshot of the rest. They are elegant, not to say fanciful constructions of stone and timber, generally of an oval shape, or at least with rounded outlines; but sometimes rambling, and varying much in detail. . . . Many of them have balconies or verandahs, and also terraces on the roof. . . . They are doorless; but in stormy weather they are closed by panels of wood, and a translucent mineral resembling glass. . . . The ceilings are usually of carved wood, and the floors inlaid with marbles, corals, and the richer stones. . . . The light easy furniture is for the most part made of precious or fragrant woods of divers colours. At night the rooms are softly and agreeably lighted by phosphorescent tablets, or lamps of glow-worms and fire-flies in crystal vases. The dishes and utensils not only serve but adorn the home. Most of the implements and fittings are made of coloured metals or alloys. Many of the cups and vessels are beautifully cut from shells and diamonds, rubies and other precious stones. Statuary, manuscripts, and musical instruments, bespeak their taste and genius for the fine arts.'

Munro's travellers had few adventures on Venus, and stayed for a comparatively short time, never stirring from the crater-country of Wŏmla. They remained long enough, however, to learn the language and study the customs of the people, and attend their most important religious ceremony, the cutting of the 'Flower of the Soul', which is very fully described. Alumion, the seventeen-year-old priestess, chosen for her beauty and serving but for a year of office, plucked the symbolic Sun Lily as the culmination of the ceremony—and she and the hero fell in love at first sight.

Marriage on Venus was a simple, straightforward affair depending entirely on the two persons concerned. So they met, and as soon as Alumion's service as priestess ended, they were married by drinking together of the pure water of a special consecrated fountain, no oath, even, being necessary in so serious a matter since the simple pledge and the knowledge of mutual love were enough to form an unaltering and lifelong union.

But Gazen and Carmichael thought that their companion had been hypnotised, and very unwisely set out from Venus one night as he slept in the Space-ship. They paid a brief visit to Mercury, and on leaving that planet from the Sunward side narrowly escaped a fiery death since the mechanism jammed owing to the heat and they barely avoided being drawn into the Sun itself. They won back to Earth in safety, however, where Gazen married Miss Carmichael; but the narrator declared that 'as soon as the ceremony is over I shall return to Venus—and Alumion'.

Four or five thousand million years from now, according to Olaf Stapledon, mankind, finding that the Moon would fall onto and destroy the Earth in a few million years, decide to emigrate to Venus. The first explorers find it an almost impossible planet: 'Its land surface, scarcely more than a thousandth that of the Earth, consisted of an unevenly distributed archipelago of mountainous islands. . . . The ocean was subject to terrific storms and currents; for since the planet took several weeks to rotate, there was a great difference of temperature and atmospheric pressure between the almost Arctic hemisphere of night and the sweltering hemisphere of day. So great was the evaporation, that open sky was almost never visible from any part of the planet's surface; and indeed the average daytime weather was a succession of thick fogs and fantastic thunderstorms. Rain in the evening was a continuous torrent. Yet before night was over the waves clattered with fragments of ice.'

Nevertheless they persevere with the ghastly materialistic tenacity of all Stapledon's races of Man, set up 'great automatic electrolysing stations', plant the islands with suitable vegetation, produce 'great floating islands of vegetable matter', and in time reclaim more land—and so make the climatic conditions less violent.

But one serious drawback comes from the native inhabitants of Venus: 'At the bottom of the Venerian ocean these creatures thronged in cities of proliferated coral-like buildings, equipped with many complex articles, which must have constituted the necessities and luxuries of their civilization. . . . Clearly they used some kind of symbolic language, based on mechanical vibrations set up in the water. . . .'

Clearly, too, these fish-like inhabitants objected to the invasion from Earth, and to the drying up of their oceans. They attacked the invaders with bombs and landmines, but they had no more chance than the Earthmen had against Wells's Martians; no providential germ came to their assistance, and the invaders exterminated them ruthlessly.

After countless further ages, more and more of Venus becoming dry land and the cloud envelope thinning away, Man developed wings and went through one of the happiest periods of his existence—before nemesis in the form of the gas-cloud approaching the Sun forces the final emigration to Neptune.

Last and First Men was published in 1930, but it does not seem to have influenced Edgar Rice Burroughs in any way when he began his series of Venerian romances with *Pirates of Venus* in 1934.

This series of four (the last, *Escape on Venus* (1946) has not so far appeared in England) is by no means as successful as his Martian adventures, and nowhere approaches the momentary inspiration of *The Moon Maid*.

His new hero, Carson Napier, is a little better educated than John Carter and his journey was made by a Space-ship propelled by rocket energy on the latest German model as recently demonstrated in fiction by Otto Willi Gail.

In spite of a certain knowledge of astronomy and mechanics, Carson, the lone voyager in his un-steerable rocket-car, failed to take the Moon into his calculations. He aimed at Mars, was pulled out of his course by our forgotten satellite, and found himself racing faster and faster towards annihilation in the Sun—just as Munro's travellers had done when their engine stuck on the wrong side of Mercury.

Cyrano de Bergerac, long before, had been drawn towards the Sun but landed on the Moon which came between at the right moment;

Carson was equally lucky, for Venus saved him from a fiery death, and he went plunging into her dense clouds, his fall lessened by parachutes in his rocket's nose until he was able to spring out and trust to his personal parachute and an oxygen apparatus.

'I jerked the rip-cord of my parachute just as the clouds swallowed me. Through my fleece-lined suit I felt the bitter cold. . . . It was very dark and very wet, like sinking into the depths of the ocean without feeling the pressure of the water. . . . As I entered the second cloud bank, there was a very noticeable rise in temperature the farther I fell. . . . I presently became aware of a faint luminosity far below.'

Down still went Carson, and dropped at length into a mighty tree, to be rescued from a giant spider by the civilized inhabitants of Amtor (as they called their world) who lived in tree-cities far above the ground. The trees might be as much as five hundred feet in diameter and six thousand high, so that they could easily hollow houses in their trunks and connect them by hanging bridges.

The tree-dwellers of Vapaja represented the civilized remnant of a great country which had been plunged back into barbarism by a communist revolution in which the ignorant masses, led by self-seeking schemers, had striven to annihilate their intelligentsia. Now the Vepajans lived a happy and cultured life in the tree-cities, troubled only by raids from their former subjects the Thorists who strove to capture them or their women in an attempt to regain some of the intelligence and learning without which they found themselves sinking into savagery and want.

Trouble also came from the Klangan or Bird-men, the half-human pirates of Venus, and from many other tribes and species whom Carson encountered in the adventures which led finally to the winning of lovely Duare the princess of Venus.

But in spite of the excellent start and the promising early chapters among the tree-dwellers, *Pirates of Venus* and its sequels deteriorates very quickly into adventures that might equally well have befallen some subsidiary hero like Ulysses Paxton in a minor Martian romance. Amtor is merely Barsoom with a little more gravity, oceans and the cloud envelope; the targo is a slightly larger variant of the spiders of Ghasta described in *A Fighting Man of Mars*; there is little difference between the Venerian basto and a Martian zitidar gone mad.

To make Mars the planet of war suited well the abilities and limitations of the creator of Tarzan: John Carter the Warlord is a credible, even a likeable figure. But Carson Napier in the planet of love and beauty seems rather a cad when not being a minor John Carter, while Duare is a pretty doll with a set of pseudo-romantic reactions, even when compared with Dejah Thoris the Martian Princess of Helium.

The stories themselves are of course exciting and ingenious: these gifts never deserted Burroughs. But apart from a momentary recollection of great trees rising to the very clouds, they leave far less impression of another world than John Munro manages to convey in the earnest, charming and quite unexciting narrative of *A Trip to Venus*.

Poorly though the earlier chroniclers may have described Venus, however, she did but hide her secret and keep her long, lonely vigil behind the impenetrable clouds until her mystery could be disclosed by C. S. Lewis in *Perelandra* (1943) with a conviction and the compulsion of sheer rightness which makes all other accounts simply impossible. The craterland of Womla might perhaps pass as one tiny island in the ocean of Perelandra at some distant date in the future; but otherwise Venus is and must remain as Ransom saw it and described it to Lewis—the new planet on which human life has but just appeared, the world of Paradise Retained.

The whole literary and spiritual achievement of *Perelandra* comes rather outside the scope of this book, but the description of the world of Venus, or Perelandra, is so much the crown of all earlier descriptions of planetary worlds that some quotation is essential; but with so well known and easily obtainable a classic as this, there is no excuse for much.

When Ransom came into Perelandra, conveyed in his celestial coffin by the Oyarsa of Malacandra, one of the Host of Heaven, he found himself at first swimming in the sea.

'Up and up he soared till it seemed as if he must reach the burning dome of gold that hung above him instead of a sky. Then he was at a summit; but almost before his glance had taken in a huge valley that yawned beneath him—shining green like glass and marbled with streaks of scummy white—he was rushing down into that valley at perhaps thirty miles an hour. And now he realised that there was a delicious coolness over every part of him except his head, that his feet rested on nothing, and that he had for some time been performing unconsciously the actions of a swimmer. He was riding the foamless swell of an ocean, fresh and cool, but warm by earthly standards. . . . The water gleamed, the sky burned with gold, but all was rich and dim, and his eyes fed upon it undazzled and unaching. The very names of green and gold, which he used perforce in describing the scene, are too harsh for the tenderness, the muted iridescence, of that warm, maternal, delicately gorgeous world. It was mild to look upon as evening, warm like summer noon, gentle and winning like early dawn.

'Yet it was a violent world too. [Suddenly] his eyes were stabbed by an unendurable light. A grading, blue-to-violet illumination made the golden sky seem dark by comparison and in a moment of time revealed more of the new planet than he had yet seen. He saw the waste of waves spread illimitably before him, and far, far away, at the very end of the world, against the sky, a single smooth column of ghastly green standing up, the one thing fixed and vertical in this universe of shifting slopes. Then the rich twilight rushed back (now seeming almost darkness) and he heard thunder. But it had a different *timbre* from terrestrial thunder, more resonance, and even, when distant, a kind of tinkling. It is the laugh, rather than the roar, of heaven. Another flash followed, and then another, and then the storm was all about him. Enormous purple clouds came driving between him and the golden sky, and with no preliminary drops a rain such as he had never experienced began to fall. There were no lines in it; the water above him seemed only less continuous than the sea, and he found it difficult to breathe. The flashes were incessant. In between them, when he looked in any direction except that of the clouds, he saw a completely changed world. It was like being at the centre of a rainbow, or in a cloud of multi-coloured steam. The water which was now filling the air was turning sea and sky into a bedlam of flaming and writhing transparencies. He was dazzled and now for the first time a little frightened. In the flashes he saw, as before, only the endless sea and the still green column at the end of the world. No land anywhere—not the suggestion of a shore from one horizon to the other.'

The first land which Ransom found consisted of the great floating islands many acres in extent, the most distinctive and original feature of Perelandra, and the most hauntingly strange and beautiful. When he had struggled with difficulty onto the earliest of these which came his way, 'his first discovery was that he lay on a dry surface, which on examination turned out to consist of something very like heather, except for the colour which was coppery. Burrowing idly with his fingers he found something friable like dry soil, but very little of it, for almost at once he came upon a base of tough interlocked fibres. Then he rolled round on his back, and in doing so discovered the extreme resilience of the surface on which he lay. It was something much more than the pliancy of the heather-like vegetation, and felt more as if the whole floating island beneath that vegetation were a kind of mattress. He turned and looked "inland"—if that is the right word—and for one instant what he saw looked very like a country. He was looking up a long lonely valley with a copper-coloured floor bordered on each side by gentle slopes clothed in a kind of many-coloured forest. But even as he took this in, it became a long copper-coloured ridge with the forest sloping *down* on each side of it. Of course he ought to have been prepared for this, but he says that it gave him an almost sickening shock. The thing had looked, in that first glance, so like a real country that he had forgotten it was floating—an island if you like, with hills and valleys, but hills and valleys which changed places every minute so that only a cinematograph could make a contour map of it. . . .

'He rose to take a few paces inland—and downhill, as it was at the moment of his rising—and immediately found himself flung down on his face, unhurt because of the softness of the weed. He scrambled to his feet—saw that he now had a steep slope to ascend—and fell a second time. . . . At long last he reached the wooded part. There was an undergrowth of feathery vegetation, about the height of gooseberry bushes, coloured like sea anemones. Above this were the taller growths —strange trees with tube-like trunks of grey and purple spreading rich canopies above his head, in which orange, silver, and blue were the predominant colours. Here, with the aid of the tree trunks, he could keep his feet more easily. The smells in the forest were beyond all that he had ever conceived. To say that they made him feel hungry and thirsty would be misleading; almost, they created a new kind of hunger and thirst, a longing that seemed to flow over from the body into the soul and which was a heaven to feel.'

The temptation to follow Ransom further through Perelandra is almost irresistible, as new, captivating, and utterly convincing scenes and experiences come to him. When he meets the Green Lady and the animals of Venus the nature of the book begins to change; and the change is completed when Professor Weston, the Earth-scientist into whom the Devil has entered (as of old into the serpent of Eden), arrives in his Space-ship, and Ransom realises that his experiences on Perelandra were to be 'not of following an adventure but of enacting a myth'—a new Genesis in 'the first of worlds to wake after the great change' of the Incarnation.

And so we must leave him on lovely Perelandra: perhaps most fittingly at the end of his first day there—'That idea of Schiaparelli's is all wrong! They have an ordinary day and night there,' was almost his first remark on his return to Earth.

'All day there had been no variation at any point in the golden roof to mark the Sun's position, but now the whole of one half-heaven revealed it. The orb itself remained invisible, but on the rim of the sea rested an arc of green so luminous that he could not look at it, and beyond that, spreading almost to the zenith, a great fan of colour like a peacock's tail. Looking over his shoulder he saw the whole island ablaze with blue, and across it and beyond it, even to the ends of the world, his own enormous shadow. The sea, far calmer now than he had yet seen it, smoked towards heaven in huge dolomites and elephants of blue and purple vapour, and a light wind, full of sweetness, lifted the hair on his forehead. Day was burning to death. . . . But before the great apocalyptic colours had died out in the west, the eastern heaven was black. A few moments, and the blackness had reached the western horizon. A little reddish light lingered at the zenith for a time, during which he crawled back to the woods. . . . But before he had lain down among the trees the real night had come—seamless darkness, not like night but like being in a coal-cellar, darkness in which his own hand held before his face was totally invisible. Absolute blackness, the undimensioned, the impenetrable, pressed on his eyeballs. There is no moon in that land, no stars pierce the golden roof. But the darkness was warm. Sweet new scents came stealing out of it. The world had no size now. Its boundaries were the length and breadth of his own body and the little patch of soft fragrance which made his hammock, swaying ever more and more gently. Night covered him like a blanket and kept all loneliness from him.'

CHAPTER FOURTEEN

TORMANCE AND MALACANDRA

URING the period covered by this book there seems to have
been no Space-trip to Uranus, though the Last Men, living two
thousand million years in the future upon the planet Neptune achieved
a 'communication with the agricultural polar regions of the less torrid
Uranus, as also with the automatic mining stations on the glacial outer
planets'. Pluto, they had found to be 'a mere ball of iron': but, under
the name of Cassandra, John Jacob Astor had dealt more fully with this
outermost planet in *A Journey in Other Worlds* in 1894.

In the same way, at the other extreme of the Solar System, Mercury
remained almost totally neglected. The Sun itself served only for
pure satire as in the case of Cyrano de Bergerac's visit; or pure
fantasy as in Sydney Whiting's *Heliondé* in 1855—no more a Space-
voyage than *Alice in Wonderland* is a journey into the interior of the
Earth.

The only visit to Mercury, and that a brief and troubled one, was
made by John Munro's Space-travellers at the end of their Trip to
Venus in 1897, when the narrator woke to find himself and the Space-
car no longer in fertile Womla but on 'a bare and rugged platform of
weathered rocks.

'The welkin was wholly overcast with dense, murky vapours, which
totally hid the Sun, and the air was excessively hot, moist, and sultry
as before a thunderstorm. Black boulders and crags, speckled with
lichens, and carpeted with coarse herbage, shut out the prospect on
every side but one. . . . I was looking away over a vast plain towards
a distant range of volcanic mountains. A broad river wound through
the midst between isolated volcanoes, curling with smoke, and thick
forests of a sable hue, or expanded into marshy lakes half lost in brakes
of grisly reeds, on the margin of which living monsters were splashing
in the mud, or soaring into the air on dusky pinions.'

Across this 'savage and primeval landscape' came 'a flying monster,
with enormous bat-like wings and hanging legs. . . . With his great
bullet head and prick ears, his beetling brows and deep sunken eyes,
his ferocious mouth and protruding tusks, his short thick neck and
massive shoulders, his large, gawky and misshapen trunk, coated with

dingy brown fur, shading into dirty yellow on the stomach, his stout, bandy legs armed with curving talons, and his huge leathern wings, he looked more like an imp of Satan than a dragon'.

This terrible creature seized Miss Carmichael in its claws and carried her away to his nest in the distant cliffs—hotly pursued by the three adventurers in their Space-car.

'A prey to anxiety and the most distressing emotions, we did not properly observe the marvellous, the Titanic, I had almost said the diabolical aspect of the country beneath us, and still we could not altogether blind ourselves to it. Colossal jungles resembling brakes of moss and canes five hundred or a thousand feet in height—creeks as black as porter gliding under their dank and rotting aisles—mountainous quadrupeds or lizards crashing and tearing through their branches—one of them at least six hundred feet in length, with a ridgy back and long spiky tail, dragging on the ground, a baleful green eye, and a crooked mouthful of horrid fangs which made it look like the very incarnation of cruelty and brute strength—black lakes and grisly reeds as high as bamboo—prodigious black serpents troubling the water, and rearing their long spiry necks above the surface—gigantic alligators and crocodiles resting motionless in the shallows, with their snouts high in the air—hideous toads or such-like forbidding reptiles, many with tusks like the walrus, and some with glorious eyes, crouching on the banks or waddling in the reeds, and so enormous as to give variety to the landscape—volcanic craters with red-hot lava simmering in their depths—while over all great dragons and other bat-like animals were flitting through the dusky atmosphere like demons in a nightmare.

'Little by little we gained upon our quarry,' overtook it as it reached its nest, and rescued Miss Carmichael after a fierce battle. Then, 'being disgusted with the infernal scenery as well as the foetid, malarial atmosphere of Mercury', they set out for Earth once more.

It might be argued that E. R. Eddison's strange dream-saga *The Worm Ouroboros* (1922) should be included here as a romance of Mercury. In the Induction in Wastdale the saga-fey narrator Lessingham, sleeping in the Lotus Room of his mysterious house, wakes to find the still more mysterious martlet waiting for him with the cryptic message 'Time is'. Rising from his bed, 'he went to the window, and the little martlet sat on his shoulder. A chariot coloured like the halo about the Moon waited by the window, poised in air, harnessed to a strange steed. A horse it seemed, but winged like an eagle, and its fore-legs feathered and armed with eagle's claws instead of hooves. He entered the chariot, and that little martlet sat on his knee.

'With a whirr of wings the wild courser sprang skyward. The night about them was like a tumult of bubbles about a diver's ears diving in a deep pool under a smooth steep rock in a mountain cataract. Time was swallowed up in speed; the world reeled; and it was but as the space between two deep breaths till that strange courser spread wide his rainbow wings and slanted down the night over a great island that slumbered on a slumbering sea, with lesser isles about it; a country of rock mountains and hill pastures and many waters, all a-glimmer in the moonshine.'

Mercury has no moon, but nevertheless, when morning dawned 'that little martlet' spoke to Lessingham: 'This is no dream. Thou, first of the children of men, art come to Mercury, where thou and I will journey up and down for a season to show thee the lands and oceans, the forests, plains, and ancient mountains, cities and palaces of this world, Mercury, and the doings of them that dwell therein. But here thou canst not handle aught, neither make the folk ware of thee, not though thou shout thy throat hoarse. For thou and I walk here impalpable and invisible, as it were two dreams walking.'

Hereafter Lessingham fades out of the picture, and with him any suggestion that Mercury is the scene of this wonderfully stirring and magical tale. It is, indeed, only so much a story of another world as is any one of William Morris's great prose romances, and it has really no more right of inclusion here than *The Wood Beyond the World* or *The Water of the Wondrous Isles*. New and brilliantly imagined though Carcë or Koshtra Belorn may be, they are surely on the same globe as Utterbol and Greenford, even as Zu-vendis and Kôr, rather than in Viritrilbia.

To some extent the same is true of Tormance, the planet which circles round the distant sun which we call Arcturus, to which Krag took Maskull and Nightspore in David Lindsay's strange and terrifying romance *A Voyage to Arcturus* (1920).

True, they journeyed in a species of Space-ship: 'Maskull beheld with awe the torpedo of crystal which was to convey them through the whole breadth of visible Space. It was forty feet long, eight broad, and eight high; the tank containing the Arcturian back-rays was in front, the car behind. The nose of the torpedo was directed towards the south-eastern sky. . . . Krag clambered past them on to his pilot's seat. . . . He pulled the starting-lever. The torpedo glided gently from its platform, and passed rather slowly away from the tower, seawards. Its speed increased sensibly, though not excessively, until the approximate limits of the Earth's atmosphere were reached. Krag then released the speed-valve, and the car sped on its way with a velocity more nearly approaching that of thought than of light. Maskull had no opportunity of examining through the crystal walls the rapidly changing panorama of the heavens. An extreme drowsiness oppressed him. He opened his eyes violently a dozen times, but on the thirteenth attempt he failed. From that time forward he slept heavily.'

Tormance is also very much of a new planetary world. Waking on it nineteen hours later, to find himself lying alone on the red sand, Maskull cannot lift his weight from the ground until Joiwind, the first person to welcome him, has given him a transfusion of her blood. 'She was tall and slight. All her movements were as graceful as music. Her skin was not of a dead, opaque colour, like that of an Earth-beauty, but was opalescent; its hue was continually changing with every thought and emotion, but none of these tints were vivid—all were delicate, half-toned, and poetic.'

As for the first landscape which Maskull saw on Tormance, 'the enormous scarlet desert extended everywhere to the horizon, excepting where it was broken by the oasis. It was roofed by a cloudless, deep blue, almost violet sky. The circle of the horizon was far larger than on Earth. . . . As they went along, the sun broke through the upper mists and a terrible gust of scorching heat, like a blast from a furnace, struck Maskull's head. He involuntarily looked up, but lowered his eyes again like lightning. All that he saw in that instant was a glaring ball of electric white, thrice the apparent diameter of the Sun. . . . Maskull would have felt inclined to believe he was travelling in dreamland, but for the intensity of the light, which made everything vividly real'.

To read *A Voyage to Arcturus* is indeed to enter a bewildering dreamland, almost a land of nightmare, but, as in Tormance, there is an intensity of light which makes everything vividly real. It is not possible, or desirable, to give a précis of this astonishing book: (it is, indeed, in print, and was broadcast on the Third Programme in June 1956): for Tormance is a world of the spirit, rather than a planet like any other before or since. Nor is it an allegory in the sense that *Pilgrim's Progress* is, for its haunting, terrifying quality lies in the fact that the meaning seems clear somewhere in the subconscious mind, but eludes the conscious with the numbing horror which we sometimes experience in seeking to recapture a dream which lingers somewhere in our being—vividly real but frighteningly incomprehensible.

C. S. Lewis, in his essay 'On Stories', describes *A Voyage to Arcturus* as 'the most remarkable achievement in this kind. . . . Unaided by any special skill or even any sound taste in language, the author leads us up a stair of unpredictables. In each chapter we think we have found his final position: each time we are utterly mistaken. He builds whole worlds of imagery and passion, any one of which would have served another writer for a whole book, only to pull each of them to pieces and pour scorn on it. The physical dangers, which are plentiful, here count for nothing: it is we ourselves and the author who walk through a world of spiritual dangers which makes them seem trivial. There is no recipe for writing of this kind. But part of the secret is that the author (like Kafka) is recording a lived dialectic. His Tormance is a region of the spirit. He is the first writer to discover what "other planets" are really good for in fiction. No merely physical strangeness or merely spatial distance will realise that idea of otherness which is what we are always trying to grasp in a story about voyaging through Space: you must go into another dimension. To construct plausible and moving "other worlds" you must draw on the only real "other world" we know, that of the spirit'.

A Voyage to Arcturus stands apart from all the other Space-flight stories described in this book; but the culmination of them all, *Out of the Silent Planet* combines what is best in their tradition with a subtle, underlying reality out of this same dimension of the spirit. After reading over fifty accounts of journeys into other worlds, *Out of the Silent Planet* still seems to hold a secure position, similar to that of *Treasure Island* among pirate stories: (there have been plenty of good ones both before and since, but to think of pirates is to think first of Stevenson's masterpiece).

Here, wrote Marjorie Nicolson, is 'the most beautiful of all cosmic voyages, and in some ways the most moving'.

In *Out of the Silent Planet* (1938), C. S. Lewis did not create a new world such as Tormance (nor need to people Space with such utilitarian planets as the Antigeos or Bokez of later 'thriller' writers): that Malacandra is Mars is as essential to the story as that, in the sequel, Perelandra could only be Venus. Nor in this, Ransom's first planetary voyage, was there any need of the celestial coffin and the angelic transport: that Ransom went in a Space-ship, the captive of the scientist

Weston and his accomplice Devine, is an integral part of the whole conception.

But the subtle difference between this and other voyages begins to make itself felt during the twenty-eight days of the flight—quietly, subtly, but none the less with the tingling sensation of the real originality:

'Ransom, as time wore on, became aware of another and more spiritual cause for his progressive lightening and exultation of heart. A nightmare, long engendered in the modern mind by the mythology that follows in the wake of science, was falling off him. He had read of "Space": at the back of his thinking for years had lurked the dismal fancy of the black, cold vacuity, the utter deadness, which was supposed to separate the worlds. He had not known how much it affected him until now—now that the very name "Space" seemed a blasphemous libel for this empyrean ocean of radiance in which they swam. He could not call it "dead"; he felt life pouring into him from it every moment. How indeed should it be otherwise, since out of this ocean the worlds and all their life had come? He had thought it barren; he saw now that it was the womb of worlds, whose blazing and innumerable offspring looked down nightly even upon the Earth with so many eyes—and here, with how many more! No: Space was the wrong name. Older thinkers had been wiser when they named it simply the heavens. . . .'

Landed on Mars, and realising that Weston and Devine have brought him by the command of a species of Martian called a Sorn, Ransom, like his captors, jumps immediately to the conclusion that the Sorn must be a typical 'monster from outer Space' probably anxious to suck his blood like a Wellsian Martian or practise on him some hideous form of vivisection like Ras Thavas the Master Mind of Mars. 'His mind, like so many minds of his generation, was richly furnished with bogies. He had read his H. G. Wells and others. His universe was peopled with horrors such as ancient and medieval mythology could hardly rival. No insect-like, vermiculate or crustacean Abominable, no twitching feelers, rasping wings, slimy coils, curling tentacles, no monstrous union of superhuman intelligence and insatiable cruelty seemed to him anything but likely on an alien world.'

To combat this vividly built up fear the obvious course would have been to step back into the Glintan or Tetarta of McColl or Wicks, even into the prophetic Shadow-Earth of *Across the Zodiac*. But with no hesitation Lewis steps boldly forward and creates his Sorns and his

Hrossa, the inevitable inhabitants of Malacandra, so unforgettable in their absolute rightness that they seem almost a discovery rather than an invention.

And alone of the imagined inhabitants of other worlds, they are four-dimensional: only on Malacandra and Perelandra are the un-Earthly bodies tenanted by immortal souls. Only these two worlds are a part of the eternal scheme of things: they, with Thulcandra, the Silent Planet of Earth, are, as it were, members of one body—previous worlds had tended more or less to be excrescences, when they were not simply disunited digits of the terrestrial limb.

Of course C. S. Lewis, the 'apostle to the sceptics', set out with a gospel to preach; set out to conquer from his own, Christian, point of view, what had always hitherto been used by the 'opposite side'. In Professor Weston he pillories the 'desperately immoral outlook' of such a writer as Olaf Stapledon and those of his way of thinking: 'He was a man obsessed with the idea which is at this moment circulating all over our planet in obscure works of "scientifiction", in little Interplanetary Societies and Rocketry Clubs, and between the covers of monstrous magazines, ignored or mocked by the intellectuals, but ready, if ever the power is put into its hands, to open a new chapter of misery for the universe. It is the idea that humanity, having now sufficiently corrupted the planet where it arose, must at all costs contrive to seed itself over a larger area: that the vast astronomical distances which are God's quarantine regulations, must somehow be overcome. This for a start. But beyond this lies the sweet poison of the false infinite—the wild dream that planet after planet, system after system, in the end galaxy after galaxy, can be forced to sustain, everywhere and for ever, the sort of life which is contained in the loins of our own species—a dream begotten by the hatred of death upon the fear of true immortality, fondled in secret by thousands of ignorant men and hundreds who are not so ignorant. The destruction or enslavement of other species in the universe, if such there are, is to these minds a welcome corollary. In Professor Weston the power had at last met the dream. The great physicist had discovered a motive power for his space-ship.'[1]

Thus Malacandra and Perelandra combine the 'other-worldness' of Mars and Venus with 'the only real "other world" we know, that of

[1] 'Man may visit the Moon by the year 2000 and colonize other planets in the twenty-first or twenty-second centuries,' an eminent rocket-engineer told a large meeting, according to *The Times* of June 8th, 1956.

the spirit'—but not merely in the microcosm of Tormance—'this little world of man'. The greatness of the theme and the universal application of the basic struggle make the adventures far more real and personal than the merely mechanical perils of John Carter or Professor Cavor: taken on this level alone the books are in a different class from any discussed in the present survey. But at the level of mere imagination and descriptive compulsion they surpass them all.

Others may come to equal or even excel *Out of the Silent Planet* and *Perelandra*: their influence is already apparent in the realms of 'scientifiction': but as the highest peak achieved since first a 'loftie traveller' set out into other worlds, this discursive pilgrimage through the Solar System of the imagination cannot do better than to end with them.

APPENDIX

*A Short Bibliography of Journeys Into Other Worlds,
Mentioned in this Book*

APPENDIX

*A Short Bibliography of Journeys Into Other Worlds,
Mentioned in this Book*

[Dates of first translations into English given in square brackets]

LUCIAN OF SAMOSATA (*circa* 120–200)
Icaro-Menippus }
The True History } [Translated by Francis Hickes .... 1634]

LUDOVICO ARIOSTO (1474–1533)
Orlando Furioso 1516
[Translated by Harington, 1591; by Hoole, 1783]

JOHANN KEPLER (1571–1630)
Somnium, seu Opus posthumum de astronomia lunari 1634

FRANCIS GODWIN (1562–1633)
The Man in the Moone: or a Discourse of a Voyage Thither. By
Domingo Gonsales 1638

ATHANASIUS KIRCHER (1602–1680)
Itinerarium Exstaticum . . . Coelestis expansi 1656

CYRANO DE BERGERAC (1619–1655)
Histoire comique des Estats et Empires de la Lune 1657
[Translated by Thomas St. Serf, 1659; by A. Lovell, 1687]
Les Oeuvres de Monsieur de Cyrano Bergerac 1662
[Translated by A. Lovell ('Worlds of the Moon and Sun'),
1687]

APHRA BEHN (1640–1689)
The Emperor of the Moon: A Farce 1687

GABRIEL DANIEL
Voyage du Monde de Descartes 1690
[Translated by T. Taylor, 1692]

ELKANAH SETTLE (1648–1724)
The World in the Moon: An Opera 1697

DAVID RUSSEN
Iter Lunare: or, A Voyage to the Moon 1703

DANIEL DEFOE (1666–1731)
The Consolidator, or Memoirs of Sundry Transactions from the World in the Moon — 1705

THOMAS D'URFEY (1653–1723)
Wonders in the Sun: A Comick Opera — 1706

SAMUEL BRUNT
A Voyage to Cacklogallinia — 1727

MURTAGH MCDERMOT
A Trip to the Moon — 1728

[ANONYMOUS]
A New Journey to the World in the Moon (2nd Edn.) — 1747

RALPH MORRIS
A Narrative of the Life and Astonishing Adventures of John Daniel — 1751

MILES WILSON (1708–1777)
The History of Israel Jobson the Wandering Jew — 1757

FRANCIS GENTLEMAN (1728–1784)
A Trip to the Moon. By Sir Humphry Lunatic — 1764

RUDOLPH ERICH RASPE (1737–1794)
The Surprising Adventures of Baron Munchausen — 1785

'NICHOLAS LUNATIC'
A Voyage to the Moon (in 'Satyric Tales') — 1808

JOSEPH ATTERLEY
A Voyage to the Moon — 1827

THOMAS CROFTON CROKER (1798–1854)
Legends of the Lakes ('Daniel O'Rourke') — 1829

EDGAR ALLAN POE (1809–1849)
The Unparalleled Adventure of One Hans Pfaall — 1835
[In 'Tales Grotesque and Arabesque', 1835, etc.]

RICHARD ADAM LOCKE (1800–1871)
The Great Lunar Hoax (in 'The New York Sun') — 1835
['The Celebrated Moon Story', ed. by W. N. Griggs, 1852]

SYDNEY WHITING ((?)–1875)
Heliondé, or Adventures in the Sun — 1855

JULES VERNE (1828–1905)
De la Terre à la Lune   1865 [1873]
Autour de la Lune   1870 [1873]
Hector Servadac   1877 [1878]

ACHILLE EYRAUD (1821–(?))
Voyage à Venus   1865

GEORGE MACDONALD (1824–1905)
At the Back of the North Wind (The Moon)   1871

PERCY GREG (1836–1889)
Across the Zodiac (Mars)   1880

[ANONYMOUS]
Politics and Life in Mars   1883

'ANDRÉ LAURIE': i.e. PASCHAL GROUSSET (1844–1909)
Les Exiles de la Terre (The conquest of the Moon)   1888 [1889]

HUGH MACCOLL
Mr. Stranger's Sealed Packet (Mars)   1889

ROBERT CROMIE (1856–1907)
A Plunge into Space (Mars)   1890

ANDREW LANG (1844–1912)
Prince Ricardo (The Moon)   1893

JOHN JACOB ASTOR (1864–1912)
A Journey to Other Worlds (Jupiter and Saturn)   1894

JOHN MUNRO (1849–1930)
A Trip to Venus (Venus and Mercury)   1897

HERBERT GEORGE WELLS (1866–1946)
The War of the Worlds (Mars)   1898
Tales of Space and Time (Mars)   1899
The First Men in the Moon   1901

EDWIN LESTER ARNOLD (1857–1935)
Lieutenant Gullivar Jones: His Vacation (Mars)   1905

MARK WICKS
To Mars via the Moon   1911

EDGAR RICE BURROUGHS (1875–1950)
A Princess of Mars   1917
The Gods of Mars   1918

EDGAR RICE BURROUGHS (1875–1950) contd.

The Warlord of Mars	1919
Thuvia, Maid of Mars	1920
The Chessmen of Mars	1922
The Master Mind of Mars	1928
A Fightingman of Mars	1931
Swords of Mars	1936
Synthetic Men of Mars	1940
Llana of Gathol	1948
Moon Maid	1926
Pirates of Venus	1934
Lost on Venus	1935
Carson of Venus	1939
Escape on Venus	1946

DAVID LINDSAY (1876–   )

Voyage to Arcturus	1920

ERIC RUCKER EDDISON (1882–1945)

The Worm Ouroboros (Mercury)	1922

HUGH LOFTING (1886–1948)

Dr. Doolittle in the Moon	1928

OTTO WILLI GAIL (1896–   )

By Rocket to the Moon	1931

CLIVE STAPLES LEWIS (1898–   )

Out of the Silent Planet (Mars)	1938
Perelandra (Venus)	1943

SCIENCE FICTION

An Arno Press Collection

FICTION

About, Edmond. **The Man with the Broken Ear.** 1872

Allen, Grant. **The British Barbarians:** A Hill-Top Novel. 1895

Arnold, Edwin L. **Lieut. Gullivar Jones:** His Vacation. 1905

Ash, Fenton. **A Trip to Mars.** 1909

Aubrey, Frank. **A Queen of Atlantis.** 1899

Bargone, Charles (Claude Farrere, pseud.). **Useless Hands.** [1926]

Beale, Charles Willing. **The Secret of the Earth.** 1899

Bell, Eric Temple (John Taine, pseud.). **Before the Dawn.** 1934

Benson, Robert Hugh. **Lord of the World.** 1908

Beresford, J. D. **The Hampdenshire Wonder.** 1911

Bradshaw, William R. **The Goddess of Atvatabar.** 1892

Capek, Karel. **Krakatit.** 1925

Chambers, Robert W. **The Gay Rebellion.** 1913

Colomb, P. et al. **The Great War of 189——.** 1893

Cook, William Wallace. **Adrift in the Unknown.** n.d.

Cummings, Ray. **The Man Who Mastered Time.** 1929

[DeMille, James]. **A Strange Manuscript Found in a Copper Cylinder.** 1888

Dixon, Thomas. **The Fall of a Nation:** A Sequel to the Birth of a Nation. 1916

England, George Allan. **The Golden Blight.** 1916

Fawcett, E. Douglas. **Hartmann the Anarchist.** 1893

Flammarion, Camille. **Omega:** The Last Days of the World. 1894

Grant, Robert et al. **The King's Men:** A Tale of To-Morrow. 1884

Grautoff, Ferdinand Heinrich (Parabellum, pseud.). **Banzai!** 1909

Graves, C. L. and E. V. Lucas. **The War of the Wenuses.** 1898

Greer, Tom. **A Modern Daedalus.** [1887]

Griffith, George. **A Honeymoon in Space.** 1901

Grousset, Paschal (A. Laurie, pseud.). **The Conquest of the Moon.** 1894

Haggard, H. Rider. **When the World Shook.** 1919

Hernaman-Johnson, F. **The Polyphemes.** 1906

Hyne, C. J. Cutcliffe. **Empire of the World.** [1910]

In The Future. [1875]

Jane, Fred T. **The Violet Flame.** 1899

Jefferies, Richard. **After London; Or, Wild England.** 1885

Le Queux, William. **The Great White Queen.** [1896]

London, Jack. **The Scarlet Plague.** 1915

Mitchell, John Ames. **Drowsy.** 1917

Morris, Ralph. **The Life and Astonishing Adventures of John Daniel.** 1751

Newcomb, Simon. **His Wisdom The Defender:** A Story. 1900

Paine, Albert Bigelow. **The Great White Way.** 1901

Pendray, Edward (Gawain Edwards, pseud.). **The Earth-Tube.** 1929

Reginald, R. and Douglas Menville. **Ancestral Voices:** An Anthology of Early Science Fiction. 1974

Russell, W. Clark. **The Frozen Pirate.** 2 vols. in 1. 1887

Shiel, M. P. **The Lord of the Sea.** 1901

Symmes, John Cleaves (Captain Adam Seaborn, pseud.). **Symzonia.** 1820

Train, Arthur and Robert W. Wood. **The Man Who Rocked the Earth.** 1915

Waterloo, Stanley. **The Story of Ab:** A Tale of the Time of the Cave Man. 1903

White, Stewart E. and Samuel H. Adams. **The Mystery.** 1907

Wicks, Mark. **To Mars Via the Moon.** 1911

Wright, Sydney Fowler. **Deluge: A Romance** *and* **Dawn.** 2 vols. in 1. 1928/1929

SCIENCE FICTION

NON-FICTION
Including Bibliographies,
Checklists and Literary Criticism

Aldiss, Brian and Harry Harrison. **SF Horizons.** 2 vols. in 1. 1964/1965

Amis, Kingsley. **New Maps of Hell.** 1960

Barnes, Myra. **Linguistics and Languages in Science Fiction-Fantasy.** 1974

Cockcroft, T. G. L. **Index to the Weird Fiction Magazines.** 2 vols. in 1 1962/1964

Cole, W. R. **A Checklist of Science-Fiction Anthologies.** 1964

Crawford, Joseph H. et al. **"333": A Bibliography of the Science-Fantasy Novel.** 1953

Day, Bradford M. **The Checklist of Fantastic Literature in Paperbound Books.** 1965

Day, Bradford M. **The Supplemental Checklist of Fantastic Literature.** 1963

Gove, Philip Babcock. **The Imaginary Voyage in Prose Fiction.** 1941

Green, Roger Lancelyn. **Into Other Worlds:** Space-Flight in Fiction, From Lucian to Lewis. 1958

Menville, Douglas. **A Historical and Critical Survey of the Science Fiction Film.** 1974

Reginald, R. **Contemporary Science Fiction Authors,** First Edition. 1970

Samuelson, David. **Visions of Tomorow:** Six Journeys from Outer to Inner Space. 1974

DATE DUE		

808.3
G797i

164658

Green, Roger L.

AUTHOR

Into other worlds

TITLE

DATE DUE	BORROWER'S NAME	ROOM NUMBER
FE 13 7	J Rippert	JA 16 79
JA 17 '89	SE 27'88	

Green   164658